Haynes

Brass Instrument

Manual

Haynes Publis'

First published in June 2013

A catalogue record for this book is available from the British Library

ISBN 978 0 85733 217 2

Library of Congress catalog card no. 2013932253

Published by Haynes Publishing,
Sparkford, Yeovil, Somerset BA22 7JJ, UK

Tel: 01963 442030 Fax: 01963 440001
Int. tel: +44 1963 442030 Int. fax: +44 1963 440001
E-mail: sales@haynes.co.uk
Website: www.haynes.co.uk

Haynes North America, Inc.,
861 Lawrence Drive, Newbury Park,
California 91320, USA

Printed in the USA by Odcombe Press LP,
1299 Bridgestone Parkway, La Vergne, TN 37086

Haynes

Brass Instrument
Manual

How to buy, maintain
and set up your
trumpet, trombone,
tuba, horn and cornet

Haynes

Simon Croft & Andy Taylor

Contents

LEFT A pocket trumpet (*Taylor Trumpets/Tim Coppendale*).

Forewords

Tony Fisher

A professional trumpet player since the age of 13, Tony Fisher has enjoyed a career most musicians could only dream of – working on stage, in the studio, on TV and radio with some of the greatest names. From touring with big bands led by such legends as Ted Heath, Fisher went on to play on soundtracks for all the early James Bond films, recorded albums with artists as diverse as The Beatles, Tom Jones, Ella Fitzgerald, Bing Crosby and Fred Astaire, and toured with Frank Sinatra – to pick just a few names from an almost impossibly long list. Formerly the director of the Bert Kaempfert Orchestra, Fisher has also delivered master classes at The Guildhall, Trinity College, The Royal Northern College, Leeds College and The Royal College of Music. In the field of jazz, he remains a regular player at venues including Ronnie Scotts and is now the trumpet player in the Humphrey Lyttelton Band, a role he filled at the late leader's request.

My father – a brass band enthusiast – introduced me to the cornet at around the age of five, and I spent the next few years in brass bands. That was really the only training I had – apart from my father insisting that I practise most days on coming home from school. Thank goodness he did, as it turned out to give me a very enjoyable and rewarding life in music.

I didn't have any formal trumpet lessons at all – there was no such thing as music on school curriculums in those days! I have been very fortunate in that I have worked in all music genres – going from the out and out jazz scene at Ronnie Scotts to the London Symphony Orchestra doing sound tracks for many films, and even recording with the pop stars of the time – the Beatles, etc.

This is a thing I should like to stress for any would-be player: be as diverse as possible. The sheer fact that I can play in all these different scenarios means that I get asked to do many different things. Instead of specialising in one form, thus narrowing down the opportunities, learn to play in as many genres and styles as you can.

As far as equipment goes – choose the instrument that is right for *you* – not because a certain player advertises a certain make! The same thing goes for mouthpieces; I have had many confrontations with teachers at colleges who insist the player uses a mouthpiece that is completely wrong for him/her. We all have different faces and muscles. Get the mouthpiece that feels the most comfortable – not one that makes it easier to play high notes!

I mention that, as most young aspiring players want to play high notes. OK, there is a time and place for that but there are many other factors that are more important. Sound quality, for example, is for me the main factor in playing the trumpet.

Also take care of your instrument – and even then, first class repairs should be high on your 'must have' list. A classic example of why this is so happened to me when I was very young and working in a touring stage show. I accidentally knocked my instrument as I walked on through the proscenium arch at the side of the stage, but thought nothing of it until I went to play the first note of my solo and *nothing at all* came out of the trumpet! I had knocked the water key off its seating and, of course, the air went straight through the lead pipe and straight out of the damaged water key. Most embarrassing. Luckily, the trumpet player in the pit orchestra saw what had happened, offered me his trumpet and it all worked out well. I think to this day that the audience must have thought it was a worked-out routine, but I can assure you it was not.

One last thing for all young players: don't be put off or upset when some days your trumpet just doesn't seem to work. We all have days like that and it is usually down to a lack of practice – or possibly some physical problem – both of which should be solved quite easily. Just keep at it, and if it all comes right and you have a life like I have had – and indeed *am still* having – the rewards are fantastic in every way.

Keep practising, best wishes
Tony Fisher

Winston Rollins

Although first and foremost known as a trombone player, Winston Rollins plays keyboards and bass, as well as being a songwriter, producer and arranger. He has performed/recorded with a dazzling array of artists on trombone including James Brown, Amy Winehouse, Joss Stone, Eric Clapton, Tom Jones, Courtney Pine, Spice Girls, Jamiroquai and Jools Holland.

Who would have thought the experience I'm about to tell you would change my life forever? As an eight-and-a-half-year-old sitting crossed legged on the floor in the school's main hall, without realising it, everything was about to change. I sat there waiting for the teacher to drop the needle on the record to play the Peer Gynt Suite No. 1, Opus 46 – otherwise known as 'Morning Mood' – as on every school morning for as long as I could remember in my short life. This didn't happen on this day.

To my surprise, in walked a group of young men and women with very shiny musical instruments. They sat down, then with a nod started to play… the sound was amazing! And I thought: I'd like to do that.

A year-and-a-half passed, and the idea of playing a musical instrument was a distant memory by now. Walking through the

corridors of school I had a disagreement with my best friend and a fight broke out between us. It was immediately broken up by the peripatetic music teacher, who threw us in a room and handed us both a trombone. His words were 'If you're going to fight, fight this'…

I was amazed; the memories of the brass band in the school hall came flooding back, and I knew I could do this. Over the next few years – with the guidance from my peripatetic teacher – I joined the Doncaster Youth Jazz Association, which had three bands at the time. This meant players had to work their way up through first the stage band, to the swing band, and then onto the Jazz Orchestra. Once I had achieved this, it was obvious that this was going to be my chosen profession, which meant I had to find out more.

As I gained experience as a young musician, I started playing with local bands, doing sessions, but also teaching the younger kids who wanted learn. But I still wanted more.

For players who were part of DYJA, there was a direct link of musicians leaving Doncaster Jazz Orchestra (as it then became known) and going on to play with NYJO (National Youth Jazz Orchestra of Great Britain). This is what I wanted to do – and live in London.

Upon moving to London, I attended Trinity College of Music, where I was exposed to my peers, who had the same outlook on music as myself. Even more, I attended the weekly NYJO rehearsals, then became a part of NYJO, as well as the Jazz Warriors and numerous other bands, which was a great achievement for me.

Being a part of this melting pot, my quest for knowledge grew even bigger. I wanted to know about the great trombone players of the past and present. This led me to discover the late great JJ Johnson, Frank Rosolino, Carl Fontana, Bill Watrous, Steve Turre, Slide Hampton, Bob Brookmeyer and Fred Wesley, to name but a few. I also attended college with Mark Nightingale, who did and still does make a great impression with me. These great players are my inspiration.

I currently work as a freelance trombone player, working right across the musical spectrum – from playing in chart-topping pop bands to playing a jazz set in Ronnie Scotts. I can find myself working in musicals in London's West End, to studio sessions of all musical styles, playing in big bands, to sitting next to a young student who needs a little encouragement to get him through. I can be writing a band arrangement – whether it's for a big band, small band or horn section – then rehearsing that chart, and playing it in a performance, probably a few hours later that evening.

All this from sitting on a cold floor one morning as a child and watching a brass band play…

Cindy Bradley

Based in New York City, trumpet and flugelhorn player Cindy Bradley released her debut album Bloom *in 2009 and has performed at numerous festivals. With a master's degree in jazz trumpet performance, gained at the New England Conservatory, Cindy has also conducted hundreds of jazz workshops at high school and community colleges all over her country.*

The trumpet became a part of my life in the 4th grade by a total fluke. The elementary school band teacher gave us permission slips to take home to our parents. I forgot mine and didn't think much of it. When they were due and I hadn't signed up, the teacher came and found me (she knew I played the piano and loved music). She told me that I could be in the school band if I circled the instrument I wanted right then and there. With no thought put into it I circled the picture of the trumpet. I used to wish that the story of how I found the instrument that I fell in love with was more inspiring, but maybe things just happen for a reason, or I got lucky.

When I was 12, I joined a community group that was a big band comprised of all kids. The groups exposed me to swing music and I heard the trumpet being used to improvise and as a solo instrument. I loved the sound. I loved bending notes and making the inflections I heard on recordings. I would go back to the school concert band and bend notes in songs and drive the director crazy. I never had a teacher that specialised in trumpet until college, but I enjoyed figuring my way around the horn more than anything.

I've done a lot of teaching and do think some people find their voice with a specific instrument. When I've had chop issues like most trumpet players run into at one time or another, I always wondered if I could pick something else up and be able to express myself in a similar way. Trumpet players in general are labelled a pretty competitive group and I've never viewed playing music that way. When people ask me what they should change about their playing, or who they should try to sound like, I always tell them that if they changed and tried to be like someone else they would no longer be themselves. I love how no two players will sound exactly alike and have always enjoyed working with other horn players.

The trumpet can create a deep love/hate relationship within a player due to how physically demanding and sometimes mysterious mastering the instrument can be. Of course I'm biased, but the huge spectrum of expression that the trumpet can create sets it apart from other instruments for me. You can never stop growing and working at it, which I think explains my deep obsession with it that I enjoy every minute of and have allowed to dictate most decisions in my life.

Giles Whittome

In addition to being a player, collector and maker of brass musical instruments Giles Whittome is a gunmaker and ballistics expert who has lived in 14 countries. He speaks French, Italian, Swahili, Swedish, and some German. He has written approximately 100 technical articles on subjects related to firearms and is also a regular contributor to The Brass Herald.

For every artisan manufacturer, there will eventually be a collector. Accumulating collections of interesting, or valuable things, or objets de virtu is almost as old as mankind – and ever since they were invented, brass musical instruments have been no exception. I was only bitten by the bug when I gave up office work and branched out into making sporting rifles, and when the capital requirement for collecting these became ridiculous for all but zillionaires, it was time to concentrate on my other love, the trumpet and its associates. At the same time, I decided that if I had a good design idea which was not available on the market, I would make it myself or get it made, and this has been the most rewarding byway of all.

One has to specialise – collecting all and any brass would

have cash, storage and display implications beyond most of us, and I decided to follow the same course as I had in firearms, that of the rare or unusual, or even plain freaky. There are collectors in the United States with literally thousands of instruments, but inevitably a large percentage of such collections comprise items which can be bought off the shelf, which to me palls very quickly and displays the size of your wallet rather than your skill or discrimination.

My own preference is for instruments which were usually dead ends in that the music they offered was too obtuse, or if they were genuinely useful, ones which failed due to the cost of manufacture – a perfect example of the latter is the compensating cornet, which cleverly eliminates the need for tuning triggers but which would cost the earth to manufacture today in cornet size, although the system is still popular in the larger brass.

To me, the ultimate example is the Wohlrab trumpet, which modern trumpeters look at in disbelief and say cannot possibly play, but it can. I believe I own the only one in England (I much hope that I am wrong) and to my mind it is a collector's dream, in that it is a truly weird aberration which actually plays quite well and is the greatest fun. This last is what collecting should be all about.

Preface

You may have turned to this page because you're wondering if this book is for you. Well, if you'd like to know about the different types of brass musical instruments, why they're designed the way they are, how they're made, how they're repaired and how you can maintain them yourself, you're in the right place.

We've written this book so that it starts with the most basic concepts and ends with the most demanding repair techniques – as far as we know, no one has ever written a book on brass quite this comprehensive before. Our intention is to make clear every aspect of brass musical instruments, even if it's a whole new world to you.

On the other hand, if you have a specific information need – like how to fix a piston valve – please feel welcome to dip straight into the bit that tells you what you want to know. This is a manual, after all.

The *Brass Instrument Manual* is a step-by-step guide aimed at:

■ Anyone who hopes to make or repair brass instruments professionally.
■ Teachers and players who need to make 'running repairs'.
■ Players who'd like to customise their instruments and mouthpieces.
■ Players at all levels who'd like to make more informed choices when purchasing or specifying their musical equipment.
■ Anyone who seeks a real understanding of how brass musical instruments work.

Thank you for picking up this book. We hope you find it a useful and enjoyable read.

Andy Taylor and Simon Croft
March 2013

Introduction

What makes a 'brass player'?

The question of what attracts a would-be player to a brass instrument rather than, say, strings – and, more specifically, leads a player to specialise in the trombone, the trumpet or tuba – is one that has barely been addressed. Yet even the most casual observer can often spot which end of a social gathering is being propped up by the brass section, and which is occupied by a genteel gathering of string players.

Both groups of musicians are from the same species, but they come in totally different shapes. They usually order different drinks and they can certainly have very different perceptions as to the optimum sound level for a conversation! You might say that brass players don't need to be washed with the delicates – and that lung-power comes in useful.

But are all tuba players stout fellows, while trumpet players behave like the leaders and trombone players are of a patient disposition? Well, that's the way it would be if we lived in a predictable world where all Geminis were chatty, all Virgos were tidy and everyone's Mum baked really good cakes.

The reality is that although playing brass is certainly physical work, players come in all shapes and sizes, across race and gender. In fact, the very diversity of brass players places demands on the instrument maker, especially when tailor-making a mouthpiece. As we will discuss in this book, players don't come in a single size, with a single set of facial features, so a 'one size fits all' approach won't work.

At this point we should add in the other major factor that accounts for the great diversity of mouthpiece designs, instrument bore sizes, preferences in materials and so on: any brass player who's dedicated to their art has in their head a sound that they're striving for. This sound will have been forged by the musical styles they've grown to love, the specific instrument they play and the sound made by the players they most admire. Again, part of the art of making a brass instrument for a specific player is getting inside their head and helping them to move towards that target tone.

That said, not everyone who takes up a brass instrument starts out with a burning desire to be the next Dennis Brain or Miles Davis. In fact many a fine player ended up on their particular instrument because it happened to be lying around the house, the music teacher needed to make up numbers, or some other seemingly random factor.

OPPOSITE: Big ambitions: you don't have to be huge to play low brass. (*Conn-Selmer*)

Samvel Avetisyan: popular Latin trumpet soloist.

John Coulton: major orchestral player.

Claude Deppa: Afro/jazz fusion specialist.

Chris Storr: chart success with top acts.

So, if you have a general hankering to play a brass instrument but you're not sure which one, how do you choose? The chapter, *The Brass Family*, should give you some pointers, in that it tells you which instruments are associated with which musical styles – and will also give you a good idea of their relative sizes.

Actually, choosing an instrument is not the major decision it may seem – in fact many musicians

Early start: this French horn is more compact than most designs. (*JHS/Gary Barlow*)

play more than one. In addition, most students of music start out with an instrument they have either borrowed or hired. As a result, 'jumping ship' needn't result in financial hardship, and an experienced teacher will soon sense if a student might be better suited to another member of the brass family.

Which brings us to a very important decision in any player's musical journey…

Choosing a teacher

A good teacher can inform through knowledge and inspire through example, guiding their students along the path towards becoming avid musicians for the rest of their lives. Unfortunately, some school students find themselves taught by a general 'music teacher', who may have little or no expertise in the instrument of the student's choosing. This can put a student off a particular music instrument completely.

This gives us an initial criterion for choosing a teacher: can they play the instrument in which you're interested? But that's not setting the bar very high. A better question might be: how *well* can they play the instrument? Not every good teacher is going to have a stellar musical career behind them, but membership of a respectable band or orchestra is a strong indication of respect from fellow musicians.

Another valid question is: how experienced is this player as a teacher? There are quite a few jobbing players out there who teach as a sideline, but the ability to convey to others the skills you've already mastered is a skill in itself. Positive indicators in this respect are past students of the teacher (especially if some have gone on to make a career in music) and professional teaching qualifications. A professional teacher will have a structured approach to learning and can prepare students for examinations at the various grades.

Somewhat more subjective is the issue of whether the student gets along with the teacher. Obviously, not everyone is lucky enough to have a choice in this, but it's sad how many adults' memories of learning to play music are centred around misery and enforced practice, rather than the joy of learning to play. There's something of a two-way street here, as for every teacher who could be criticised for taking too regimented an approach, there are probably ten students who need to understand that a desire to 'play like Wynton' has to come somewhere down the line after 'develop embouchure and learn scales'!

Individual teachers with good reputations can be located through musical instrument stores. These establishments have a vested interest in helping their customers learn to play well, because they're potentially creating repeat business for decades

Ton Aben: trumpet enthusiast.

to come. Many larger stores provide lessons on the premises, and these are generally likely to be well run. Music schools are another good source to investigate, especially as there will probably be a large number of former students who can vouch for their experience.

For all that, it should be acknowledged that there are large numbers of dedicated and inspirational teachers doing a fine job of nurturing fledgling talent within the mainstream educational system. Such schools are easy enough to spot by the level of after-school activity and the number of students who elect to get involved.

Buying a brass instrument

For the would-be player, buying a first instrument is definitely a step best taken with the help of a teacher or experienced player. The world is littered with brass instruments that look really nice but don't play very well and probably never will. Unfortunately, until you can play, there's no way to sort the 'lookers' from instruments of genuine quality. (Alas, when you're learning to play you need all the help you can get, as it takes a really accomplished player to get a good sound from a cheap instrument.)

Arguably, the worst strategy for buying your first instrument is to buy a 'bargain' from an online store you don't know anything about. That can be a route to scoring a 'looker'! The message here isn't 'don't buy online'. Our point is only to buy online if you know exactly what you're buying, and who's selling it.

Unfortunately, even buying a shiny, new, big-brand model that's been recommended to you may not be as safe as it seems. There are unscrupulous operators in the Far East selling illegal fakes that look like the famous makes but certainly won't play like them. If you want to buy online, it's best to stick to established retailers. These are generally stockists offering a range of brands, and have a 'bricks and mortar' operation based somewhere that you can actually visit, or at least call.

At the other end of the scale, buying through your teacher can be a good option. Depending on where you live, if you're in full-time education you may be able to buy your instrument new at an attractive price through the school or college. Even if this isn't possible, busy teachers often have a number of students who are ready to upgrade, and can therefore recommend a used instrument with which they're familiar.

Buying a used instrument has up-sides, but also potential pitfalls. A wise buy second-hand means (a) a better instrument than you could otherwise afford, and (b) one that should hold its value, should you want to sell it or trade up in the future. However, unless you're buying from someone you know, or a specialist dealer that has a good reputation, it puts the onus squarely on you – or whoever you take along – to decide whether the instrument is worth the asking price.

A specialist dealer, rather than a general musical instrument shop, can offer considerable advantages to the brass player. General music stores don't tend to keep much brass overall, but a good specialist will be able to offer a varied selection of suitable instruments. It's also worth pointing out that specialist dealers usually have their own repair facilities and would rather add value to an instrument by refurbishing it, instead of pushing it out of the door in dubious condition.

Buying privately is really for experienced players and collectors who know exactly what they're looking at. Even then buyers need to be on their guard. In particular, beware people selling an expensive instrument they don't seem to know much about. While it's possible it really was found in Uncle Albert's basement, it could equally well be stolen.

Why cheap instruments can be bad value

These are some of the more common failings with instruments built down to a very low price:

- Soft, low-grade brass – dents easily and has dull tone.
- Low-grade solder – means braces will easily break away.
- Leaky valves – make the instrument hard to play.
- Uneven internal contours – degrades tone and intonation.

In short, there are brass instruments out there that represent a poor start for any music student.

Advantages to buying new

- ■ Factory-fresh condition.
- ■ Wide range of models to choose from.
- ■ Latest design/technology.
- ■ Full guarantee.
- ■ Possible educational/group purchase discount.

Disadvantages to buying new

- ■ You might pick up a better instrument second-hand for the same money.
- ■ Equally, expect to lose a fair bit when you sell/trade up.

Advantages to buying used

- ■ You can afford a better model, compared to paying new price.
- ■ Potentially you can sell/trade up without losing money in future.
- ■ Some older instruments are collectable.

Disadvantages to buying used

- ■ No guarantee, unless you buy from a specialist dealer.
- ■ Some old instruments are worn and practically useless.

A specialist dealer, like Paxman Musical instruments in London, offers expert advice as well as a wide range of models.

A dealer's receipt is always reassuring, especially if it's made out to the actual seller.

A considerable part of this book is devoted to the things that can go wrong with a brass musical instrument and the ways these problems can be repaired. Rather than go into detail in this chapter, we'll point out some of the possible defects and their general cost implications.

Many of the more obvious problems are also the ones that are easiest to fix, while problems related to the valves don't impact on the look of the instrument but can be costly to put right. For example, broken stays and dents spoil the look of an instrument but are often fairly easy repairs, providing the extent of the damage is moderate overall.

Easy things to check for include: slides aren't jammed; valves run freely; valves and levers don't have excessive play or make excessive noise; and the instrument passes air in all valve positions. Checking if the valves leak excessively is advisable. A 'quick and dirty' way of finding this out can be referenced under 'Valves, measuring air tightness', in the index at the back of this book. Making worn valves airtight again is a complicated process and is only worth carrying out on an instrument of significant value.

Valves that are sticking may simply be a sign that the instrument hasn't been played for a while. However, without cleaning the valves and casings, then re-lubricating, it's difficult to know for sure. Piston valves are particularly vulnerable to mechanical damage caused by seemingly minor mishaps, such as a stray mouthpiece in the case hitting one of the valve casings. Again, this kind of damage can be repaired, but

the cost needs to be factored in when assessing value.

Removing extensive denting and pitting involves considerable restoration, especially if it requires replacing original lacquer and/or plating. Some players cherish these battle scars, while others prefer their instrument to look as close to new as possible. Even on a purely cosmetic level, this is likely to involve many hours of skilled work. Beyond this, tubing that's thinned over the years to the point where it collapses on being touched – or has actually split – means that patching or replacement will be required.

Because good quality repair and restoration is labour intensive, you can expect a large bill to fix an instrument that's seriously worn-out. When it comes to hourly rates, musical instrument repairers are generally quite modest compared to some of their counterparts in more high-tech sectors. Nonetheless, it's important to understand that the repair pro is largely working by hand, whereas the musical instrument factory has the benefit of machinery and mass production using semi-skilled labour. These are major reasons why so many mid-level brass instruments from the past are now beyond economic repair. In simple terms, there are factories turning out new models for less money today than it takes to fix the old ones. That's not the whole story, though.

For instance, improvements in materials technology mean that the 'key' that holds a piston valve in alignment on an old-style trumpet is made of metal. When that key wears the reciprocal groove in the valve casing, the result is increasingly noisy operation. The solution is a complicated sequence of soldering, replacement and filing, which is covered elsewhere in this book. It's not a job for the inexperienced, or the faint-hearted, unless the instrument is already close to scrap in value.

Today's piston valves use a different system where the 'key' component is made of plastic. As this plate invariably wears before any metal part of the valve assembly, it can be replaced by anyone who's prepared to carefully unscrew the various valve parts then reassemble them in the right order. Not only that, but the valve should work better than the old-style metal key system!

When it comes to brass and marching band instruments, there's another reason why a find from Uncle Albert's basement might not be as useful as you'd hoped, and it's all about tuning. Today we're all used to the idea that the A above middle C on a piano is 440Hz in frequency, but this only became an international standard in 1955. Weirdly enough, this idea was first incorporated into the Treaty of Versailles signed in 1919

A new student outfit, such as this one from Odyssey, removes a lot of uncertainty from that first purchase. (*JHS/Gary Barlow*)

after the end of World War One, making it possibly the only time a musician helped to define the conditions for ending a war.

Prior to that, bands and orchestras in parts of Europe were using a pitch of A = 452.5Hz, while the US 'military high pitch' was even higher at A = 457Hz. What this means to the buyer of a vintage brass instrument is that it may not play in standard pitch. Alternatively, it may have been modified at some point in the past, which reduces its authenticity as a period piece.

As a general rule vintage instruments are a bit like vintage cars – fascinating reminders of our past and frequently beautiful to behold, but not at all the best models to learn on!

The right instrument for you

Every musical instrument dealer comes across well-heeled customers who can afford a top-notch instrument, even though their playing skills aren't very advanced. Often these are successful individuals who've taken up playing again after a break of some years. Typically they want to own the same horn as their musical hero. This isn't always a good idea. Although learning on a high quality instrument is a real advantage, many modern 'signature' models are built for performance parameters few amateurs have the technique or lung-power to deliver. These instruments are all but unplayable to the non-virtuoso. A better choice for most players is an instrument of smaller bore and lighter construction, which is why all brass instrument manufacturers offer such models.

The brass family

This chapter introduces the many instruments in the brass musical instrument family and names the parts of these instruments. These will be referred to throughout the remainder of this book.

As we'll see in the next chapter, all brass musical instruments work on the same basic principles, and much the same can be said of the materials they're made from and the techniques used to build them.

So why are there so many brass musical instruments, if they're basically variations on a theme? The most obvious answer is pitch; if you want to put together a brass ensemble that sounds full and rich, you'll probably want instruments in different registers, ranging from bass through baritone, tenor, alto and so on. On that level, a tuba is essentially a giant bass bugle with valves (or a bugle is a miniature tuba without the valves…).

But the relative pitch of each instrument is only part of the story. Factors such as 'tone' and 'timbre' form a major part of the difference between one brass instrument and another.

In terms of the notes they can produce, there's a considerable overlap between the trumpet, cornet and flugelhorn, for instance. However, for reasons we explore in later chapters the timbre is quite different.

Explaining these differences in writing isn't easy. The classic observation is that writing about music is like dancing about architecture!

LEFT A family of Vincent Bach trumpets (*Conn-Selmer*)

Orchestra

Superficially, little changes in the world of orchestral brass from one century to the next. Appearances, however, can be deceptive. Brass players are tending to be drawn to a bigger, darker tone than in the past, meaning that instruments once considered suitable only for jazz are starting to appear in orchestras. In addition, advances in materials technology have seen the subtle substitution of durable and consistent synthetics for organic materials such as cork and felt.

French horn. (*Paxman Musical Instruments/Nik Milner*)

Trumpet. (*Conn-Selmer*)

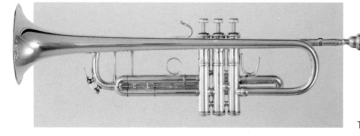

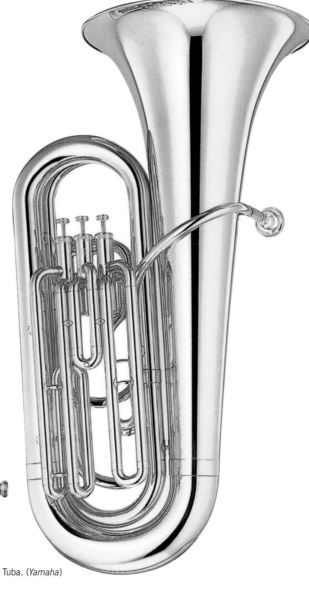

Tuba. (*Yamaha*)

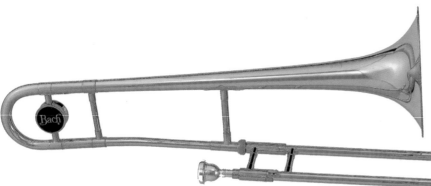

Trombone. (*Conn-Selmer*)

Brass band/marching band

One of the wonders of the brass band is that arrangements of such complexity – often with considerable light and shade – can be produced by a group of people pursing their lips and blowing down metal funnels. Anyone who'd never heard a brass band would surely never imagine that it could produce such a unique and evocative sound.

Soprano cornet in E♭. (*Yamaha*)

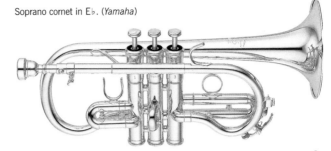

BELOW AND RIGHT:

Cornets in B♭. (*Conn-Selmer and Yamaha*)

The King cornet above is a typical US design, whereas the Yamaha cornet in silver on the right conforms to the European tradition. Notice the differences in the way the tubing is bent, especially the way the spout of the Yamaha cornet exits the valve block and enters a 'shepherd's crook' shape.

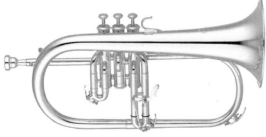

Flugelhorn in B♭. (*Yamaha*)

In the US especially, marching bands have a line-up that's different to a European brass band. In addition to unique instruments, notably the sousaphone, US variants, shown on the next page, are often configured so that the bells are pointing directly at the audience. Suffice to say, the results can be very loud.

RIGHT: Horn in E♭ (also known as an alto horn in the US, tenor horn in the UK and Althorn in Germany). (*Yamaha*)

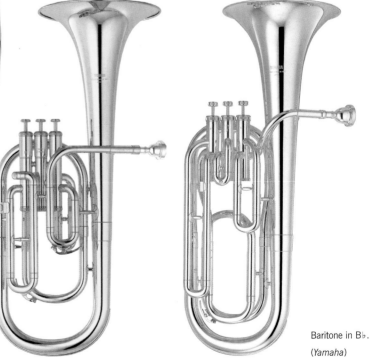

Baritone in B♭.

(*Yamaha*)

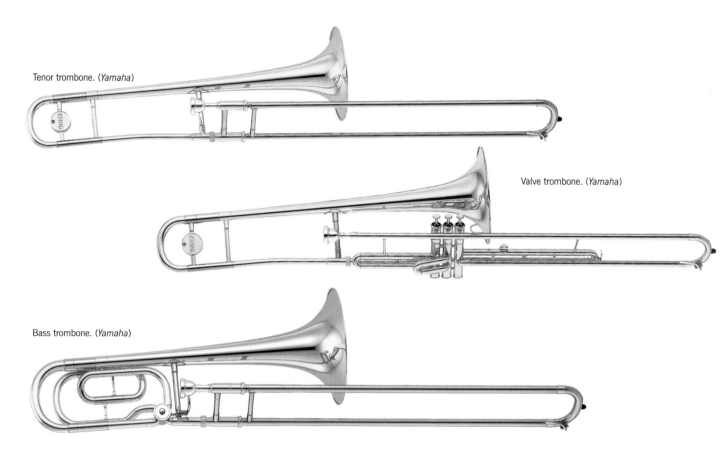

Tenor trombone. (*Yamaha*)

Valve trombone. (*Yamaha*)

Bass trombone. (*Yamaha*)

Euphonium in B♭. (*Yamaha*)

Tuba E♭ and B♭. (*Yamaha*)

Sousaphone. (*Conn-Selmer*)

Instruments that are typically based on piston valves in the UK, North America and elsewhere are often produced with rotary valves in mainland Europe. This typically applies to trumpets, but also tubas and other brass instruments. In addition, the geometry of the tubing runs is often different, forming a distinctive 'lozenge' shape, compared to the straight-sided oval shape found in many parts of the world.

Trumpet. (*Conn-Selmer*)

Mellophone. (*Conn-Selmer*)

ABOVE AND LEFT: US-style marching instruments with audience-facing bells. (*Conn-Selmer and Yamaha*)

Mainland European tenor horn and tuba with rotary valves. (*Gebr Alexander*)

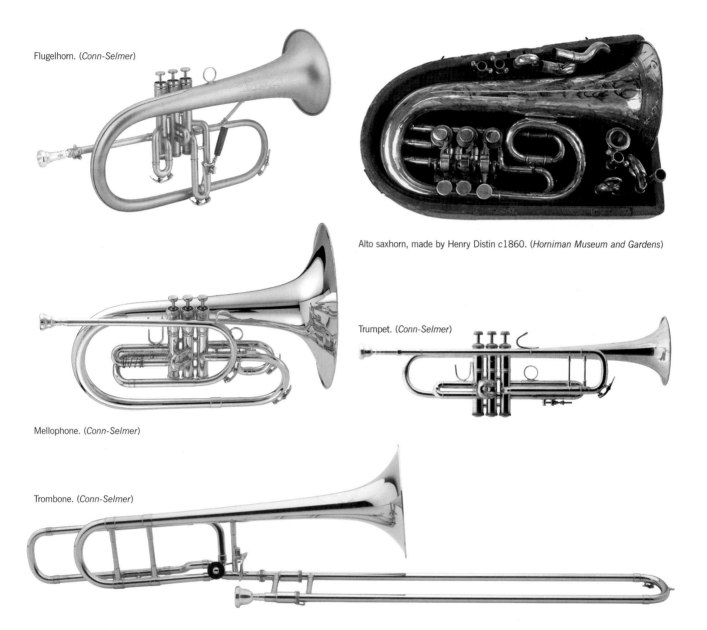

Flugelhorn. (*Conn-Selmer*)

Alto saxhorn, made by Henry Distin c1860. (*Horniman Museum and Gardens*)

Mellophone. (*Conn-Selmer*)

Trumpet. (*Conn-Selmer*)

Trombone. (*Conn-Selmer*)

Jazz

Of all musical genres, jazz is arguably the one where trends in brass musical instrument construction have changed most rapidly. Players have tended towards instruments and mouthpieces of heavier construction and bigger bores, leading to a corresponding increase in volume and projection. In addition, jazz players are generally happy to flaunt the differences between their horn and the instruments of the past, opting for new geometries to the tubing, radically different bracing techniques and deliberately oxidised or flamboyantly lacquered finishes, rather than traditional shiny brass.

Some lesser-known brass instruments

There probably never can be a 'complete' book of brass musical instruments, because there have been so many over a period of thousands of years and all over the world. Some have fallen by the wayside because they've been largely superseded by a better design. This is certainly true of instruments that use a series of crooks to facilitate key changes. While horns of this type continue to be made and used to play the music of their day, they've been largely rendered obsolete by instruments equipped with valves.

Then there are instruments that are perfectly good but

occupy a very similar niche
to an established instrument,
and consequently never quite set the
world alight. It's probably fair to include
the saxhorn family in the category. Patented
by Adolphe Sax (he of saxophone fame), the
saxhorn exhibits a pleasingly mellow sound.
However, its tapers place it in the
tuba/bugle family. Indeed, the tenor
version of a saxhorn is impossible
to distinguish from an alto horn/
althorn in any definitive way.

Bugle. (*Giles Whittome*)

Other instruments are limited
in application by the repertoire
that's been written for them.
As the name suggests, the
Wagner horn, or Wagner tuba,
was designed for that particular
19th-century German composer.
Sitting somewhere between a
French horn and a tenor tuba,
the instrument is essential when
performing Wagner's *The Ring
of The Nibelung*. Although other composers – notably Brukner,
Strauss and Stravinsky – have also adopted the instrument,
the total number of works remains small, so the instrument is
invariably played by French horn players who 'double' on the
Wagner tuba.

Wagner tuba.
(*Gebr Alexander*)

tonal quality. At the same time, horn makers started to offer
sets of crooks. While these offer nothing like the versatility of
valves, they do enable the horn to be played in different keys, by
introducing further lengths of tubing.

During the last quarter of the 20th century the hand horn
underwent something of a revival in interest. As a result, not
only is there a substantial body of music written for the hand
horn, but it is continuing to grow, as composers and players
rediscover the simple pleasure of working with an instrument of
such purity.

Valveless instruments

Although valves are a relatively modern innovation in the history
of brass musical instruments, it should not be assumed that all
valveless brass is obsolete. The trombone – of course – relies
for the most part on its slide to reach specific pitches, but there
are other instruments where the player's lips are almost the sole
device for reaching notes.

The most common of these is the bugle, one of the simplest
brass instruments and best known for its role in the military,
where bugle calls remain a form of communication. The bugle
is limited to the notes in the harmonic series (see next chapter
for an explanation) and all bugle calls employ no more than
five notes.

The horn as a musical instrument began life as the *cor de
chasse*, which is simply French for a hunting horn. In order
to expand the useful range of the instrument, players in the
mid-18th century started to use their right hand to adjust the
throat size of the bell, thereby greatly improving intonation and

Hand horn, also known as a
natural horn. (*Gebr Alexander*)

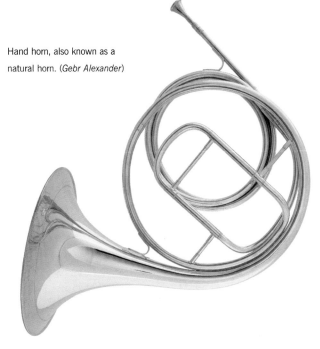

A selection of wooden Denis Wick mutes. (*Conn-Selmer*)

Mutes

No account of brass musical instruments would be complete without at least a mention of mutes. As the name implies, one function of a mute is to reduce the acoustic output. This may be as an artistic device, to enable the brass parts to blend more successfully in sotto voce passages, or simply to allow practice without attracting the attentions of enraged neighbours!

But another key function of a mute is to alter the timbre of the instrument. For example, it's hard to think of Miles Davis' signature tone without instantly also thinking of the distinctive sound of the 'wah-wah' Star Mute by Emo Harmon that Miles so often employed.

There are many different types of mute and the choice continues to expand. As will be noted in the Chapter *Modern Innovations*, Yamaha has succeeded in producing a practice mute that not only deserves the title 'silent' but uses digital electronics to enhance the practice experience. Here we list the most commonly accepted categories:

- **Straight** mutes are available for almost every brass musical instrument, from the trumpet to the tuba. Located in the bell by thin strips of cork to allow some sound to pass, the hollow mute is often cone-shaped and produces a somewhat metallic sound.
- **Cup** mutes perform a similar function to straight mutes but have a lip that goes over the rim of the bell, producing a more muffled tone.
- **Solo-tone** mutes are arguably a variation on a straight mute but are longer and contain baffles that absorb the lower end of the spectrum, producing a more cutting tone. This type of mute has also been labelled 'Clear-tone' by makers Humes & Berg and was mainly fashionable in the 1930s–50s.
- **Wah-wah** mutes have a solid ring of cork around the neck, so that all the air is forced though the mute. For added variation, the front of the mute features a metal cup, the effect of which can be set by sliding it in and out. Some players, notably Miles Davis, prefer to remove the cup altogether.
- **Buzz-wah** mutes originated with an improvised trick by King Oliver, who in the 1920s held a kazoo into the bell of his trumpet to achieve a distinctive tone. Commercial versions were soon produced to satisfy the demand from other players who wanted 'that sound'.
- **Bucket** mutes are unusual in that they clip to the rim of the instrument, which can make rapid attachment problematic. This type of mute muffles the upper frequencies, making for a softer sound.
- **Derby** or **hat** mutes were originally exactly what they appear to be – bowler hats. Of all the common mute types, hat mutes are unusual in that their position can be continuously manipulated to produce some distinctive effects. Because of the sound this produces, hat mutes are sometimes erroneously referred to as wah-wah mutes.
- **Plunger** mutes work in a similar way but are capable of producing an even more vocal effect. Although plunger mutes are sold as such in musical instrument outlets, they can be obtained from a builders' merchant or hardware store. The only material difference is that the version used by plumbers has a wooden handle, which is best removed for musical applications.
- **Practice** mutes vary considerably in their complexity, but all are designed with the same intention – to minimise the sound level from the instrument and so permit practice in environments where it would otherwise be unacceptable. For this reason they're sometimes known as hotel mutes, or whisper mutes.
- **Stopping** mutes are used only on the French horn, where they perform a very specific purpose – as a substitute for hand stopping. This is particularly useful for sustained passages containing low notes, which are very demanding on the player's technique. Most stopping mutes have the effect of raising the pitch of the horn by a semitone (half step). French horn players therefore regard the device as a 'transposing mute', as compared to the 'non-transposing' straight mute.

Nearly all mutes have an additional characteristic to some degree or another – they disrupt intonation. How pronounced this unintended effect is depends greatly on the skill of the mute maker, as well as that of the player.

Naming the parts of a brass instrument

Before learning how to maintain brass musical instruments, it's a good idea to learn the names of the constituent parts. For one thing, it'll make the rest of this book a lot easier to understand.

NB: Readers who are new to the world of brass musical instruments may be surprised to discover how many component parts an instrument can be reduced to, often using nothing more specialised than a small screwdriver.

That isn't to say that it's a good idea to take an instrument apart 'just for fun'. Once components such as valves are out of their casings, they're much more prone to damage. It's also important to realise that putting an instrument back together correctly requires more knowledge than it took to take it apart.

Ultimately, of course, we want to encourage readers not to be afraid of taking musical instruments apart; but you'll be quite a few pages further into this book before we get to that stage.

The parts of a trumpet

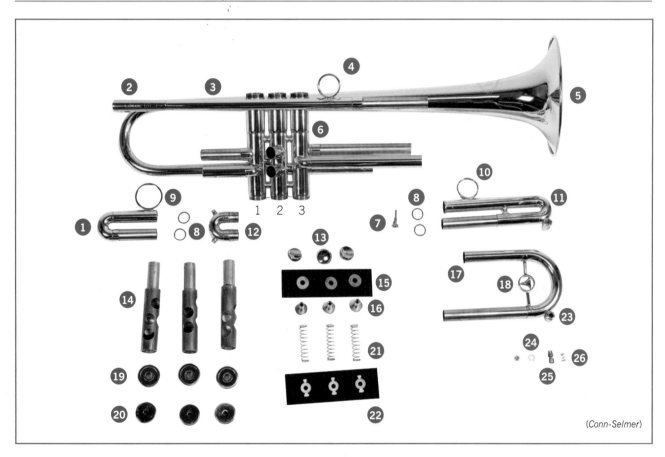

(Conn-Selmer)

1	First slide	8	Slide 'O' rings	15	Felt	22 Valve guide
2	Receiver	9	Slide ring	16	Valve stem	23 Water key
3	Leader pipe	10	Slide ring	17	Main tuning slide	24 Water key circlip
4	Finger ring	11	Third slide	18	Brace	25 Water key valve
5	Bell	12	Second slide	19	Top cap	26 Water key spring
6	Valve casing	13	Finger button	20	Bottom cap	
7	Third valve stop screw	14	Valve	21	Valve spring	

The parts of a trombone

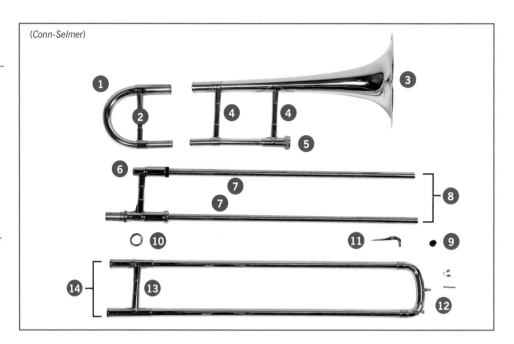

(*Conn-Selmer*)

1 Tuning slide
2 Counterweight (not found on all trombones)
3 Bell
4 Braces
5 Bell lock nut
6 Mouthpiece receiver
7 Rails
8 Inner slide
9 Protector for knob/bumper
10 Slide lock ring
11 Water key
12 Knob/bumper
13 Hand brace
14 Outer slide

The parts of a French horn

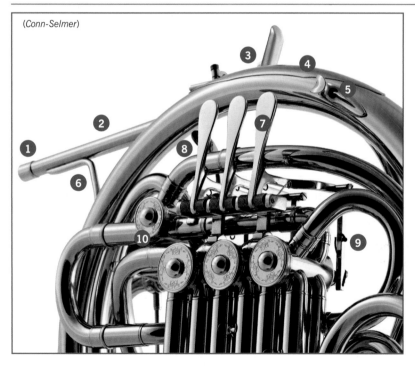

(*Conn-Selmer*)

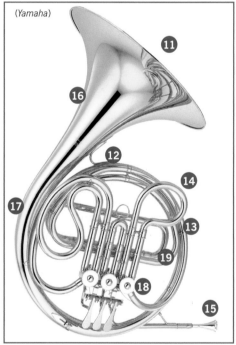

(*Yamaha*)

1 Chemise	6 Stay	11 Bell	16 Throat
2 Mouthpipe	7 Valve lever	12 Main-stay	17 Spout
3 Hand-rest	8 Thumb lever	13 Branch	18 Rotary valves
4 Guard	9 Linkage	14 Slide/crook	19 Main tuning slide
5 Finger support	10 Valve cap	15 Mouthpiece	

A cupboard of curiosities

At this point, the more knowledgeable reader may be thinking 'The brass family is bigger than this chapter suggests.' Indeed it is. Although there are larger collections of brass musical instruments, the 40-plus instruments owned by Giles Whittome provide a unique insight into the art of the instrument maker, from whimsical design ideas that never caught on, to breath-taking testimonials to contemporary craftsmanship.

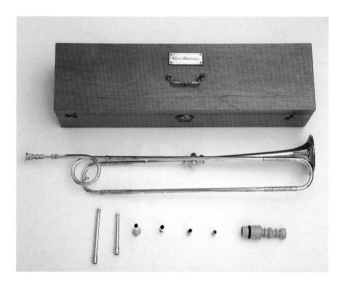

Solid silver natural trumpet – Whittome/Taylor, contemporary

This luxurious example is of a presentation natural trumpet. The crooks and tuning shanks are all of sterling silver, the bell is 100% pure silver and the garland, pommel and ferrules are silver, plated with gold to nearly ten times the normal thickness. The case is oak, lined with velvet, and the 18th-century-type mute is in olivewood. The mute raises the pitch by a semitone, so a tuning bit must be inserted to compensate.

The bell was made not by forming on a lathe, but by coating a mandrel with an electrophoretic release agent, then by electroplating until the desired thickness of 0.4mm was achieved. Electroplating with an alloy poses technical difficulties, but the pure silver used for this bell posed no problems and gives a purity of tone.

Cornet – Eclipse/Whittome, contemporary

This singular and striking instrument started with Giles' desire to design the perfect cornet, not just sonically, but visually.

'There were certain features which I thought a cornet ought to have. The first thing was a garland, which for some reason assists sound projection – that's the ring round the bell,' reveals Giles. 'The other is interchangeable mouthpipes. It's got three with different levels of resistance – high, medium and low – and one that takes a trumpet mouthpiece if you've got extended high register work.

'I wanted copper, because I love the sound of copper, and I wanted a trigger to operate the main tuning slide, so it didn't matter which valve you had down. It's got all of that, plus loads of bits and pieces.

'It plays like an absolute dream. It's also one of the most beautiful instruments I've ever seen. It's a lovely thing and it really works too. Instead of braces, we have snakes. All that was done for me by Eclipse.' (Eclipse is a brand name used by UK manufacturer First Class Brass Ltd.)

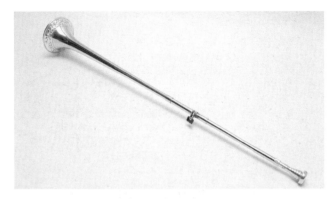

Post horn – Webb/Taylor/Whittome, contemporary

This is one of three fine ornamental post horns belonging to Giles, and he had a hand in its manufacture.

'The bell and the garland were made by John Webb,' Giles reveals, in reference to the renowned instrument maker, who recently donated his own collection of about 250 vintage and rare brass instruments to the Royal Conservatoire of Scotland. 'It was going to be part of a trumpet but I decided I wanted a post horn. Andy Taylor put on the other bits for me.'

Natural trumpet – Whittome, contemporary

This natural trumpet is one where Giles really made his own stamp as a maker, choosing to stay as historically authentic as possible. Readers wondering how a player and collector could gain the necessary skills should remember that Giles is also a top-flight gun maker, whose work changes hands for many thousands of pounds.

'I wasn't allowed any machine tools at all, so it was a question of hand soldering, hand hammering and what have you,' he says of his self-imposed discipline. 'For the bell, we had a mandrel and you start with a piece shaped like that [indicates rudimentary cone] and you hammer and hammer and hammer, until eventually it flares and assumes the desired shape. I must have hammered that bell 3,000 times.'

Natural trumpet – John Webb, contemporary

In addition to being struck by the great beauty of this natural trumpet, readers may wonder what the four round shapes are on the bow in front of the crook. As Giles explains, they are a solution to the intonation problems associated with valveless instruments, which by definition can normally only produce one harmonic series: 'There are two notes in the natural trumpet series which are out-of-tune, but by putting holes in the trumpet in certain places and uncovering them, just for those two notes, you can bring in notes from another series, which fill the gap.'

Cornet – Carl Boosé, c1856

'There's a story attached to this one. It was made by a German called Carl Boosé, who emigrated to England in the first half of the 19th century, and he was such a good musician that within about ten years he was bandmaster of the Scots Guards. He also made instruments, including this one.

'I restored it fully, with all the toys and bits and pieces in it,' says Giles, although he admits it was already a collector's dream in terms of condition. 'Even the lining in the case is completely original and unscratched. It's just like new.

'The extraordinary thing is, an article was written about that in the International Trumpet Guild magazine, and I got a letter a little later saying: "This was made by my great, great

grandfather; I am the sole surviving Boosé." And the letter was written from 100 yards away from where I practise every Wednesday in Long Melford [Suffolk, England]. I went to her house and played it to her. She was practically in tears!'

Soprano flugel – in the style of Cerveny

'It was probably made by Cerveny in Czechoslovakia, but there's no name or serial number on it,' explains Giles. 'Leigh McKinney, who runs Eclipse, has a Czech wife and he knows quite a bit about Czech instruments.

'It's a pretty little thing, this flugel, and a really rare bird. I've had dozens of these in my life and they've never played in tune, but this one plays in perfect tune, so I'm sticking with this one.'

If the finish on a brass instrument can ever be described as 'delicious', then the frosted effect on this one certainly fits the bill.

'They call that "scratch and bright". You wipe the instrument before plating with a 3M (Scotch-Brite) cloth, to scratch the surface, while leaving selected bits bright for contrast.'

G piccolo – Gustave-Auguste Besson, *c*1875

'You get professionals in here, and if I say "Which instrument would you beg, borrow, steal…?" if I gave you the choice, large number go for this one. G piccolos are wonderful for Bach cantatas in C and D. That was invented by Gustave Besson in 1875, and has never changed. Everybody says "What a huge bell for a piccolo", but that is frankly the reason it plays in tune.'

Compensating cornet – Boosey and Hawkes, 1898

'It's probably the most valuable instrument here, apart from the silver one,' Giles offers. 'See all the extra bits? You don't need triggers. It automatically retunes itself, which is quite astonishing.'

The compensating system was developed for Boosey & Hawkes by David James Blaikley in 1874, and was a considerable breakthrough, due to the improved intonation it made possible. So how does it work?

'Well, if you've got valves one and two down, the air's going a certain way. If you then press three, valve three is supposed to lower it a tone-and-a-half. But you're no longer working with the original length of instrument, you're working with that [indicates additional tubing]; so the tone-and-a-half that was appropriate for the original instrument is too little for the now longer instrument. So this system redirects air back through the first valve and, see, there are two third slides … and there are two first slides, so they introduce extra lengths of tubing when all the valves are used together.'

Four-valve trumpet – John Webb, contemporary

This instrument has been 'heavily reworked' by Giles himself. 'With the fourth valve you can play the ultra-low notes, like the Mahler low F – a perfectly pitched F, which you cannot play on any normal trumpet,' he adds.

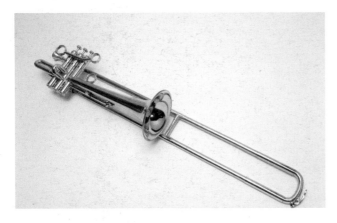

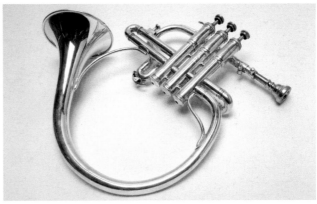

Slide trumpet – Whittome/Taylor, contemporary

The design is by Giles and the instrument was built at Taylor Trumpets.

'This is what the Americans call a Firebird, which is a trumpet-come-trombone; but, unlike anything the famous Maynard Ferguson ever made, it's got the full seven positions on the slide. I call it the trumpone, for obvious reasons.

Larry Ramirez, Ferguson's designer, tried and tried, and wound up with a telescoping slide – a slide within a slide, which, of course, is a wonderful recipe for air leaks and disaster. He made two and I think they were both junked,' says Giles of Ramirez's seven-position design. The original Firebird proved to be more enduring and was used at times by Don Ellis and James Morrison, as well as Ferguson himself.

'I've managed to crack it,' Giles enthuses. 'One is now in use by Steve Bernstein, the only person to make his living from just the soprano trombone. This is the only other one.'

Reverse bell cornet – Whittome/Eclipse, contemporary

'American marching bands had a big stint of "over the shoulder" weapons in the 1880s. They marched in front of the regiment, who kept complaining "We can't hear!", hence the reverse bell,' says Giles of the inspiration for his design.

'We butchered an old Irish cornet for the purpose. It was a Richards of Dublin cornet, which was picked out of a skip, and given to me. In the States they're nearly always rotary valves, but I thought one with piston valves would be nice.'

The finger buttons are fashioned from matching silver threepenny bits, each with the head of King George V.

Orpheon – Whittome/Taylor, contemporary

'That is a copy of a Besson orpheon, which is a bell-vertical version of the B flat soprano cornet,' Giles reveals. A clean, original example would be extremely difficult to find and would probably date from the end of the 19th century.

F piccolo trumpet – Whittome/ Eclipse, contemporary

'This was made to my design, with a third valve trigger and no stays, simply gold snakes. The whole thing is thickly plated in 24-carat gold. Allison Balsom likes it too,' Giles reveals. 'She was very kind; she said it was warm in the middle register. That's quite a nice thing to say about a piccolo, because they very rarely are.'

Valide – Whittome/Taylor, contemporary

'This is a valve-come-slide trombone. Valides – valide trombones – were quite popular in the States at one stage. You've got this great big slide sticking out at the front, so you'll see all the other slides point backwards, to maintain the balance in the hands.'

American jazz musician Brad Gowans is credited with the original valide design, a version of which was produced in limited numbers by the Getzen Corporation in the 1940s–50s.

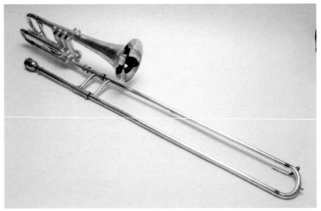

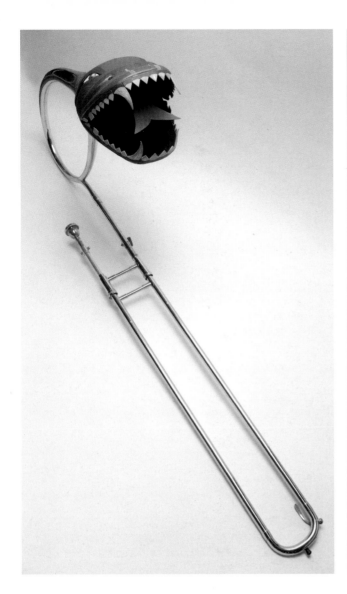

Making mouthpieces the prehistoric way

Giles makes his own mouthpieces, although he has a considerable collection from many makers. He prefers period-correct ivory when making designs with a vintage flavour and has an ingenious way of circumventing the legal and moral nightmare that would come from using elephant tusk – he travels to Siberia and sources ivory from woolly mammoths. Despite the fact the species died out in that region 10,000 years ago, the frozen climate of Siberia has ensured that many remain in ice as organic matter, rather than fossilising, as they would in more temperate climates.

So what's the material like to work with? 'Absolutely marvellous,' Giles enthuses, 'vastly better than elephant ivory. Superb, stable, non-chipping, non splitting...'

As for non-metallic mouthpieces: 'Oh, there's loads. I make them out of boxwood – that's a natural trumpet mouthpiece. I make them out of paduac, a Brazilian red hardwood.'

It should be pointed out that it isn't illegal to trade in antique ivory or mammoth tusk, as these are from animals long dead. It's trading in recent ivory that's illegal, because this will inevitably have been poached from an animal that has died as a result.

'You end up having these wonderful arguments with the Customs people,' says Giles. 'They say, "You can't bring in ivory." Actually, mammoth ivory is specifically exempted under the CITES rules (the regulations established by the Convention on International Trade in Endangered Species). It's like Monty Python's Parrot Sketch: "It's not endangered, it's bleeding extinct!"'

Buccin – Whittome/Taylor, contemporary

'The idea for the buccin was French, because their army urgently needed re-manning. As you can imagine, being in the army wasn't quite the honoured profession it had been after the Battle of Waterloo.

'So they used to send the bands out through the streets, with these marching up the front of the band. The idea was that the village youths – 14- and 15-year-olds, suitable for recruiting – would be so taken with the flapping tongues, dragon-head and the weird braying noises that they made, that they'd sign up.

'Whether it worked, I have no idea,' Giles concludes, 'but the buccin was written for by Berlioz in his *Messe Solennelle* of 1824, for example.

'I had the famous Jim Morrison play it, and he said: "Ooh, over the top of the stave it's everywhere..." The harmonics go sadly awry because the sound waves can't make out where the end of the bell is – is it the start of the mouth, or the end of the mouth? So it all gets a bit fuzzy when you get near top C.'

Twin belled cornet – Boosey & Hawkes, 1898

'The use of it lies mainly in the fact that you can have a mute in one bell and switch instantly between the muted and unmuted sounds,' explains Giles. It would seem that few players shared his enthusiasm, as this model is even more rare than 'echo' cornets from the late 19th century, which are examined in more detail in the chapter on the brass family.

However, examination of the Internet might lead readers to imagine there are many more of these instruments in circulation than is the case. Giles explains why:

'I take master classes at the Brass Band Summer School and I take this along. Dozens of quite well-known players have played it, and like having their photo taken with it. Then they upload them on to the Web to show their friends.'

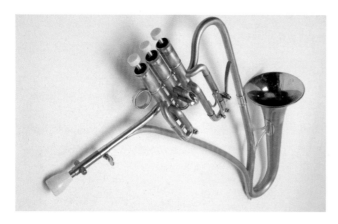

Normaphon Flugel – Taylor Trumpets, contemporary

'This is a perfectly standard flugel but just made in alto saxophone format. Again, mammoth ivory mouthpiece and valve tops. Paul Mayes – who's a brilliant professional trumpeter – said what he liked about it was you could get so close to the music!'

Slide trumpet – John Webb, in the style of 1830

'This is the original slide trumpet; it's a very usable instrument. The slide trumpet was the last gasp of the non-valve and non-hole instruments. It wasn't fully chromatic, but even so, Thomas Harper in the 19th century was always in demand for the *Messiah*, which he did perfectly on these.

'They're normally pitched in F and you put crooks in to bring them down in pitch. That's got an E♭ crook in at the moment. This particular design dates from around 1830, but you might be surprised to hear that in 1910 there were a lot of trumpeters who still played them.'

Trombugel – Whittome/Eclipse, contemporary

'This was put together by me and Eclipse just for fun. It's the valve section of a tenor horn, the bell of a trombone, and the tubing of a flugel. So I call it a "trombugel",' says Giles. Perhaps unsurprisingly, it sounds somewhat like a flugelhorn.

Soprano sousaphone – Jupiter, contemporary

'They made very, very few of them, then suddenly there was a large demand for them and an owners' club has sprung up. I was emailed by a guy in the States, who said, "Is it true you have one? Please tell me all about it," and so on.'

Jupiter – a brand that sits at the more affordable end of the spectrum – has also produced a soprano mini-trombone. Attempts to find information on either of these instruments online is somewhat hampered by the multitude of references to Jupiter soprano saxophones – as well as sousaphones and trombones – all of which form part of the company's current output.

German crookless trumpet – Carl Wohlrab, c1950

This trumpet is probably one of the finest examples of an engineering solution that sets out to eliminate something that was never a problem, and in so doing introduces a whole range of problems that are essentially insurmountable.

In order to eliminate valve tuning crooks, or slides, the Wohlrab solution is to employ valves of about the diameter of 12-bore shotgun cartridges. Through the use of internal partitions, these contain the additional tubing length that would have otherwise required slides. It doesn't take a great deal of imagination to realise that these valves must be devilishly difficult to manufacture.

For all that, Wohlrab was a high-quality maker of classical trumpets, rather than a deluded crank who imagined he knew something about musical instruments. His crookless design is by no means a disaster, as tone and intonation pass muster. Due to their relative rarity, the crookless design tends to sell for much more than Wohlrab's more conventional trumpets.

Pinto trumpet – Olds, 1970s

At the other end of the spectrum to the Wohlrab crookless design is the modular Olds Pinto, also briefly available as

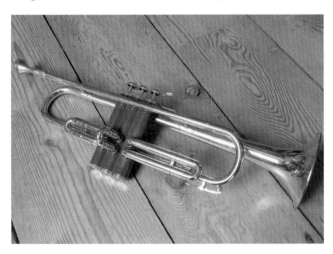

the Reynolds Ranger. As Giles explains, 'This is an amazing machine where the valves are completely interchangeable. You can dismount the whole trumpet – just undo two screws and the bell and leader pipe come off. The slides are interchangeable, everything is interchangeable. The whole valve section is plastic, but of course there are metal liners. It's much cheaper to make it that way. They made quite a few of them, but they're very rare now.'

R. Dale Olson filed the US patent in 1974 while director of research for F.E. Olds and Son. Not only did the valve block design eliminate some time-consuming manufacturing processes, but the modular nature of the horn also meant that it was easy to swap and discard any component which became damaged in the factory.

'It's quite nice to play, surprisingly,' says Giles, before adding

cautiously that 'Due to the odd arrangement of the valves, which all have to be the same, there's a protuberance sticking into the air column, which does slightly restrict the airflow.

'Olds claimed in their publicity material that the protuberance restricting the airflow increases the speed of the air, and therefore improves the tone, which is the finest example of making a virtue out of a horrible necessity that I've ever heard. It's a total lie. I don't know if anyone ever believed it. It's a wonderful example of what ad men can do if unrestrained.'

Alas, the design survived for no more than three years, killed off not because it had no merit but due to the chaotic environment at F.E. Olds, which was owned by a succession of parent companies.

Flumpet – Taylor Trumpets, contemporary

'As is obvious, this name is a combination of flugel and trumpet, the other choice being trugel, which doesn't sound so good,' Giles considers. 'It was always obvious that the tones of the two instruments might give rise to a blended sound, and indeed the instrument sounds smooth, lacking the occasional harshness of the trumpet but adding some of its flexibility to the flugel. This example benefits from a copper spout, which is well suited to the flumpet.'

Many people claim to have invented the flumpet but Giles considers the potential offered by the instrument 'so obviously desirable' that a number of makers could have developed the idea independently. He says he can remember his trumpet tutor, the great Jack Mackintosh – 'The Cornet King' – telling him that he had played on a flumpet music specially written for the instrument before World War Two.

The fundamentals – and some partials

Many people are uncertain about how a brass musical instrument works, or even of the differences between brass and woodwind. In this chapter we take a brief look at the history of brass and its design basics, then delve inside the instrument to find out what's really going on.

The earliest brass musical instruments weren't made of brass. That may seem like a contradiction, but it's true. What defines an instrument as belonging to the 'brass family' is the way the sound is produced. This is by pursing the lips and 'blowing raspberries'.

Technically, a brass musical instrument is sometimes classified as an 'aerophone', meaning that it produces sound by vibrating air. Some might prefer the term 'labrosone', meaning 'lip-vibrated instrument' – after all, the source of the vibration is the player's lips. Acousticians and scientific types sometimes use the term 'lip reed', while North American musicians understand the term 'brass wind'.

Whichever description you prefer, it's probably fair to say that we've firmly established which family of musical instruments we're talking about. Before we look at the function of various parts of a modern brass instrument, let's go back a few thousand years and see where the whole thing began.

Producing a buzzing sound through lip vibration is a simple idea and – as anyone who's watched a baby can confirm – it's one that comes along at a very early age. So the idea of making

LEFT If we could actually see sound vibrating the air it would look something like this. (*Based on a picture supplied by Conn-Selmer*)

The didgeridoo still played by native Australians is basically the same instrument as depicted in cave drawings.

Meanwhile, in Europe, people discovered that blowing down animal horns or conch shells made useful rallying calls in hunting and military settings, as well as for purely cultural purposes. Similarly, traditional variations on the fundamental idea of a brass musical instrument can be found all over the Asian continent, where they're widely used in religious festivals. Many of these are spectacularly embellished, often using an embossing technique whereby patterns are formed in the metal by hammering it with a pointed tool from the inside.

All brass musical instruments rely on some type of mouthpiece and they nearly all use a tapered tube (although some didgeridoos are cylindrical, and all valved instruments have some cylindrical tubing in them). That apart, the diversity of horn types – and the immense geographical distances over which they're found – strongly suggests that any number of our ancestors came up with the idea independently.

This early English hunting horn was used to create a rallying call. (*From the collection of Giles Whittome*)

Found in Tuscany, this trumpet dates from the Etruscan period, dating it somewhere between 400BC–200BC. (*The British Museum*)

an enjoyable noise by blowing down objects may predate humankind's emerging metalwork skills by thousands of years.

Possibly the earliest musical instrument is the didgeridoo, which can be seen being played by indigenous Australians in cave paintings dating back more than 1,500 years. Didgeridoos are likely to go back in time much further than this, not least because the manufacturing process is so simple. Some of the work is traditionally done by termites, which prefer to first eat the softer inner core of branches, leaving the would-be didgeridoo player to simply fashion a mouthpiece of beeswax and decorate to taste.

Of course, termites don't distinguish between didgeridoos and any other piece of branch. So although there were almost undoubtedly didgeridoos prior to the ones shown in the paintings, they would long ago have been reduced to dust by the same creatures that helped to fashion them.

Trumpets made at least partially from copper or bronze still exist from ancient Egypt. Two were found in the tomb of Tutankhamen, making them more than 3,000 years old. Others are clearly depicted in battle scenes dating from the same period.

Amazingly, the surviving Egyptian trumpets are still in playable condition, making them the oldest musical instruments that it's still possible to hear exactly as they'd have been heard all those thousands of years ago.*

---

* For the record, the famous 1939 BBC recording of these instruments is likely to greatly exaggerate their capabilities. The first thing bandsman James Tappern noticed when called upon to play the ancient trumpet was the lack of a mouthpiece. With no historic replica on offer, he substituted his own, which was undoubtedly better engineered than the original. However, the fact that a modern mouthpiece shank fitted the receiver of an instrument 3,000 years old is in itself remarkable.

This trumpet from Tibet is made from a human thighbone and silver. It dates from the 19th century. (*The British Museum*)

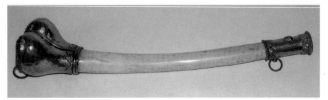

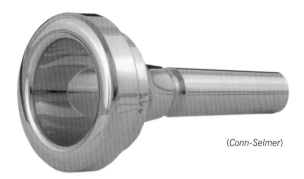
(Conn-Selmer)

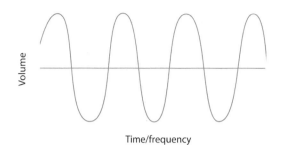

Fig 1: Sound waves are often depicted like this. In the physical world, the peaks and troughs on the graph are actually high and low air pressure.

What does the mouthpiece do?

Mouthpiece design is discussed at length in the chapter *Design and Manufacture*. For now it will probably suffice to note that the two most important functions of the mouthpiece are (a) to provide a supporting rim for the lips, so that the player can form the 'embouchure' required to produce vibrations at a specific frequency; and (b) to provide a small chamber that the player effectively seals with the lips, so that the only route for the air pressure is through the throat of the mouthpiece and into the leader pipe (or mouth pipe) of the instrument.

In simple terms, a mouthpiece that makes it easy to play the high notes makes it harder to play the low notes and vice versa. However, that hardly begins to do justice to the many variables there are in mouthpiece design, or the overwhelming significance of the mouthpiece to the player. Most players will happily try out someone else's instrument but they'll invariably use their own mouthpiece, because it's the one they feel comfortable with.

The importance of this physical interface between player and instrument is why it so often becomes an endless search for the Holy Grail of a mouthpiece that 'plays even better' than the last one. There's no such thing as the 'perfect' mouthpiece, although some will be considerably better suited to an individual's embouchure and playing style than others. Alas, there are players who spend years amassing hundreds of mouthpieces before coming to this very conclusion. (See how much money this book has already saved you?)

However, it's unwise to trivialise the importance of selecting a suitable mouthpiece, or having one made if the mass market is unable to offer a suitable one. While most students start off with a mouthpiece of generalised proportions, an experienced teacher or mouthpiece maker should be able to observe the signs that a mouthpiece isn't the best fit for a student, and recommend alternatives.

What's happening to the air inside the instrument?

Some people are misled by the fact that the player is blowing down the instrument, and so think that the resultant sound is somehow blown across the room to the listeners' ears by the air. That's not what's happening.

To better understand what's really going on inside the instrument, it's useful to understand how sound propagates in the outside world. Most people are familiar with the sort of diagram shown in Figure 1. Here, the more oscillations there are in the waveform left to right, the more vibrations there are a second, which is another way of saying the musical pitch would be higher. Similarly, the broader the waveform is top to bottom, the louder the sound would be.

Although that's certainly something like the way a single note would look on an oscilloscope, if you could actually see sound waves in the air they'd look more like Figure 2 (see previous pages). What's happening is that air molecules are being pushed together into areas of high pressure (compression) and pulled apart into areas of low pressure (rarefaction).

This tells us that sound isn't propagated by air rushing across the room. Rather, the vibration set up in one air molecule excites the molecules next to it, and so on, until the *sound*

A practical test

You can prove to yourself that the vibration from your lips creates areas of high and low pressure inside your instrument. If you take another look at Figure 1, you'll see that there must be some points where the pressure is equal to room pressure – the points where the wave is bisected by the straight line going through the middle.

Where those midpoints are situated within the tubing that forms an instrument will depend on frequency (*ie* how high or low the note is). You'd imagine, then, that some of those notes might have a zero-pressure point that coincides with the exact location of a water key, and you'd be right!

Try playing with the water key held open and you'll discover that some notes are completely unaffected by what should be a disastrous 'leak'. From this we can conclude that the air pressure inside the instrument is equal to the air pressure in the room at that point in the tubing.

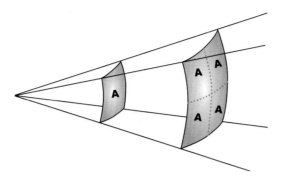

Fig 3: When the distance sound travels through free space doubles, it has a quarter of its original energy, because the number of air molecules it's vibrating is four times greater.

Fig 4: The way sound travels from a bell can be compared to the way light comes from a car headlight, rather than a table lamp.

wave crosses the room. Something similar happens if you wave your hand around in a bowl of water; the waves cross the bowl but the water pretty much stays where it was. (And when the wave hits the edge of the bowl, the wave bounces back, which is exactly how sound behaves in a room. As we'll see, the air inside a horn does something similar as well.)

Air is very good at transmitting sound. Depending on how dry the air is and how far above sea level you are, sound will travel about a mile in five seconds (343.2m a second).

By now you may be thinking: 'So I bet air inside a brass musical instrument behaves just like the air in a room.' To an extent you'd be correct, but let's introduce another fact about the way sound propagates through air.

Everyone knows that the further away you are from a sound source, the quieter it is. That's mainly because, if there's nothing in the way, sound propagates outwards in a spherical shape. If you take a look at Figure 3 you'll see how intuitive this notion is.

The further the sound wave is from the source, the more molecules it has to excite in order to keep going. As a result, the wave is dissipated, or, to put it another way, the energy is progressively diluted the further it travels. In fact the sound loses a quarter of its original energy for every doubling of the distance between the sound source and the listener, because the area it covers is four times greater. (This is known as the 'inverse square law'.)

But the air inside a brass musical instrument isn't in 'free space'; there's a solid barrier between it and the outside world, formed by the tubing. As a result, the sound pressure built up by the player blowing out through his/her lips has nowhere much to go but forward. Which is one reason why brass instruments are so loud! (Actually, the sound pressure doesn't just go forward, which is why we mentioned the water in a bowl.)

Figure 4 gives you a visual analogy for sound waves in free space versus inside a brass instrument. Imagine you have one 100W bulb fitted to a domestic table lamp and another one fitted inside a car headlight, with a reflector at the back. The table lamp will send out a soft light in all directions, while the car headlight will shoot out a beam all the way down the road.

The partial truth

It's obviously a priority for any player that the instrument 'feels' right and makes it as easy as possible to play. In a brass musical instrument, much of that feel comes from the backpressure, or impedance, presented to the player's lips.

This brings us back to the point touched on earlier that not all the energy in the system is going from the player's lips to the bell – some is actually going the other way in the form of what are technically 'counter-propagating waves'. These provide a kind of reinforcing 'information' to the player that he/she is producing the appropriate frequencies (*ie* musical pitches).

So how does that work? Well, the notes that a brass musical instrument of specific length can produce are limited to the natural harmonics that can be created by changing lip tension and air pressure. More lip tension and faster air produces higher notes, whereas less lip tension and slower air produces lower notes.

These harmonics are known to brass players as 'partials', and are created when the sound wave that forms the fundamental frequency sub-divides within the instrument's tubing. Figure 5

Fig 5: This visual representation of the harmonic series shows how the division of the standing wave of air divides into ½, ⅓, ¼ etc, corresponding to the musical intervals of an octave, a fifth above that, a fourth above and so on. No frequency in the harmonic series corresponds exactly to a musical interval and some are very noticeably 'out of tune'.

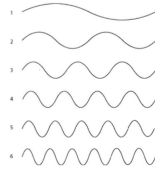

shows the partials being formed and the musical intervals that result. Figure 6 shows those intervals on a stave.

There's a certain amount of leeway either side of the exact frequency, whereby a note will sound but will be sharp or flat of the centre pitch. But these 'counter-propagating waves' aren't uniform in strength, they have 'peaks'. It's probably not such a surprise to discover that the feedback to the player's lips is strongest when the harmonic is an accurate division of the speaking length of the horn. Therefore, players can *feel* if the partial is forming correctly, even if they can't hear.

The family tree

It would be tempting to think that providing the partials are formed correctly, the notes must be in tune. Unfortunately, nothing could be further from the truth! For one thing, those partials are not quite the gift from physics to music that they might seem. As the panel called 'Bad-tempered brass' explains in more detail, some of the partials in the natural harmonic sequence are quite a long way off the corresponding pitches used in most Western music.

But some brass instruments are considerably more out of tune than others. This section divides brass instruments into two families and sets about explaining some of the intonation issues associated with each.

The traditional system for dividing up brass instruments described them as either 'cylindrical' or 'conical'. We think this is potentially confusing, and also technically wrong, because all brass instruments with valves have a certain amount of parallel-sided tube, which by definition is 'cylindrical'.

Arguably the easiest and most accurate way to understand the fundamental design differences is to look at the members of the 'horn' family on one side and the 'bugle' family on the other.

The horn family includes trumpet, cornet, French horn and, to a large extent, the trombone. (Although the trombone has a lot of cylindrical tubing due to its slide, the tapered sections are largely exponential.)

The bugle family includes flugelhorn, tenor horn, baritone euphonium and tuba – in short, most of the instruments found in a brass band. Although the 'tuba family' is also a recognised term for the bugle family, it's from the bugle that later instruments, such as the tuba, were developed. We prefer the term 'bugle family', because the tuba is basically a giant bugle with valves. It seems counter-intuitive to say that the flugelhorn is a soprano tuba! (In design terms, that's exactly what it is, though.)

Figure 7 illustrates the most immediately obvious difference between the two families. While the horn family has a modified exponential increase along its taper, the bugle family has a

Fig 6: The harmonic series as it appears when assigned to the nearest musical pitch.

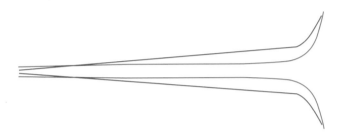

Fig 7: The horn (red) and bugle (green) families have different tapers. Theoretically, a horn has an exponential taper with a cylindrical section in the middle, while the bugle has a continuous, linear taper, with a flare at the end. In reality both these schemes are subject to design modifications to enhance performance, as well as the practical need to accommodate valves and slides.

Bad-tempered brass

For the sake of making some of the basic concepts regarding the intonation of brass instruments easier to understand, in the section called 'The partial truth' we discuss the harmonic series as if it were one and the same thing as the notes found in Western musical scales. In reality, they're different.

The Western chromatic scale has been modified into 12 equal semitones, which are slightly out of tune with many of the harmonics, especially the 7th but also 11th and 13th intervals. 'Equal temperament' is a compromise that allows, for instance, keyboard instruments to be played in all keys. In other settings, such as an a cappella vocal group, it's likely that equal temperament will be discarded in favour of creating harmonies that are 'spot on', rather than just close.

While most musicians are aware of intonation issues and work around them in whatever way best suits the musical setting, it isn't necessary to have a deep understanding of the underlying mathematics before appreciating the finer points of brass musical instrument design. We simply raise the issue because it's there – and because it means that musicians and musical instrument designers alike are engaged in a constant negotiation between the laws of physics and music as we'd like to hear it.

Figure 6 shows how the harmonic series looks when notated. In reality, some of the notes in the series – notably the 7th, 11th and 14th – are almost a quarter of a tone out.

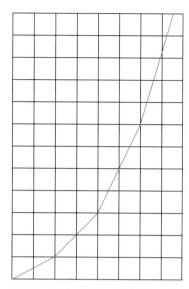

Fig 8: In theory, the flare of a horn is logarithmic. To put it a simple way, the amount of taper multiplies as you go along its length, producing the distinctive curve you see here.

straight-sided taper with a flare on the end. While a straight-sided taper is an easy enough concept to understand – for every increase in length, the tubing undergoes a constant increase in diameter – some readers may wonder what we mean by 'exponential'. An exponential curve is logarithmic, or, to put it another way, multiplies along its length.

One way to see this is to take a piece of squared paper. Starting at the bottom left, draw a line that goes right by two squares and up by one square. From there, draw a line that goes right by two squares and up by two squares. Then, from there, draw a line that goes right by two squares and up by four squares… You'll end up with a crude approximation of a horn flare.

All this is theory – brass instrument designers are in the business of making *musical* instruments, not *scientific* instruments. As a result their drive is to make their products sound and feel better to musicians – and that means bending

the rules! In fact, many modern designs challenge even the basic distinctions we've set out between the two brass families – to the extent that it's best to regard them as generalisations, rather than a categorical explanation of a specific musical instrument. Many of the adjustments made to the tapers in order to change the volume, tone or intonation of the instruments are too small to be seen. That said, anyone looking at a tuba should be forgiven for saying the bell doesn't look as straight-sided as our description of a giant bugle implies.

The other major difference between the two families of instruments is that the bugle, or tuba, family has the bulk of the instrument, wherever possible, tapered. The only parallel-sided tubing is found through the valve block, on the valve slides and through the main tuning slide. On a tuba the slides are often stepped in bore, so although they are of necessity cylindrical, one side is bigger than the other. Therefore, the continuous taper is maintained as far as it can be.

Instruments in the horn family have a distinctive feature in addition to the exponential-style bell taper. They have a lot more cylindrical tubing within their overall length. For instance, a trumpet is roughly half-cylindrical and half-tapered from mouthpiece to bell.

In comparison, a cornet is only about one-third cylindrical. A cornet is also approximately 1mm smaller at the start of the leader pipe and slightly bigger at the bell, whereas a trumpet is bigger at the start of the leader pipe and ends with a slightly smaller bell. Therefore the rate

BELOW: In contrast to the flugelhorn, the trumpet is a member of the horn family. Almost half its length is parallel tubing and the flare at the end more or less exponential. (*Conn-Selmer*)

RIGHT: As a latecomer to the family, the tuba is logically and technically a giant bugle. That said, it would be simplistic to pretend that the bell corresponds exactly to the straight-sided taper suggested by theory. (*Yamaha*)

Despite its name, the flugelhorn is a member of the bugle family. Note the almost continuous taper from mouthpiece to bell. (*Conn-Selmer*)

of taper is different. While these points of difference might not mean much to the non-player, they're essential to the character of the two instruments.

More partial considerations

This discussion of the two families brings us back to partials, because the horn family – with its exponential flare and cylindrical tubing – copes better when it comes to intonation. The length of cylindrical tubing actually makes the instrument more stable in the way it produces its partials. Conversely, a straight-sided instrument with little cylindrical tubing is extremely inconsistent in its intonation. This is why a flugelhorn is so hard to play in tune.

Examples of the difference between horns and bugles can be found in both musical and design practice. For instance, a trumpet player is likely to 'lip' some notes to adjust the partial to the correct musical pitch and may use a ring slide on the third valve, to temporarily lengthen the tubing to get the low D and C# in tune. A similar arrangement is often used on the first valve.

In comparison, a 'compensating' system is used for tubas, baritones and euphoniums, whereby an additional valve is depressed in combination with the main ones, so routing the air through extra tubing. This allows compensating instruments to play with accurate intonation in the octave below their open second partial, which much of the repertoire for these instruments demands. For the larger members of the bugle family, pushing out a relatively short slide with a lever simply wouldn't be compensation enough.

While it's often been said that 'the tempered scale and tapered tubes are not natural bedfellows', we don't mean to imply that horns are 'better' than bugles. As we've said before, these are *musical* instruments, not *scientific* ones. Part of the

Slide rings aid trumpet intonation.

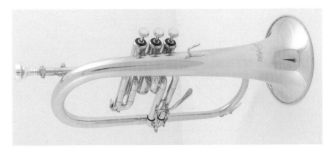

Flugelhorns suffer from many intonation problems, but without them they wouldn't sound like a flugelhorn any more. (*Conn-Selmer*)

musical character of some instruments comes from the fact that they don't play in tune. It's partly the player's dancing around the exact note that gives an instrument such as a flugelhorn its lyrical, almost vocal qualities.

Equally, it would be a mistake to imagine that modern brass design is necessarily moving towards a state of artistic perfection. Musicians working in an increasingly competitive, amplified environment have been pushed to play higher, faster and louder. That in turn puts the pressure on manufacturers to design 'high-performance' instruments where subtlety isn't high on the list of priorities. Many players have vintage classics they treasure and love to own, but as working musicians they have to deliver whatever the gig demands – and that means picking the right instrument for the job.

What does the bell do?

Most people grasp that the bell 'makes the instrument louder', but there's a more specific way of describing its action. In order to make sense of its primary function, we need to look at the instrument as a complete system, starting back at the mouthpiece.

Within the cup of the mouthpiece, the pursed lips are vibrating. Although the amount of movement is small, so is the cubic capacity of the cup, so the changes in pressure are large. To put it another way, inside the cup the air *displacement* is small, even though the pressure changes are large.

By the time the sound has reached the other end of the instrument, the situation has reversed. Now the pressure changes are small but the amount of air displaced is large. Without the full conversion process, the sound output will be greatly reduced. A simple way to demonstrate this is using a French horn with a detachable flare. Unscrew the flare from the rest of the bell and the volume drops dramatically.

In general terms, the bell helps to make the conversion from high pressure/small displacement to low pressure/high displacement as consistent as possible.

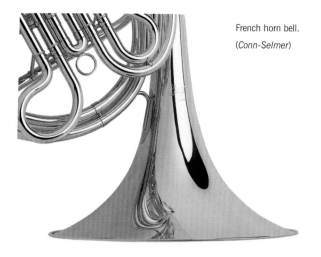

French horn bell.
(*Conn-Selmer*)

Trumpet bell.
(*Conn-Selmer*)

The role of the bell in this respect is similar to the role of a horn in a concert loudspeaker system. In both instances they control the directivity of the sound, as well as the ratio between the pressure level at the source (how hard the player is blowing across those lips) and the sound pressure level in the room (how loud the horn sounds to the audience).

However, this is a considerable simplification of the bell's role in a musical instrument. The bore of the bell and the material it's made from have a considerable impact on the volume and tone the instrument produces. The effects of varying these two parameters are discussed in detail in the chapter *Design and manufacture*. For now it's enough to note that the ringing of the metal resonator that's the tubing of the instrument is an important part of a brass musical instrument's tone – and the bell has a major part to play in establishing its 'signature' sound.

The bell also has its part to play in intonation. Due to its extended range, the French horn potentially has greater intonation problems than other members of the horn family, but players have learned to compensate by using their right hand to effectively modify the profile of the bell by changing hand shape.

Many horn players find that using a mute makes it harder for them to intonate accurately. The primary reason for this seems to be because the tactile feedback provided by the waves returning to the lips by correctly formed notes is at least somewhat disrupted. A scientific study conducted by Gregory Formosa at the Department of Mechanical Science & Engineering, University of Illinois, has shown quite convincingly that cheaper mutes – perhaps designed without taking that feedback effect into account – perform measurably less well in this respect. The inference is that the bell has quite an important role in the overall intonation of the instrument.

Another way of looking at this is that, for any given note, there's a point – or 'threshold' – in the bell taper where the tubing ceases to support the resonating air column and the remainder of the flare acts merely as a megaphone – *ie* it directs the sound, rather than aiding the formation of the note.

In his 1978 work *The Horn, The Horn*, Paxman Musical Instruments' designer for many years the late Richard Merewether describes this threshold as 'lying back towards the finger-hook for the middle-C, as written for F-horn, and constantly progressing out to the to the bell's mouth as higher notes are sounded. By the high written G, it has arrived at the player's hand.' Merewether argues that this explains the ability of right-hand techniques discovered in the 19th century to extend the usable upper register of the horn; the player is in effect reprofiling the bell to a narrower bore. This idea is wholly consistent with the fact that smaller bore instruments (and we're primarily discussing the taper of the bell here) are well centred and don't wander in pitch as much as larger bore instruments.

What do the valves do?

The first brass musical instruments had no valves. As a result, the maximum number of notes they could produce was limited to the 'partial' notes of the harmonic series. To make things worse, the higher up the harmonic series you get, the closer together they become, so it becomes correspondingly harder to hit the intended note. (We've also highlighted above the poor intonation of some partials.)

In order to give composers the greater selection of notes they craved, an early solution to this was a system of 'crooks'. These are additional lengths of tubing a player could add manually to the instrument in order to change its key. However, this was hardly a process to undertake between notes, so instruments still weren't chromatic. Rather than being able to play any note or scale, they were simply able to swap one set of limited options for another.

Some of the solutions to this problem were frankly ridiculous, from both an engineering and a musical point of view. While it's glaringly obvious to the casual observer that an instrument with multiple bells and a mechanism like a Gatling gun at its centre is never going to catch on, a surprising number of these monstrosities were the subject of patents.

One idea that appears to have some merit is the use of air holes and keys, rather like a saxophone. Although this scheme was employed on the now largely neglected serpent, a significant drawback is that the instrument was difficult to play. If you imagine fitting, say, a French horn with air holes and keys, you'll soon see what an incredibly complicated machine you'd be creating.

Only one 'pre valve' design for increasing the available range of notes remains in widespread use today – the slide. The sackbut and the Renaissance trumpet both date from the early to mid 15th century. Of the two, the sackbut has the larger bore and is probably the most legitimate precursor of the modern trombone.

The solution that stuck for most brass was, of course, the one that gives players the greatest agility – introducing additional

Disc valves, or 'Patent Lever Valves', were patented by John Shaw in 1838 but enjoyed only short-lived popularity due to their tendency to stick. Air-tightness was also undoubtedly a problem. (*Horniman Museum and Gardens*)

The serpent employed air holes and keys like a clarinet or saxophone, but the arrangement proved unwieldy.

With a continuous taper and no flare, neither intonation nor volume would compete with modern brass instruments. The serpent was invented in France around 1590 to play with church choirs. (*Horniman Museum and Gardens*)

Using Heinrich Stölzel's valve system, this J.H. Ebblewhite cornopean from 1835 is a precursor to the modern cornet. Note the way tubing exits from the bottom of the valve casings. (*From the collection of Giles Whittome*)

lengths of tubing through a series of valves that would spring back to their original position when released.

Labelling anything 'the first' is always a little dangerous, as someone could come along with an earlier example, but a gentleman by the name of Heinrich Stölzel designed an instrument with two valves in 1814. Stölzel was a professional horn player, and it's interesting to learn that his intention was not simply to render crooks obsolete – he hoped from the start to create a chromatic instrument.

Valve types by design

By far the two most common types of valve used in musical instruments are the piston valve, found in instruments including the trumpet, and the rotary valve. British readers will tend to associate the rotary valve with the French horn, but in Continental Europe it's commonly used on a wide range of

Piston valves can be found on trumpets and all of the instruments of the brass band in the bugle family. (*Conn-Selmer*)

Rotary valves are most commonly found on French horns but can be used on any brass instrument, as examples from mainland Europe show. (*Paxman Musical Instruments*)

Axial valves offer unimpeded airflow but are relatively bulky and heavy, so have been used almost exclusively on trombones so far. Note the unorthodox entry and exit points for the tubing on this Bach unit. (*Conn-Selmer*)

instruments, from the trumpet to such relative rarities as the Wagner tuba (described in the previous chapter).

Over the last 30 years a new generation of rotary valve has emerged – the axial free-flow designs. As their name implies, these offer unimpeded airflow regardless of the position of the valve rotor, which equates to a more consistent feel for the player. Due to their size, weight and the complicated tube layouts they demand, axial rotaries are used almost exclusively on trombones at present. But their radical departure from the classic cylindrical valve geometry hints at future applications. Detailed descriptions and diagrams showing air-flow are given for rotary, piston and the less common Vienna system in the chapter *Design and manufacture*.

Although each employs a different mechanical approach, nearly all valves have one thing in common: when in the up position the air passes straight through, and when in the down position the air passes through an additional length of tubing. This additional stretch of tubing is equipped with its own slide where practical, so that it can be fine-tuned separately from the main slide that tunes the entire instrument.

Valve configurations

Common to much of the brass family is a core arrangement of three valves, which introduce a tone, a semitone and a tone-and-a-half respectively. This basic arrangement may be supplemented in a number of ways. For instance, many French horn players prefer the double horn design, whereby a thumb-lever switches the airflow between either an F horn or a B♭ horn. In a full double horn there are independent slides for the F and B♭ sections, with the three main rotary valves of a 'double deck' design.

There are a number of other variants to the French horn's configuration, including the somewhat simpler compensating double design and the considerably more complex triple descant horn. The latter requires a three-deck valve. Some players dislike this arrangement because the resultant instrument is heavy, while others avoid it because studio sessions carry a 'doubling' fee for musicians who carry two instruments.

Not all brass is based on the three-valve format. For instance, there are French horns with as many as six valves, while some

of the bigger bass instruments can have five.

At the other end of valve configurations, the modern bass trombone is similar to a tenor trombone but has two valves, one pitched in F and one in G♭. When combined, these valves put the instrument into the key of D. The fact that two valves are currently the normal maximum on a trombone, combined with the way the weight is distributed on the player's shoulder, help to account for the success of the relatively large axial valves on this instrument.

In the past, single valve trombones were popular, with the valve adjustable to produce F, E or E♭. As most trombones are based around a slide, many don't have a valve at all, as is the case with most tenor trombones.

Other instruments with a fourth valve include tubas, euphoniums and piccolo trumpets. As mentioned earlier, the additional 'compensating' valve lowers the pitch by an interval of a fourth and is used to correct the sharpness of the valve combinations 1+3 and 1+2+3 (whereby 4 replaces 1+3, and

The whole story?

With the exception of those straight cornets used for royal ceremonies, brass instruments are coiled for the convenience of the player. Otherwise getting on the bus with a euphonium could be a very challenging experience!

Now, here's an interesting puzzle. If you were able to unravel all the instruments in the brass family and lay them side by side you'd soon come to an astonishing conclusion. The difference in length between the 'high brass' such as trumpets and flugelhorns and the 'low brass' such as the trombone, tuba and euphonium isn't half enough to explain the difference in register. We've chosen our words carefully here because the answer to this puzzle is that the high brass are 'half-tube' instruments, while the low brass are 'whole-tube' instruments.

Whole-tube instruments have a big enough bore relative to the tube length to enable the fundamental tone to be created. (By this we mean they allow an accurately pitched note to be played with ease.)

Half-tube instruments have a smaller bore relative to their length, with the result that the lowest note that can usefully be reached is the second partial (which can also be termed the 'first overtone').

This division between instruments isn't the same as the bugle and horn family differences noted elsewhere.

2+4 replaces 1+2+3). While it's possible to use all three of the main valves and the fourth, the increased range comes at the price of severe intonation problems. Again, this isn't the only scheme; on some instruments the fourth valve provides a two-and-a-half tone extension, allowing it to be played chromatically down to the pedal notes.

This brings us neatly enough to flagging up what might be regarded as the secondary benefit of valves. The primary benefit that valve pioneer Stölzel was fighting for 200 years ago was chromaticism – the ability to play the notes of any scale. But along with this came the promise of improved intonation. Many experienced brass players use alternative fingerings (ie valve combinations) when more accurately intonated notes can be found on a different tube length. This avoids the more troublesome partials.

For obvious reasons, the reliance on alternative fingerings is especially common on the instruments that can most benefit from it. We've already mentioned the larger members of the bugle family but should also add C, E flat, D and piccolo trumpets, along with the French horn.

The relative ranges of brass musical instruments

NB: We offer this chart as a general comparison of the range each instrument offers. In reality there's a significant difference between the normally accepted 'written' range for an instrument and its 'actual' range. Over the years improvements to instrument design and performer training techniques have greatly extended the usable range of many of the brass instruments shown here. As with so many areas of musical endeavour, performance standards regarded as extraordinary by one generation of players become merely the benchmarks for those that follow.

So to finish

The traditional finishing process for a brass musical instrument is created by rubbing the outer surface with progressively finer grades of emery cloth before buffing it to a high shine with an abrasive 'soap' applied by a soft but rapidly rotating cloth wheel.

While this is undoubtedly attractive when the instrument is new, a process of oxidisation will start to dull the finish. In itself this isn't especially detrimental to the instrument, but more serious corrosion can eventually eat through the thin walls of the instrument itself. How quickly this happens depends to some extent on the level of usage and whether the instrument is dried down after use. However, a major factor is the body chemistry of the player. Some people seem to have exceptionally acidic

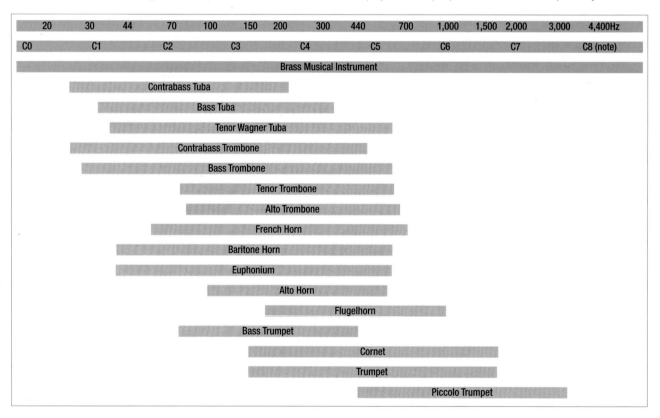

sweat, and we've come across individuals who can turn an instrument almost lobster pink just through prolonged contact with the brass.

Brass and military bands generally prefer their instruments to be silver-plated. This gives the instrument a tough outer finish. Although it isn't completely resistant to oxidisation, it cleans quite readily back to a high shine.

An alternative, or supplement, to plating is lacquer. The term 'lacquer' covers a number of formulations, of which the most hardwearing cure chemically, rather than by air-drying. Those that simply dry through the evaporation of a solvent can make a repairer's life difficult. On one hand, the more delicate lacquers scratch quite easily during de-denting procedures; on the other, they can discolour or even catch fire when a soldering torch is brought near them. This can escalate a simple soldering job into a full strip-down and re-lacquer. It isn't pleasant telling a student with a once-immaculate trumpet worth £150 that replacing the burned lacquer will cost more than the instrument did in the first place. (Strategies for minimising lacquer damage during repairs are covered in the section on 'Professional repairs').

The finish applied to brass instruments has no noticeable effect on the tone. Hence any suggestion that an instrument with chocolate-coloured lacquer is going to produce 'dark, smoky tones' comes straight from the marketing department. We're not saying the instrument *won't* produce those tones, just that the lacquer isn't the reason for it.

That said, appearance matters to a lot of players, so the quality of the finish is important. Certainly, anyone who hopes to sell a lot of instruments would be silly to ignore this fact. Brightly coloured lacquers have helped to attract a new generation of brass players, who might otherwise have decided that an electric guitar or a drum kit was a more exciting option.

Professionals are often equally concerned with the look of their instrument. Not only is there the issue of how it looks to them, there's the question of the impression it leaves on the audience. Jazz players are particularly image-conscious, although not all of them would care to admit it. Some prefer a cool, 'I've played this baby for a thousand years' look, which can be achieved by oxidising the instrument in a controlled way and/or using satin lacquers. Others prefer the hot-rod ethos of fancy graphics, or a luxurious combination of silver and gold plate.

In the end, musicians are individuals. If they wanted the same tone, the same feel and the same look as each other, there'd be only one trumpet, one flugelhorn, one cornet … and what a dull world that would be.

Jazz musicians often prefer the under-stated, worn-in look rather than anything so shiny it looks as if it's come straight off the production line. That said…

…every jazz musician is different, and they're certainly not all following the same dress code, as Cindy Bradley shows. (*Taylor Trumpets*)

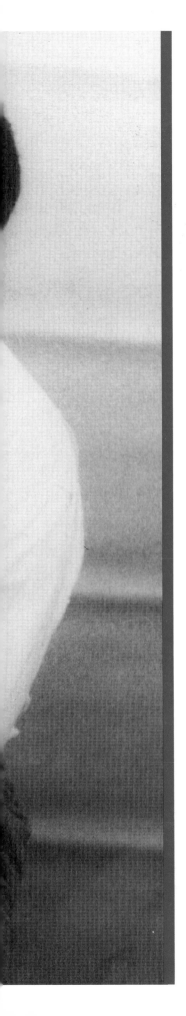

Iconic instruments

The last 100 years or so have thrown up a select number of instruments that collectors crave and players desire as a means of emulating their musical heroes from the past. There can never be a definitive list of these, but here's a personal selection.

LEFT. The most expensive trumpet in the world: Dizzy Gillespie's Martin Committee with upturned bell sold for $55,000.

ABOVE Miles Davis stuck with one trumpet throughout his career – a Martin Committee.

French Besson

All modern trumpets can trace their roots back to the French Besson models made from the 19th century to the mid-20th century. These instruments were directly copied by Elton Benge, amongst others, while makers including Vincent Bach and F.E. Olds have used the Besson design as their starting point.

The story of Besson brass musical instruments began in 1834, when a young Gustave-Auguste Besson rented a small shop in Paris in order to begin to apply what he'd discovered in the emergent science of acoustics to the design and manufacture of musical instruments. Amazingly, not only did the business grow rapidly but the Besson 'prototype mandrels' were still considered definitive by musical instrument designers more than 100 years later.

Due to demand, Besson opened a branch in London in 1851 and, as a 1958 Besson catalogue shows, a complete range of instruments came to be distributed in the US through C. Bruno & Son. These instruments were supplied not just to leading individual musicians but to entire bands and orchestras in universities and colleges.

By this time triggers on the first and third valves to aid intonation were a common feature on Besson trumpets. Remarkably, the valve guides used at this time were made of Teflon, a material virtually unheard of until it was popularised through its use as a non-stick pan coating in the 1960s. (Despite a popular belief that Teflon was developed by NASA during the space race, it is in fact a Dupont brand name for PTFE, a material discovered by accident in 1938.)

Equally, Besson's top-of-the-range trombones featured ultra-lightweight outer slides, as well as rotary valve change to the key of F, plus a slide to E. Again, these were very innovative features in 1958.

Besson alto and tenor horns were available with the tilted bells preferred by American marching bands as well as the upright bells on models described as 'English bore'. A similar diversity was available in its tubas, and the company also offered two models of sousaphone.

Although it's the French Besson trumpets that are arguably the most directly copied of the company's designs today, it shouldn't be forgotten that the 'automatic compensating' system it developed remains a standard feature in the intonation systems of modern brass band instruments.

As with many brass musical instrument brands, the history of Besson is a complicated one. Throughout the 1980s and until the late 1990s many – but apparently not all – Besson trumpets were made by the American maker Kanstul (or at least, workers from that company). However, the story is further muddied by

Mellow yellow: the cover of the Besson 1958 catalogue.

the fact that the initiative to re-create the classic French Besson designs came in 1983 from what was then the company called Boosey & Hawkes Buffet Crampon Inc.

(As an interesting historical aside, a 1958 Besson catalogue specifically showcases 'Hydraulically drawn, wrinkle-free tubing'. When one of the authors visited the now sadly defunct Boosey & Hawkes factory in London in the late 1970s, hydraulic presses were still absolutely key to consistent, high-volume manufacture.)

Probably due to the confusion regarding the origin of the later Besson instruments, many a fine horn has been sold for

An adjustable finger ring was another feature by 1958.

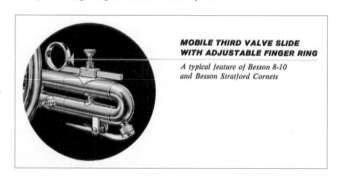

MOBILE THIRD VALVE SLIDE WITH ADJUSTABLE FINGER RING

A typical feature of Besson 8-10 and Besson Stratford Cornets

An H.B. Jay Columbia Cornet-Trumpet is not only a fine instrument to play, it's a looker too, as this example belonging to cornet expert Nick DeCarlis shows. Note the interchangeable leader pipes to accommodate trumpet and cornet mouthpieces respectively. (*www.vintagecornets.com*)

In the same year, Besson trumpets featured a first valve trigger, in addition to the third valve slide ring. This was almost futuristic in 1958.

what are frankly 'bargain basement' prices. The most desirable instruments are those made in France.

Harry B. Jay Columbia Cornet-Trumpet

Ask almost anyone to name the instrument played by Louis Armstrong and they will reply 'trumpet' without a moment's hesitation. However, the answer is only partially correct, because he actually began his career playing cornet, and only switched to trumpet in the late 1920s. When Armstrong landed a prestigious job playing cornet on a riverboat in the early 1920s he was able to afford a truly fine instrument, so he bought a Harry B. Jay Columbia Cornet-Trumpet model.

The choice of model was probably significant to Armstrong's development because the model designation derives from the fact that it was supplied with interchangeable leader pipes – one suitable for a cornet mouthpiece and the other for a trumpet mouthpiece. It has been speculated that Armstrong made the switch to a trumpet mouthpiece on the H.B. Jay, then made a permanent switch to trumpet when he discovered the extended upper register now available to him.

These instruments remain reasonably collectable, although not to the extent of the Louis Armstrong signature trumpet. As an aside, it's sometimes assumed that 'Columbia' is part of the

unique model designation, whereas the word actually appears on all H.B. Jay instruments, including low brass. Given that the instruments were made in Chicago, we may never know why.

Selmer Louis Armstrong Special trumpet

Launched in 1933, this model is essentially the same as the Selmer Challenger that Louis Armstrong had started using the year before, but renamed and with fancy engraving to help

The Selmer Louis Armstrong is essentially a fancy version of the Challenger, but as player associations go it doesn't get much better than this 1933 model. (*From the collection of Richard Church*)

Another very similar model is the Selmer Nat Gonella Special. The one seen here has been lovingly restored. (*From the collection of Marc Caparone*)

Whether it was really the work of several players, or designed by one man alone, the Martin Committee trumpet is almost revered for its dark, smoky tone.

RIGHT Close-up of a Gonella Special bell from a fine example of the trumpet belonging to Chris Tyle, who played with Nat Gonella on occasion. (*http://tyleman.com*)

the maker capitalise on the association. Nonetheless, this Selmer is an extremely significant horn, as it accurately represents both the vehicle Louis used to drive the trumpet to hitherto unheard-of heights and the aspiration of a generation of players who would follow in his footsteps.

Today, an original Henri Selmer Louis Armstrong Special in good condition is a collector's piece with a high price tag. For players with slightly less-deep pockets, but a hankering for the authentic tone, it's worth knowing that Selmer also offered a similar horn named the Nat Gonella Special in honour of the Louis Armstrong-inspired trumpeter, bandleader and singer from England. These tend to command a little less in the marketplace.

Martin Committee trumpet

First produced in the 1940s (but predated by the Handcraft Committee, which appears in a Martin catalogue in 1938), the most sought-after of Martin trumpets derives its name from the 'committee' appointed to contribute to its design. Eminent names on the committee included Elden Benge, Foster Reynolds, Vincent Bach and Renold Schilke, although Schilke would later claim that he alone actually designed the instrument.

Many great jazz trumpeters have favoured the Martin Committee. This includes Miles Davis, who continued to play a Committee throughout his varied and innovative career. Chet Baker, Al Hirt and Maynard Ferguson are all associated with the Martin Committee, but the most universally recognised example

undoubtedly belonged to the legendary Dizzy Gillespie, who played a Committee with a specially upturned bell from 1954 (as well as King instruments, among others).

By Gillespie's own account, his trumpet first gained an upturned bell due to an accident in 1953, after two dancers bumped into the instrument when it was on its stand. The jazz legend apparently liked the sound, and so became the player of the most distinctive horn in the history of music. However, British journalist Pat Brand later claimed that Gillespie had tried out a trumpet with an upturned bell in England as early as 1937. Although he is mainly associated with Martin instruments, Dizzy also played a King Silver Flair with upturned bell from 1972 and had played King Super 20 trumpets since 1947. He was given a Schilke in 1982. Dizzy's unique Committee was sold at a Christies auction in 1995 for $55,000.

The most valuable Martin Committee trumpets are those with serial numbers between 140,000 and 210,000. Depending on whose date estimates you believe, this equates approximately to the years 1940–58. However, this calculation is somewhat contradicted by the observation that players generally believe the instruments declined in quality after 1956.

Martin was to repeat the Committee concept for trombones in the late 1930s, when it appointed nine players to the committee that helped to define the model it released in 1939. This was a few years after the same concept had been applied to the Martin Committee range of saxophones.

After several changes of ownership, Conn-Selmer eventually acquired the Martin brand in 2004, but production ceased in 2008.

Vincent Bach Stradivarius trumpet

An eminent orchestral trumpeter in his own right, Vincent Bach was virtually forced into mouthpiece making after a botched 'improvement' by a repairman rendered his own mouthpiece unplayable.

After a period of remodelling existing mouthpieces and making some of his own, Bach started mouthpiece production from his own premises in 1918. Bach trumpets followed in 1924. They were well received, and it was apparently due to players referring to them as 'a real Stradivarius of a trumpet' that led to the adoption of the name as a brand shortly thereafter. (The trademark application was filed in 1925.)

Unlike some of the instruments we've highlighted in this chapter, the widely respected Bach Stradivarius range contains many variants and is associated with a great number of leading players in both the classical and jazz fields.

After approximately 40 successful years in the musical instrument business, Vincent Bach sold his company to Selmer in 1961, when he was 71 years old. The company continues to follow and develop Bach's original designs, while his mouthpieces essentially created a standardised set of dimensions by which other mouthpieces are gauged today.

Rightly or wrongly, it's the Bach trumpets that were made in New York before production moved to Indiana in 1965 that are the most highly regarded, and this is reflected in the price they command today. (Production at the Indiana plant suffered severe setbacks, notably a three-year strike that started in 2006 and saw only around a third of the original workers return when it ended.)

However, from a collector's point of view it's of critical importance in which New York location a Bach trumpet was made. The company moved from New York City in 1953 to Mount Vernon, New York. It's the trumpets made in New York City that are regarded as the crème de la crème.

As an approximate guide, Bach trumpets bearing a serial number lower than 11,000 were probably made in New York City, but readers are advised to

Vincent Bach (right) discussing manufacturing detail. (*Conn-Selmer*)

learn considerably more about the distinguishing features of these instruments before purchase. (Identifying totally original instruments is made harder by the fact that during World War Two the Bach company was forced to 'mix and match' components in response to a much reduced parts inventory. It takes experience to tell a trumpet that left the factory with parts from more than one model, as opposed to one that's been assembled at a later date.)

The third Bach factory, which was based in New York City from 1928 to 1952. (*Conn-Selmer*).

King Silver Tone/Silver Sonic trombones and trumpets

While many manufacturers started out making trumpets and only branched out into trombones as part of a general diversification, trombones were central to the H.N. White Co product range from the very start. Indeed, it is said that Henderson N. White personally made the slide on every trombone the company sold from 1894 to 1908.

'King' only became a brand after it appeared on bells as 'The King' on H.N. White's instruments. (*Conn-Selmer*)

His design collaborator was a Cleveland trombone player by the name of Thomas King, and Henderson engraved the earliest bells with the words 'The King' as a tribute to the local player. So it was that King became a brand of trombone, trumpet, and soon a whole range of brass musical instruments. (The company later diversified into woodwind, then strings, and gained something of a reputation for the quality of its double basses before selling this division to the Kay Bass Company in 1965.)

As this image from 1940 illustrates, H.N. White had grown by that time into a large and successful instrument maker. (*Conn-Selmer*)

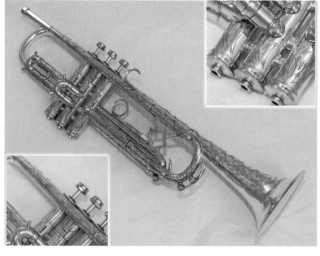

In the second half of the 1920s H.N. White introduced sterling silver bells to its trombones, achieving enhanced tone, with greater clarity, along with a generally more pleasing quality. With their elaborate engravings, these vintage Kings were also arguably some of the best-looking bells ever produced. The Silver Tone bell became available on many instruments in the King line-up but was rebranded Silver Sonic in 1950.

Silver-belled King instruments generally remain eminently collectable, not just because they're beautiful but

King Artist No 2 Silver Tone Liberty trumpet, 1938. (*H.N. White Company LLC*)

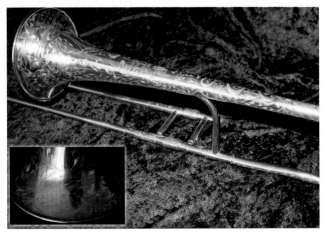

King Artist Special trombone, fully engraved, 1920–38. (H.N. White Company LLC)

also because they're very playable instruments. This applies to King saxophones as well as trumpets and trombones.

As noted elsewhere, legendary trumpeter Dizzy Gillespie played a King Silver Flair trumpet from 1972 and throughout the 1980s. This instrument was subsequently presented to the Smithsonian Institute, where it is on display.

Although associated with many players, the King Silver Tone trombone is notable as the instrument of choice for bebop innovator J.J. Johnson, arguably the first player with sufficient speed and articulation to bring the trombone to this style of music. An immensely influential player, J.J.'s career spanned from the 1940s until the late 1990s, although he was better known as a composer of film music during the 1970s and '80s. He died in 2001.

Today H.N. White King trombones are still played in bands all over the world. Following Henderson's death in 1940, his wife and daughter ran the business successfully for 25 years before selling it in 1965. Today the brand is part of the Conn-Selmer group.

Olds Recording trumpet

The date on which Frank Ellsworth Olds made his first brass musical instrument is apparently lost to time, but it was almost certainly a trombone. A patent number that appears on early Olds trombones can be dated to 1912, giving us the first definite point in time.

By 1928 experimental work on a trumpet had begun, but Frank was never to see it go into production, as he died suddenly. It was under his son Reginald's leadership that the company produced its first trumpets the following year.

During the 1930s Olds produced many highly regarded trumpets, of which the most iconic is arguably the Recording model we're highlighting here. Players who own an Olds Recording trumpet frequently comment on the many styles of music to which the instrument is suited and often express the opinion that if it's only possible to own one trumpet, this is the one to have.

It seems likely that the Recording model was one of the later additions, which made the timing of its launch unfortunate, since production at Olds and other musical instrument makers across the US was all but halted by World War Two.

By the early 1970s F.E. Olds & Son was part of the giant musical instrument conglomerate CMI, owners of famous brands including Gibson and Epiphone guitars. In 1979, having failed to find a buyer at an acceptable price, CMI decided to shut down the Olds factory and sell off the assets. In so doing the company inadvertently ensured that the Olds Recording trumpet would become one of the most sought-after and treasured trumpets in the world.

Buyer beware! After this time the Olds name was sometimes used on instruments imported into the US. These are generally held to be of much lower quality and their value today would be a fraction of the 'real thing'.

This entry in a 1947 Olds catalogue makes it clear that the Recording model is aimed at players working in the motion picture industry.

Although it's the 'Ladyface' saxophones that are most commonly found, examples of brass with this distinctive engraving includes trumpets and even sousaphones.

Conn 'Ladyface'

Unlike our other iconic instruments in this chapter, the 'Ladyface' description refers to a style of engraving, rather than a specific model. In fact it doesn't even define a specific musical instrument, as Ladyface engraving can be found on period trumpets, trombones and saxophones.

Although Conn instruments were frequently adorned with an attractive engraving, it's the ones that feature a lady which command the best prices (in much the same way that a pretty woman is a popular subject for a tattoo, or the decorative artwork on a hot rod). However, there are other factors that determine how collectable a Ladyface instrument might be.

Some of the engravings were originally quite crudely executed, while others have more artistic appeal. (Generally speaking, the ones from the late 1930s and 1940s are the most finely done, whereas by the 1960s many had taken on what can be most kindly described as a level of abstraction.) In addition, any unlacquered bass instrument is likely to have had the engraving eroded and softened by decades of cleaning, and this will also affect value.

Oddly enough it's the Ladyface instruments that look clean and clear that are most sought after, even if they no longer play particularly well. To an extent they've become collectable and 'iconic' beyond their practical value as musical instruments.

Couesnon flugelhorn

A particular favourite of American jazz trumpet players in the 1950s, the Couesnon flugelhorn remains a desirable instrument today, due to its sweet tone. Many players assume that Couesnon, a French company, is now defunct. That isn't so, but it's fair to say it's seen a considerable decline in its fortunes since 1911, when it employed around 1,000 workers and occupied 11 separate manufacturing units.

The origins of the company go all the way back to 1827 but the Couesnon family took over in 1883, by which time the manufacturer had already established a good reputation for its percussion and woodwind, as well as brass. The company continued to grow in reputation and stature, winning many awards and exporting extensively into the US, often under the brand of local musical instrument retailers, or distributors.

By the 1930s Couesnon was such a prolific supplier of musical instruments to the massive marching band market in its native France that it almost enjoyed a monopoly at the high-quality end of the market. (Oddly, its trumpet factory in Paris was located next door to the F. Besson trumpet factory, and it must be said that offerings from the two makers are difficult to tell apart.)

The music scene in the 1950s and '60s was markedly different to the pre-war years and it's at this point that the Couesnon story takes a distinct downturn. Despite its best efforts to attract orchestral and jazz players, the Couesnon brand failed to gain any significant market share, so as the marching band market dwindled so did the maker's fortunes.

This is a relatively 'late' example of the flugelhorn, dating from 1965, by which time Couesnon's fortunes were on the wane.

By the 1960s the company was effectively breaking up, as factories were sold off in the face of falling revenue. Worse was to come in 1968, when a fire badly damaged its main factory, destroying not only a key part of its manufacturing capability but also historic records regarding models, serial numbers and the like.

The once lucrative US export market was all but closed to Couesnon in 1978, when major musical instrument manufacturer Gretsch (today operating under the umbrella of Fender Musical Instruments Corporation) cancelled its distribution agreement.

Since 1999 the Couesnon name, factory and remaining tooling has belonged to a small family-owned company called PGM, which started out in the drum-making business. PGM Couesnon – as the company is now known – has around 25 employees and makes only brass band instruments. This includes three models of flugelhorn.

At the time of writing the flugelhorns are available in small numbers in several countries including the US but, as they're handmade, there's a waiting period of a few months. When jazz players first realised the potential of Couesnon flugelhorns they were easy to find, and could honestly be regarded as 'cheap'. Today they're sought-after, and prices for truly playable examples have risen, although they're still affordable compared to the more modern horns aimed at professional players.

Double bell euphonium

Almost uniquely in this chapter, we're heralding this instrument as iconic, without specifying a brand. Although many top makers offered a double bell euphonium at one time, they're today something of a curio and reasonably collectable, regardless of which maker's name appears on the bell.

A particularly attractive example was offered by N.H. White under the King brand. The company's brochure of 1932 explains: 'The double bell euphonium gives the player two horns in one. The small bell horn has much of the trombone tonal character, while the larger has the true baritone voice.' (These are, perhaps, slightly curious claims, in that the baritone has a predominately cylindrical bore whereas the euphonium has a larger, predominately conical bore. Equally, players have expressed the opinion that the smaller bell sounds more like a baritone, or perhaps a B flat tenor horn than a trombone – which is perhaps not surprising, given that it has almost nothing in common with a trombone.)

In addition to providing tones appropriate to low and high registers, the two bells can also be used for special effects, as with the echo cornet featured elsewhere in this chapter.

Double bell euphoniums were popular in the early 1900s. This example was made by Frank Holton and belongs to Gerard Westerhof.

Innovative though the idea was, it was no cheap gimmick. No one seems to know when the first King double bell euphonium was made but it can certainly be seen in the N.H. White catalogue of 1911, and a very much refined version was still ostensibly in production in 1965; but demand is likely to have been minimal by that time, as it had substantially fallen from favour.

The C.G. Conn company is credited with producing the first double bell model in the 1880s and it was well received by bandleaders of the time. Although he was not the first to adopt it, John Philip Sousa is probably today the best-known composer and conductor to have favoured the instrument. (As an historic aside, founder Charles Gerard Conn was rather fond of producing unusual instruments and made the first sousaphones for Sousa's band before transferring his attention to oddities, including the largest horn in the world – approximately 10m in length – as well as the largest drum.)

Other manufacturers to have offered a double bell euphonium include Holton, York, Buescher and Besson, although the last are exceptionally rare. In terms of value, any in playable condition will be at the top of the pile, but a five-valve Conn would probably be the most desired (these being a four-valve configuration, with a diverter valve for the bells).

This handsome Lehnert echo cornet dates from around 1895 and comes from the collection of Wayne Collier. (*Nick DeCarlis, www.vintagecornets.com*)

Echo cornet

As with other double bell instruments, the first echo cornets date from somewhere around 1880. At this remove it's probably impossible to say who built the first example, but F. Besson is a good contender. There are also surviving examples from Boosey & Sons, Brown & Sons, Conn, Courtois, Holton and

Engraved instruments don't come much prettier than this late 19th-century Higham echo cornet. (*Nick DeCarlis, www.vintagecornets.com*)

others. Other makers certainly featured an echo cornet in their catalogues but it's uncertain whether they had any takers, given that it has always been a somewhat specialist instrument.

No cornet maker is likely to have been intimidated by the prospect of an unexpected order for such an instrument, as the cornet is basically as standard but with an added diverter valve for a smaller bell with an integral mute, the effect of which is not unlike playing through the classic Harmon mute. The combination of reduced volume and a more subdued tone from the second bell makes for quite a convincing repeat, or echo effect.

There are minor variations on the theme: most have the muted bell facing forwards and most allow the muted echo bell to be detached when it isn't needed (which, to be honest, is most of the time). Probably because of the somewhat limited application for this instrument, the manufacture of echo trumpets was pretty much over by 1920 and it's unlikely in this age of digital effects that there will be a mass revival. Nonetheless, it remains a unique and strangely affecting instrument that almost any cornet player would like to own.

Jazzophon trumpet

One look at this instrument tells you exactly why you'd want one – visually, it's cooler than an art deco cocktail shaker with ice in it. As a musical instrument it's probably not the most practical

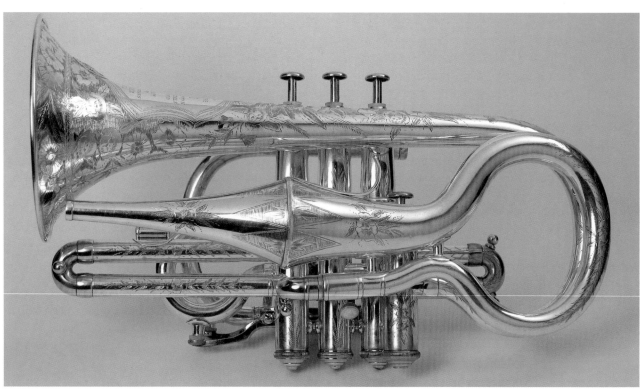

Cooler than a cocktail: this Wunderlich-branded Jazzophon has a trigger-activated wah-wah mute. (*From the collection of Gerard Westerhof*)

Rarer than rocking horses: the Normaphon is even harder to find than the double-belled Jazzophon. This alto Normaphon dates from around 1926, and was patented by Richard Heber, but sold by C.A. Wunderlich. (*From the collection of Gerard Westerhof*)

choice, which accounts for why even the players of the 'jazz age' couldn't bring themselves to buy it in any significant numbers.

Although stylistically the Jazzophon owes much to the saxophone, it's essentially the trumpet version of an echo cornet but dressed for a wild night at The Savoy. It has two bells, of which one is 'normal' and the other is fitted with a trigger-activated wah-wah mute.

As with any engineering solution that creates more problems than the apparent limitations it sets out to solve, the Jazzophon was ultimately destined to a footnote in history – but what a stylish-looking footnote that is.

Surviving examples of the Jazzophon from around 1930 can be found branded C.A. Wunderlich, but that was probably a distributor, rather than its maker. Others are often unbranded. Finding the precise origins of the instrument is harder than it might appear, however. Richard Oskar Heber was producing a range of brass musical instruments under the Norma brand at the time. The Normaphon – a single-bell instrument shaped liked a saxophone – was its solution for bands that wanted to look as if they had a saxophone player but could only find capable brass players. (The Normaphon was also considerably cheaper than a saxophone.) C.A. Wunderlich was a distributor for the Norma range.

It would be very convenient to believe that Heber made/developed the Jazzophon for C.A. Wunderlich, but the truth is more complicated. The first known advertisement for the Jazzophon dates from 1926, this from a Czech manufacturer and distributor. Another advertisement followed shortly afterwards, from another company in the region that was also a manufacturer and distributor. However, both advertisements were predated slightly by the granting of what was the German equivalent of a short-term trademark for the Jazzophon, to Franz Xaver Hüller.

Like others in this story, Hüller was based in Graslitz, an area on the then Czech/German border that was known as the 'music store' into the first quarter of the 20th century, due to its prolific output of musical instruments. On that basis, working out 'who-done-it' is probably impossible when it comes to the Jazzophon; there are simply too many characters with the ability, the opportunity and the motive.

Alas, Jazzophons are so rare that an estimate of value is extremely difficult. As there are few surviving examples, any sale price would be determined by an equally select group of collectors.

Typical Kruspe design features include a 'reverse' thumb valve and a flattened bow curve to the main tuning slide. (*Mike Corrigan www.horndr.com*)

Kruspe French horns

Ed. Kruspe was founded in 1834 in Erfurt, Germany, by Karl Kruspe and his two sons, Eduard and Friedrich. The family name can be found in the town records as far back as 1530. New Kruspe horns can still be bought from German dealers but availability is limited.

Kruspe (pronounced 'crispy') were widely used in North America in the first part of the 20th Century, until World War Two disrupted distribution. Although Kruspe offered a number of models in that period, the Horner model was, at the very least, a considerable influence on the design of the Conn 8D model, released in 1937.

In fact, Kruspe is in many ways the father of the modern horn, as he created the first double horn in 1897. (However, the design is credited to Edmund Gumpert, a professional horn player.) Although the new F/B♭ created controversy at the time, it proved to be the future of the French horn.

The Kruspe signature tone is big and dark compared to other horns, and some players describe the sound as having 'gravy' as a result. This can be attributed in part to the larger throat of the Horner model (named after Anton Horner, born 1877, who was for many years principal horn of the Philadelphia orchestra).

Typical design features include a 'garland' around the bell, although not all models have one. This originally reinforced the bell, which on early models has no bell wire. Some players believe that this reinforcement also helps to focus the tone from the bell, which is typically very thin. Despite this delicacy of construction, there are playable Kruspe's that are more than 100 years old.

Players sometimes fear that a Kruspe horn is in worse condition than is actually the case. This is because the maker tended to use more protective guards than is usual, and these can sometimes be mistaken for patches over sections that have worn through.

One of the reasons for this is the distinctive 'reversed' thumb valve, which places the mechanism at the front and leaves little room for the thumb lever. Hence the thumb of the player tends to remain in contact with the wall of the spout, with the obvious potential for accelerated corrosion and wear.

A clue that a Kruspe is an early model is the distinctively flat bow to the main tuning slides, compared to the later bows which are more rounded. Although the date of the changeover is hard to pinpoint, it seems to occur during the 1930s.

Kruspe fans who regard themselves as players first and collectors second sometimes advise that the instruments in pristine condition are often the least desirable. The reason is simple: not every vintage Kruspe is a great player – and the ones that don't play so well are the ones that tend to have been left in the case for prolonged periods of time.

Monette 149

Identifying a single Monette model as 'iconic' will always be controversial for the simple reason that every model developed by the David G Monette Corporation is arguably worthy of this accolade. However, for many players the tipping point from the traditional trumpet designs that had been slowly refined over a couple of centuries, to a new style of instrument came around 1986, when Wynton Marsalis transitioned from using a Bach Stradivarius trumpet to a Monette MB-149 (the medium bore version of the instrument).

With its raw brass finish, the Monette 149 was sufficiently

Wynton Marsalis with his unique Monette Prana Decorated trumpet, which was the first one made and has decorations, symbols and icons special to Marsalis' life.

distinctive to be identifiable to non-players, while players were drawn to a much greater projection than they had experienced from trumpets in the past. The characteristics of the instrument come in part from a generally heavier construction, which tends to reduce sound dissipation, increasing the sound level directed at the audience.

That said, David Monette is known for his holistic approach, not just to the design of the instruments his company builds but also to the relationship between the player, the instrument, the acoustic space presented by the venue and the audience, amongst other factors. (As noted elsewhere in this book, Monette mouthpieces have also been the subject of many innovations, including integral mouthpiece/trumpet designs, notably the Raja and Samadhi models.)

Due to the long association between Monette and Marsalis, it is sometimes assumed that the MB-149 was designed for him, or that Monette primarily designs for jazz players. In reality, neither of those things is true. The first Monette catalogue dates from 1983, and it reveals that the 149 was designed for players Joe Giogianni (whose extensive credits include lead trumpet with Blood, Sweat and Tears) and Charles Schlueter (who was for 25 years the principal trumpeter with the Boston Symphony orchestra). The first Monette trumpet developed specifically for Marsalis was the darker, thicker-toned MB-100 in 1988, although it was by no means the last, as the picture bottom left, shows.

A largely self-taught trumpet player from Michegan, Monette was inspired to enroll as an apprentice musical instrument repairer at the Allied Music School, in Wisconsin. His subsequent work as a repairer at musical instrument stores built him a reputation amongst professional trumpet players and those who championed him included Fred Sautter, principal trumpet player with the Oregon Symphony Orchestra, and Doc Severinsen, bandleader and trumpeter for the Tonight Show. Prior to founding his own company, Monette worked as a consultant to CG Conn.

One man's iconic collection

Richard Church is a trumpet and cornet player based in the UK. Although he has played in brass bands, orchestras and dance bands over a span of half a century, he today plays New Orleans jazz almost exclusively. Many of the pictures in this chapter are amongst the highlights from his collection of 30 horns, many of which are trumpet/cornet pairs.

'My passion as a cornet and trumpet player is now New Orleans style jazz, though I started in brass bands some 50 years ago, progressing into orchestras, dance bands etc,' says Richard. 'At that time, the names of Bunk Johnson, Kid Howard,

Player and collector Richard Church.

Dede Pierce, Kid Thomas and Percy Humphrey meant nothing too me. But as I discovered them on CD, through the help of other musicians, a whole new world opened up.

'It was then that I wanted to use the same (now vintage) instruments that they had. With help from Andy Taylor, I first got the King Silvertone trumpet, which was soon paired with a King Silversonic cornet.

'It was quite strange that every time I got another horn, along came its brother,' Richard says. 'I bought a Buescher Truetone 400 off the Internet and took it to Andy for refurbishment. When he saw it, he remembered an absolutely battered Buescher trumpet that he'd acquired in the States, but had done nothing with. Well, eventually it was restored to as-new condition, and they now make a lovely couple!'

Although Richard's stated intention is not to buy any more horns, they seem to keep on finding him. For instance, the Selmer Louis Armstrong Special was discovered in a loft.

'All my horns are played at gigs,' he says, adding: 'The problem can be which one to take!'

Buescher 400 True Tone cornet, 1949 (left), and trumpet, 1950.

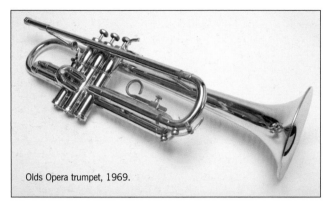

Olds Opera trumpet, 1969.

Olds Opera trumpet, 1969.

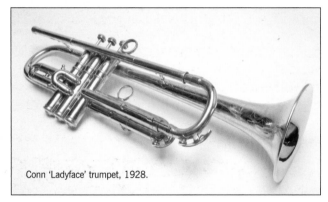

Conn 'Ladyface' trumpet, 1928.

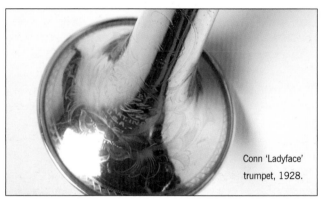

Conn 'Ladyface' trumpet, 1928.

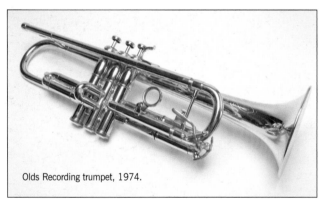

Olds Recording trumpet, 1974.

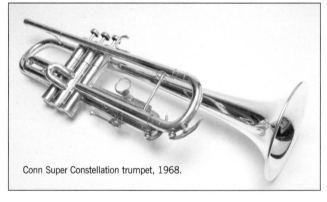

Conn Super Constellation trumpet, 1968.

Taylor/Bach hybrid trumpet.

Olds Super cornet, 1952.

King Silver Tone trumpet, 1935.

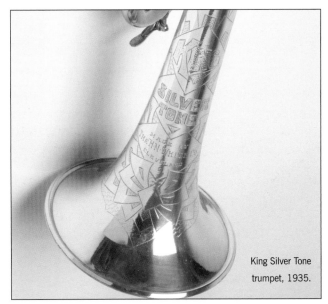

King Silver Tone
trumpet, 1935.

Olds Super trumpet, 1952.

Olds Super
trumpet, 1952.

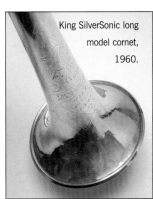

King SilverSonic long
model cornet,
1960.

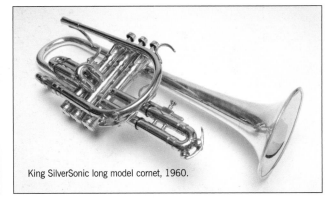

King SilverSonic long model cornet, 1960.

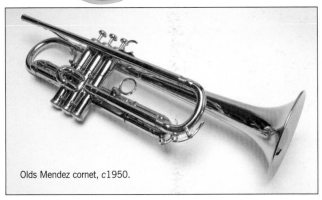

Olds Mendez cornet, c1950.

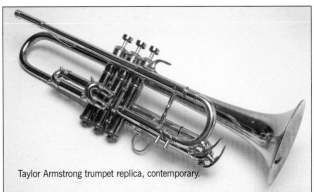

Taylor Armstrong trumpet replica, contemporary.

Olds Recording Cornet, 1965.

Conn New Wonder cornet, 1925.

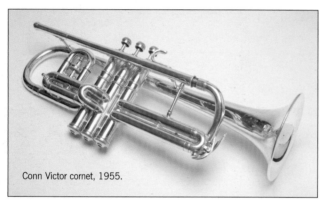

Conn Victor cornet, 1955.

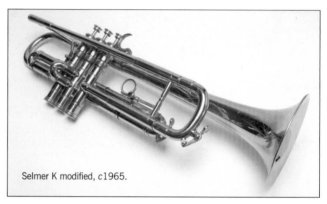

Selmer K modified, c1965.

Conn cornet, 1924.

Conn cornet, 1906.

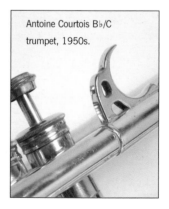

Antoine Courtois B♭/C trumpet, 1950s.

Antoine Courtois B♭/C cornet, 1950s.

Antoine Courtois B♭/C trumpet, 1950s.

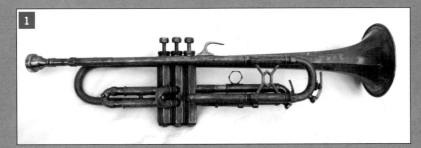

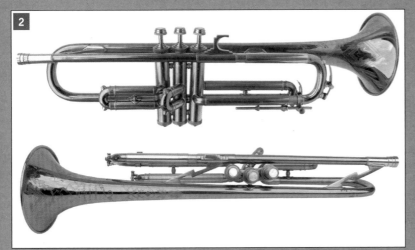

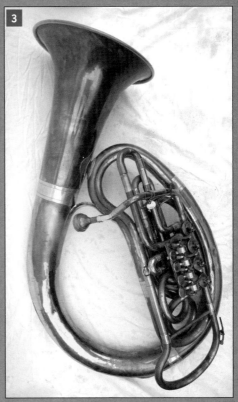

Too rare to be iconic

One of the paradoxes of collecting is that the very rarest items are beyond valuation, for the simple reason that they seldom, if ever, appear on the market. But whether they're unrecognised 'pawn shop prizes', or the subject of fierce bidding battles in the world's auction houses, they often have one thing in common: they're so cool, some people just have to own them.

1 This trumpet is branded Arigra, and was made by Anton Riedl of Graslitz (now Kraslice in Czechoslovakia). As the octagonal art deco design suggests, it dates to *c*1930. (*From the collection of Gerard Westerhof*)

2 An ultra-rare Lew Davis trumpet. Not much is known about Lew as a musical instrument designer, but he was a highly respected trombone player in the 1930s. He and his brother Ben Davis, a leading saxophone player, were major shareholders in the Selmer London retail operation, so it is likely that this instrument was built by Selmer, or a subsidiary (*Trevor Jones Brass & Woodwind Ltd*).

3 A four-valve helicon in B♭ by Eduard Riedl senior, also from Graslitz. (*From the collection of Gerard Westerhof*)

4 Dating from the start of the 20th century, the Saxtrombone was designed by the ever-inventive Adolphe Sax. It has six valves – one for each note. This one was built by D. & P. Lebrun of Brussels. (*From the collection of Gerard Westerhof*)

Modern innovations

Modern materials, along with computer-aided manufacture and consumer expectations, have changed everything, from the wine 'cork' to almost every aspect of today's cars. Brass musical instruments are no exception to this trend, and the changes range from subtle improvements in design for the classical sector to a new generation of flamboyant horns for players who want to be as 'loud' in every respect as their guitar-toting or drum-bashing counterparts.

LEFT Bumper slickers: neoprene lasts longer and is more stable than cork. *(Paxman Musical Instruments)*

Guiding light: nylon valve guides are easier to replace and are quieter in operation.

Nylon valve keys

The key is the component that prevents a piston valve from rotating in its casing. Compared to the old-style metal valve keys, the newer plastic keys are quieter. They are also easy to replace, whereas the old system requires a repair pro to not only fashion and solder in a replacement key but also to re-cut the key slot once it becomes worn. (See the section on Professional Repairs, for more detail.)

Non-corrosive valve pistons

Vincent Bach claims the credit for introducing the use of non-corrosive Monel metal to make the bodies of piston valves. Widely used in brass instrument valves and trombone slides today, Monel metal is extremely hardwearing. A trademark of the Special Metals Corporation, Monel is composed of up to 67% nickel, copper and some iron and other trace elements (typically aluminium and titanium). Although the characteristics of Monel are very desirable from the point of view of the completed instrument, it's difficult to work, as it's inherently harder than nickel silver and hardens still further when subjected to pressure.

Show me the Monel: from a Vincent Bach brochure. (Conn-Selmer)

More recently some valve manufacturers have turned to stainless steel, which is now available in a considerable range of grades, some of which are comparatively easy to work. Another metal that's found its way into valve making is titanium, an extremely light and durable material that's also resistant to corrosion. Titanium has something of a reputation for being difficult to machine but

PISTONS

The use of non-corrosive Monel metal for pistons was pioneered by Vincent Bach. Carefully aligned ports, enclosed bronze springs, and hand-lapped fit assure years of light, trouble-free action. Nylon guides eliminate valve noise.

there are many grades of titanium alloy, some of which are considerably easier to work than others. In addition there have been significant advances in tool technology in recent years, which has increased the rate at which material can be machined.

Neoprene bumper 'corks'

Many manufacturers have substituted synthetic materials such as neoprene rubber for cork, or felt. This has a number of advantages including durability, consistency of material and the fact that it's impervious to moisture, so won't expand or contract (see page 66).

Yamaha Silent Brass System

Available for a variety of instruments, the Yamaha system is a significant breakthrough for brass players because it allows for silent practice in places where the noise level would otherwise be unacceptable. In fact the mute part of the system is so effective that Yamaha also provides a personal headphone amplifier, which connects to a pickup inside the mute. The amplifier contains digital electronics that can simulate room acoustics, plus a CD input for play-along practice. An important factor in the design of the system is that the mute allows for even and consistent intonation.

An open trumpet doesn't perform like a closed one, so a practice mute is best viewed as a supplement to playing in a 'normal' environment, rather than as a substitute. Notes are rather easy to hit with a practice mute in place, which can lull

Yamaha personal studio: presumably if you plug the headphone jack into a PA you get the loudest 'mute' in the world. (Yamaha)

students into a false sense of security if it's used as the sole way of playing for extended periods. Rather like a young cyclist who's just had the stabilisers removed, players need to readjust their technique as they discover that it's up to them to keep balance!

Axial flow valves

These recent innovations have significantly improved the airflow in trombones with F extensions. By using a conical valve, makers including Laetzsch, Greenhoe, Millervalve, Kanstul and latterly Vincent Bach with the Infinity valve have been able to reduce the amount of deflection in the airflow, compared to the tight bends found in a conventional rotary valve. René Hagmann has taken a slightly different approach, achieving axial-type air-flow with a cylindrical valve. (Credit should also go to Orla Thayer, who invented the Thayer Axial-Flow Valve in 1976, albeit with some help from Zig Kanstul. The patent on his invention has now expired.)

Many players describe trombones fitted with axial flow valves as more free-flowing to blow, and as having less unwanted tonal variation when the valve is engaged, compared to rotary designs. The use of axial flow valves in musical instruments is confined almost exclusively to the trombone, mainly because they're too bulky to be used on other instruments.

Many trombone makers offer a choice of valve types, a fact that serves to illustrate the strength of player preference for one or another. Some players actively prefer the increased resistance the conventional rotary valve provides in the lower register, and some also criticise the mechanical vulnerability of the more open layouts, these being designed to minimise tight bends in the tubing.

Go with the flow: a brace of Hagmann valves. (*Servette Music Ltd*)

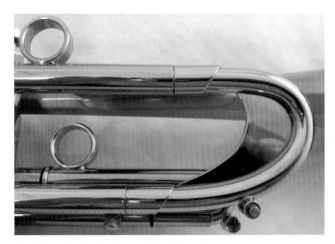

Key feature: the Amado water key is basically a valve.

Amado water key

The push-button design of the Amado-style water key eliminates one aspect of the conventional water key that's prone to failure – the cork. Essentially a miniature piston valve, the Amado water key has only one significant vulnerability, and that's the same as all valves; without lubrication, it will seize up. Some players have failed to grasp this fact and have – unfairly, we think – branded the key unreliable.

Heavier construction

The move towards a louder, high-performance style of playing has led to increasingly more rigid bracing in the high brass, with trumpets in particular seeing a move to sheet bracing. Because these braces are attached to far longer lengths of the instrument's tubing than the small flanges on conventional braces, the effect is to inhibit vibration in the tubing itself (which is essentially lost energy), thereby delivering a higher degree

Call for reinforcements: bracing has tended to get heavier.

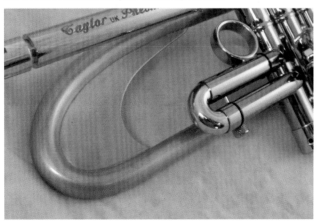

of volume and articulation. Other parts of the instrument to become heavier include mouthpieces, receivers and valve caps.

David Monette must take considerable credit for introducing a heavier style of construction to instruments that have become popular with trumpet players in symphony orchestras, and those working on TV/film soundtracks, as well as many leading players in the jazz world.

At the risk of pointing out the obvious, the price to be paid for this heavier engineering is a generally heavier instrument, which is consequently more fatiguing for the player to hold, especially for extended periods. For this reason the designer needs to be particularly careful to ensure that the trumpet balances well at the valve section, so that the holding hand isn't constantly struggling to maintain the instrument in the correct position.

Integral mouthpieces

In a further bid to maximise energy transmission through the instrument, some are now equipped with a permanently attached mouthpiece. This isn't an option recommended for players who have yet to settle on the right mouthpiece for them!

Alternative strategies in the bid to achieve greater rigidity include lengthening the mouthpiece shank and receiver to increase the contact area, and the use of a mouthpiece that screws in, effectively locking it in place. In addition to making it possible to exchange the mouthpiece, these approaches also make the instrument easier to clean.

David Monette is undoubtedly the maker most associated with the integral mouthpiece, but the latest RAJA line instruments from the David G Monette Corporation use a threaded mouthpiece, as the man himself explains on the www.monette.net web site:

"Our new, threaded integral mouthpiece RAJA instruments have made our latest RAJA designs affordable at just a modest cost over our regular tapered, detachable mouthpiece models.

These are the best of the best - with all the advantages of our previous RAJA instruments but with the flexibility to change mouthpieces when needed. We offer them

An open and shut case: screw-bell horns are easier to carry. *(Paxman Musical Instruments)*

Ball games: mini-ball linkage is easy to adjust and cheap to replace. *(Paxman Musical Instruments)*

in lighter weight models, and in two heavier, sheet braced weights - the new RAJNA weight, and also the full-weight traditional RAJA weight."

Detachable horn bells

When it's in its case a French horn can make for a bulky package, so it's no surprise that many players prefer an instrument with a detachable bell, which allows the instrument to be stored in a less unwieldy case. In addition to making the horn easier to carry, it spares the player from advertising to the world that he/she is carrying around an expensive musical instrument.

Ball and socket linkage

Some players of instruments fitted with rotary valves prefer a mechanical linkage, as this arrangement is a little more robust than string linkage, which can snap unexpectedly if not properly maintained. However, mechanical linkages can become noisy if the pivot points are allowed to become loose. Tightening the old-style mechanical linkage requires a range of tools – and considerable experience on the part of the repair technician if over-tightening is to be avoided. The contemporary 'mini-ball' linkage is adjusted with a screwdriver and the components are inexpensive to replace if wear has become excessive.

Non-symmetrical mouthpieces

Harrison Mouthpieces of Vancouver offers a range of Wedge mouthpieces that aren't symmetrical. That is to say, they must be orientated when inserted into the instrument, because the shape formed up-and-down is different to left-to-right. The benefits claimed include more even response in all registers, better articulation and greater comfort, amongst others.

This idea is not totally new. J.W. Cauffman & Co made a somewhat oval-shaped mouthpiece back in the 1940s, and there have been other manufacturers that decided to go down

this route. However, the limitation in the past was the complexity of manufacture. Whereas a conventional mouthpiece

Thick end of the wedge: Dr Harrison's design is non-symmetrical. (*Harrison Mouthpieces*)

can be shaped with considerable precision on a lathe, an asymmetrical mouthpiece requires computer-controlled manufacture for accurate and repeatable production.

In addition, earlier oval mouthpieces were designed to be played with the long axis placed horizontally, and the contours of the rim were intended to increase surface contact and evenly distribute pressure around the rim circumference in order to improve comfort and endurance. Superficial examination of the Wedge rim might lead one to assume that the Wedge is similarly designed. However, with the Wedge mouthpiece the oval is placed vertically, and the contours are designed to reduce surface contact and unevenly distribute pressure around the rim circumference. This opposite approach is claimed as the basis for the Wedge's superior performance, and was key to the granting of the Wedge US patent, No 7,893,333 B 2.

Despite the level of work entailed in developing and making such a design, Wedge mouthpieces are quite affordable, particularly the entry-level models, which are formed from plastic. The designs are the work of Dr Dave Harrison, a physician and also a trumpet player for more than 40 years. Since their launch in 2007 Wedge mouthpieces have gained an impressive range of testimonials.

The triple French horn

Many players discovered the practical benefits of 'double' horns, which combine a three-valve F horn and B flat horn.

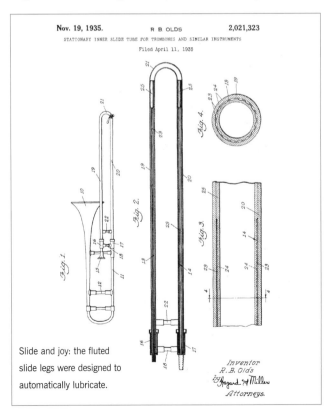

Designing such an instrument is a considerable challenge because careful compensation of the tube tapers and lengths is required for the instrument to perform well in all three registers.

Paxman Musical Instruments is credited with producing the world's first

Triple treat: the latest Paxman Model 83F is more compact than previous triple designs. (*Paxman Musical Instruments/Nik Milner*)

viable triple horn that could be played in F, B♭ and F alto. These feature two thumb levers; one for the F alto and the other to switch between F and B♭. The valve section has three sets of airways and slides, so it's possible to tune all three registers independently for each valve. Two fundamental designs of the instrument exist, one being a full triple and the other a compensating design, which requires a less complicated tubing arrangement. Beyond this, there are variations in material, bore size and valve configuration. In all versions of the Paxman triple, titanium valves are now employed to keep the instrument to a manageable weight.

Some musicians prefer not to use a triple horn on recording sessions because they get paid a 'doubling fee' if they produce a second horn to play the higher parts!

Fluted slide legs

An innovation found – as far as we know – only on vintage Olds trombones, the grooving applied to the inner slide legs is designed to eliminate sticking by making the slide self-lubricating. The idea is that the grooves act as reservoirs for the slide oil, which then bathes the rails when the slide is operated. A secondary benefit is the exceptional rigidity of the slide rails. Reginald B. Olds was granted a patent on this design in 1935.

Nov. 19, 1935.   R B. OLDS   2,021,323
STATIONARY INNER SLIDE TUBE FOR TROMBONES AND SIMILAR INSTRUMENTS
Filed April 11, 1935

Inventor
R. B. Olds
Hazard & Miller
Attorneys.

Slide and joy: the fluted slide legs were designed to automatically lubricate.

Design and manufacture

Anything that can be made can also be repaired, or modified. Knowing how the key parts of a brass musical instrument are made is an important foundation when deciding the best way to go about a repair – especially when the best way forward is to fabricate a new part rather than attempt to rescue the old one.

Material considerations

Brass isn't the only metal used in the construction of 'brass' musical instruments. In fact, even instruments that are predominantly made from brass often have chemises, stays, slides and other parts made from more durable nickel silver. Many of the most common alloys used in brass musical instruments are, however, either brass with the percentage of copper to zinc modified, or with a third metallic element added. These changes affect both the hardness and the colour of the resultant alloy.

Standard 'yellow brass' is an alloy comprising 70% copper and 30% zinc, whereas nickel silver comprises 63% copper, 27% zinc and 10% nickel. (Despite the name, nickel silver contains no silver whatsoever.) The third common alloy used in musical instrument making is 'gold brass', which typically comprises 85% copper and 15% zinc. All three alloys are used to make leader pipes, bells and other parts of the instrument.

LEFT Soft soldering is used to attach ferrules and flanges to tubing. Hard solder is used to make joins in the brace itself and to attach the finger rings to the flange. (*Conn-Selmer*)

ABOVE This instrument from Taylor Trumpets clearly shows the difference between the nickel silver used on the slide, receivers and garland, the yellow brass used on the leader pipe and flare, and the copper used on the spout.

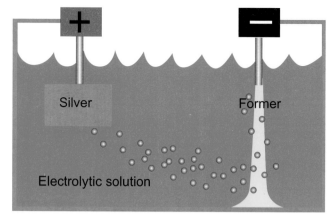

The electroforming process is the same as electroplating, in that material leaves the anode and is attracted to the cathode is a process known as 'electrodeposition'.

Players are also likely to encounter instruments made of gilding brass, red brass or rose brass. Manufacturers use all three names, and the alloys can contain anything from 85–90% copper. The 90% copper alloy tends to be called red brass, because at that percentage the result is coppery in colour. Rose brass tends to be used to describe one of the two lesser copper mixes. Pure copper – as opposed to an alloy – is a popular choice for flugelhorns.

Solid silver is sometimes used as the bell material for trumpets, trombones and also saxophones. The King Silversonic range is a case in point. Although some players swear by the tone silver bells produce, it's an expensive option and can be a risky business for the maker. Most bells and spouts are formed from sheet, but a percentage of these inevitably fail to make the grade and end up in the scrap box. With silver sheet costing much more than most other alloy alternatives, over-thinning the metal during manufacture is an expensive mistake.

For this reason, manufacturers tend to prefer the less risky technique of electroforming the entire bell from silver plate on a metal mandrill, or former. Once the bell has built up sufficient thickness in the tank, it must still be cleaned, a rim put on the flare and the spout bent to the required shape. Fortunately, electroformed bells bend quite nicely because the silver is pure plate, so it's soft and there's no seam to crack.

Many players express a preference for one material over the others but some wrongly attribute characteristics to the metal that rightfully belong to the bore of an instrument. The size of the bore – especially as the taper approaches the bell – has a tremendous effect on the tone of an instrument. Unless a player has listened to and analysed a considerable quantity of instruments there's likely to be some confusion between the two, as well as a considerable number of other variables. The late Richard Merewether, a fine professional horn-player and designer of world-class French horns for Paxman Musical Instruments (where both authors trained), addressed this subject in a brochure from the 1970s.

'Individual players have a predilection for one alloy or another, yet the difference between metals (in horns otherwise identical) is not so pronounced as that heard when two players blow the same horn in turn. If any generalisation can be made about alloys aside from human considerations, one would submit that yellow brass makes for a warm sonority, that gold brass gives a delicious, veiled sound persisting even into fortissimo, whereas nickel silver brightens and, so to say, condenses the tone into a crisp clarity.

'A body of opinion, seemingly contradicting this last statement, stems from the fact that the first nickel silver horns widely distributed were of much larger bell-taper than the brass ones then in common use. A considerably "darkened" tone-quality was attributed to the alloy (wrongly we think) rather than to a radically different bell profile.'

So far, the metals we've discussed are used primarily in the main tubing of an instrument. For the parts that are subject to mechanical wear or stress it's preferable to use more durable materials.

Nickel silver with a 10% nickel content is malleable enough to form bells, but an alloy with 15% nickel silver is arguably better for tuning slides, as it's extremely hardwearing. The downside for the maker is that it burrs when lathe-turned and blunts tools quickly. That said, it looks almost like chrome when polished and resists corrosion better than brass.

The one instrument that puts the main slide through an absolutely punishing amount of wear and tear is, of course, the trombone, as the slide is in almost constant use. Here even nickel silver isn't hard enough, and cupronickel (also known as copper-nickel or cupernickel) is the material of choice. This is an alloy of copper that combines nickel with strengthening elements, such as iron and manganese. A typical mix is 75% copper, 25% nickel, plus a trace amount of other metals.

Cupronickel is not only extremely hardwearing, it's also highly resistant to corrosion. However, it's also difficult to work, being more like stainless steel in its consistency and overall reluctance to bend or cut. For this and other reasons, trombone slide repair is often a job for the specialist, rather than the interested amateur.

Even more hardwearing and resistant to corrosion is stainless steel itself, the formulation of which is achieved by adding 10–11% chromium. This metal is sometimes used in the manufacture of upmarket trumpet and flugelhorn valves, as well as custom mouthpieces.

Titanium is a very durable but lightweight metal that's used in high-quality rotary valves, especially in double and triple horns, where the additional weight is a significant factor. However, this material requires specialist cutting tools and will only be found on instruments built for professional players.

Mouthpiece design

It's probably impossible to over-emphasise the importance of the mouthpiece to a brass player and the quality of the music they produce. While most brass players are happy to try new models of instrument, they'll tend to do so with 'their' mouthpiece – at least in the first instance. And while some players stick with their 'first love', others embark on an endless quest to find the perfect mouthpiece for them.

Although there are some differences between the high and low brass, due to size – and there are specific types of mouthpiece associated with specific instruments – much of what there is to learn about mouthpieces is, fortunately, universally applicable. We say 'fortunately' because there's a lot to know, so the more application there is for what you've learned, the greater the incentive to get stuck into the detail!

One potential variable in mouthpiece design is the length, which will affect tuning and intonation. In reality this dimension has a standard of close to 88mm for a B♭ trumpet, as this has been found to work well. A common trick is to shorten the mouthpiece slightly, as this makes the instrument play a little sharp. For lead players – or those who struggle with the upper register, or tend to play flat – this is an easy fix. However, there's more to shortening a mouthpiece than simply cutting a section from the shank, for reasons that will become clear when we consider other aspects of mouthpiece design.

(The mouthpiece for a C trumpet is around 6.5mm/¼in shorter than that of a standard B♭ trumpet. Some B♭ players

use a C mouthpiece to sharpen the upper register. For the benefit of readers who may be curious, placing a B♭ mouthpiece into a C trumpet isn't particularly beneficial.)

The cup and rim are most important aspects of mouthpiece design as these are the elements in contact with the player's

The parts of the mouthpiece.

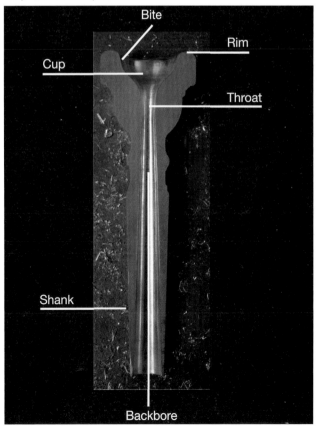

A variety of Vincent Bach trumpet and trombone mouthpieces. (*Conn-Selmer*)

face. Mouthpiece catalogues often use somewhat subjective phrases such as 'soft', or 'flat', or 'cushioned', when describing the attributes of mouthpieces. In order to understand how changing a mouthpiece creates these characteristics, it's necessary to identify exactly which part of the mouthpiece affects each one.

The 'bite' is the part of the mouthpiece where the curve of the rim meets the onset of the bowl that forms the cup. The contour of that transition can be soft, or it can have an 'undercut'. The term is slightly misleading, because the amount of metal cut away is negligible, but it feels to the player that the cup falls away at that point.

A little bit of bite – especially on a shallow mouthpiece – gives the inner part of the lip increased grip. A softer transition, that is more rounded at that point, doesn't give that grip. But everything you change on a mouthpiece is a process of action and reaction. For every enhancement, the player will pay the price somewhere else.

Rim

A rounded inner rim is probably less tiring to play on. You can get through the entire gig with the same feel. If you have the bite on the inside, it's almost like artificial grip. All the time the lips are in form, it's fine, but the minute the muscles start to relax and the player loses grip they'll find they're really fighting the instrument.

Classical players, who need to remain in control over long periods of time, tend to play with a slightly more rounded contour at this part of the mouthpiece. Someone who really wants to 'bang it out' will probably go for more bite but if their lip goes as they're coming up to that super-high G, there will be no chance of recovering in time. Endurance considerations

are definitely the downside of a mouthpiece with a pronounced amount of bite.

There are also tonal considerations. A rounded transition from the rim to the cup will generally produce a softer, warmer tone, and with more control. Bite in a mouthpiece gives more attack. It's like a set of sports tyres that will make sure the car stays on the road.

The roundness of the rim across the middle section is primarily an issue of comfort. Some players like the profile to be fairly flat, others prefer it very rounded – and many players have a preferred profile somewhere in between. A semi-flat profile is a popular option.

A 'cushioned' rim is slightly wider externally, allowing the round-off to be gentler than would otherwise be the case. Although this is theoretically more comfortable, spreading the pressure of the rim over a greater area of the face with a cushioned rim has a downside. Typically, the player will unconsciously press the mouthpiece to their face harder in order to achieve a proper seal. This causes fatigue at an earlier stage than the player might have hoped. So the comfort of the cushioned rim comes at the cost of reduced endurance. In the end, however, personal preference is the biggest factor when fashioning the external profile of the rim.

Some mouthpieces have an edge on the outside of the rim, as well as a bite on the inside. While a rounded cup is appropriate for a trumpet, players tend to select a mouthpiece with a more pronounced outside edge for the cornet. A cornet is less reliant on pressure, so the player shouldn't press so hard. The harder rim profile soon sends a warning sign to any student who forgets this! Unkind though it seems, a mouthpiece with a hard edge is a constant, tactile teacher when it comes to contact pressure.

A cornet player tends to produce a softer, almost creamy

From left to right (in exaggerated form): rounded rim, cushion rim and rim with bite.

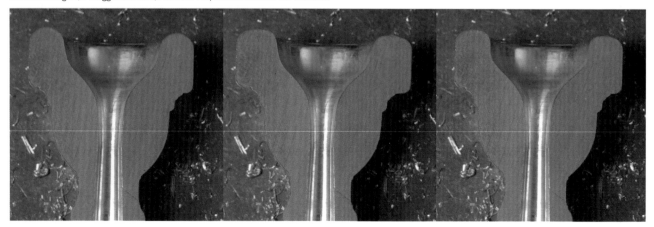

sound, precisely because he/she presses against the mouthpiece relatively softly. This tends to mean that a cornet player approaches the trumpet somewhat like a cornet. Regardless of the mouthpiece they choose for the trumpet – which is likely to have a rounded rim edge – the cornet player's embouchure has already been developed by the mouthpiece they learned on.

Conversely, a trumpet player confronted with a cornet will tend to stick with the 'pushier' embouchure they've learned from the instrument they started on. Unsurprisingly, the result is a cornet that sounds like a trumpet.

For the most part this explains the difference in tone between US and European cornet players. US players tend to come to the cornet having already formed their embouchure on the trumpet, whereas European players typically learn the cornet as a first instrument. As a result, US cornet players have a distinctly trumpet-like edge to their playing. In case this is taken as a criticism, it should be added that there's considerable mutual admiration between the US and European cornet and trumpet playing communities.

Equally, on some high-note mouthpieces – such as those made by Schilke – what we might call the 'table', or tilt, of the rim is different to most mouthpieces. Whereas the rim generally slopes away towards the external edge, on a mouthpiece designed for higher-register trumpet playing it can slope down towards the cup. This places the strongest grip at the outside of the rim and focuses the energy into the middle. It's not always very comfortable but it can help the player to deliver the required performance.

Cups

Two general descriptions of cup profile are C or V, the latter being the preferred cup for French horn and flugel. As the terms imply, C cups are more rounded and bowl-like, whereas V cups are more straight-sided.

(On cornets and bigger mouthpieces, such as used for the tuba, this part of the mouthpiece is often referred to as 'the bowl', because that's exactly what those large, C cup mouthpieces look like. Because the tuba is such a large instrument and requires a commensurately large amount of air, a V cup tuba mouthpiece is totally unheard of. Similarly, there are no tuba equivalents to the shallow C cups used on lead trumpet mouthpieces.)

Until the 1950s V cups were the norm across many brass instruments. Although it might be supposed that a V cup would be the more efficient design for channelling air into an instrument, the C cup gives the player a small reserve of air, and a certain back pressure, that works better for most instruments.

The Taylor mouthpiece on the left has a V-shaped cup, while the one on the right is C-shaped.

The advantage to the player is enhanced tactile feedback, or, to put it another way, they can feel what they're doing more easily. This has the benefit of better tuning. That said, a V cup produces a distinctive, warm tone and is the preferred option for French horn players.

The deeper a cup is, the broader the tone will be, overall. The payoff is range, because a deep C cup makes it more difficult to play in the higher register, which is an important consideration for many players of high brass instruments. On the other hand it makes for a rich tone and aids the production of notes in the lower register.

Shallow C cups aid the production of notes in the higher registers. Such mouthpieces don't have a great deal of internal volume, in the sense of cubic air capacity, but do produce an immediate response. There's no 'give', or elasticity, in such a small volume of air, so it will go 'straight down the hole'.

However, there's a limit to how far this strategy can be followed, because there comes a point where the player's lip 'bottoms out' by impacting the bowl itself. Where that limit is varies from player to player, and a major variable in this respect is the ethnic origin of the player. This is considered in the panel entitled 'Ethnic issues'.

Depth is just one parameter. The wider the diameter of the rim – as measured across the internal surface of the mouthpiece wall – the bigger the tone, potentially, and the greater the available volume. 'Wide and shallow' is the modern design formula for many lead trumpet players.

But as the internal area expands, so the control demanded of the player increases, because more of the lips now form the 'speaking area'. This is a payoff many more experienced players are prepared to accept, because the rewards in terms of fatter, fuller tone are considerable. Conversely, students typically start off with a narrower than average mouthpiece, as it's easier to control.

One of many paradoxes found in mouthpiece design is that some players graduate from a narrow diameter to a wider one, only to return to the narrower one in later years. Essentially, they learn the embouchure control required for a wider mouthpiece but reach a stage in their career when they decide to opt for a narrower one again, because the marginal gains in tone/volume no longer seem worth the continual physical exertion.

A natural question to ask at this point is, 'If a wide mouthpiece makes for bigger tone and a shallow mouthpiece makes for a better upper register, isn't a wide/shallow mouthpiece the ultimate design?' While this has undoubtedly been the trend in trumpet mouthpiece design, it must be stressed that the practical range of this strategy is small.

The cup transitions into the throat at the bottom of the bowl. While most modern mouthpieces have a C cup and French horn mouthpieces use a V cup, the flugelhorn mouthpiece has a combination of the two. Close to the rim it's certainly a C cup, but as it nears the throat it takes on the depth of a V cup. Many cornet mouthpieces are much the same. Older flugelhorn mouthpieces, in contrast, are very similar to those of the French horn. However, the introduction of a deep C makes the flugelhorn more user-friendly to trumpet players, who constitute the majority of flugelhorn players (although some are primarily cornet players).

Some of the richest flugelhorn tones are arguably produced by French horn players, used as they are to a V profile mouthpiece. This gives them an embouchure that's perfect for the flugelhorn. To this extent, French horn players would seem the best suited to playing flugelhorn as a second instrument, but this seldom seems to happen in reality. This may be because the flugelhorn is seen mainly as a jazz instrument.

A similar design approach can be seen today in other mouthpieces, including those for trombone and high-note

Ethnic issues

As anyone who regularly makes mouthpieces for jazz musicians will know, the embouchure of the typical black player is different to that of a white player, because their lips are somewhat bigger. Therefore, they need a mouthpiece that's right for their face, not a hypothetical player with Caucasian features.

Unfortunately, many teachers and manufacturers fail to address this issue. This leaves a lot of black students learning on mouthpieces that aren't ideal for them, often causing them to make adjustments to their embouchure as a result.

It's very important when making custom mouthpieces to understand that getting the right fit for your client's physical build and playing style is the key to the whole exercise. Otherwise, they might as well just walk into a store and buy one.

Whether you're making a mouthpiece, or simply helping someone to choose one, it's worth bearing in mind that very shallow cups and larger lips don't work well together because of the tendency for the lips to hit the back of the cup and choke the note completely.

Similarly, the rim size should be taken into account when matching mouthpiece to player. Smaller lips and smaller rims can work well together because there's still a proportion of the rim that's supported by the less fleshy areas of the face surrounding the mouth.

Players with larger lips are likely to find the same mouthpiece uncomfortable because the entire rim is being supported by the fleshy part of their lips. In addition, a lot of the muscle control lies in the areas of the face surrounding the lips. For these reasons it's not uncommon to see black players positioning the mouthpiece slightly to one side.

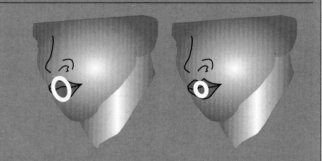

For it to be comfortable, a mouthpiece needs to be supported by the areas around the mouth, as shown on the left. If a mouthpiece is mainly supported by the lips – as shown on the right – it will rapidly become uncomfortable.

Possibly because brass instruments were developed in the early years against a background of largely white musical development – for instance, for orchestral music – a large proportion of mouthpieces are still of essentially Caucasian proportions. While the larger mouthpieces used on the lower brass make any ethnic distinction largely meaningless, on an instrument such as the French horn the difference is close to critical.

Generally, for the high brass a black player will need more support across the rim – which equates to a broader, 'cushioned' rim wall – along with a slightly increased rim diameter to give better support. The same logic applies to white players who have more generously proportioned lips.

Music teachers should assess, very early on, whether each student has a suitable mouthpiece. After all, no responsible sports teacher would dream of sending students out on the track with shoes that were too small for them.

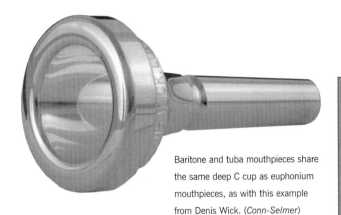

Baritone and tuba mouthpieces share the same deep C cup as euphonium mouthpieces, as with this example from Denis Wick. (*Conn-Selmer*)

trumpet playing. (Tenor trombone mouthpieces can be found with either V or shallow C cup profiles. Although the mouthpieces are big, players still need to reach high notes.) Typically, makers opt for a shallow C cup, with a certain amount of bite and a relatively flat table, which then transforms into a V as it nears the throat. This hybrid design approach allows for a very fast transfer of air, due in part to the reduced capacity of the chamber.

(It should be noted that this isn't simply the subjective impression of a player – research has led to the development of similar profiles in seemingly unrelated areas, such as the design of water nozzles for fire engines. In fact, water is a very good medium when attempting to model the movements of air, as it exhibits somewhat similar characteristics but has the great advantage of being visible.)

As with all mouthpiece parameters, there comes a point where introducing too much V into the throat end of the cup is counterproductive. As the air capacity increases, the mouthpiece becomes harder to control. There's simply too much air.

At the other extreme, an acute transition between the cup and the throat throws up its own problems. The lack of continuity between the two parts of the air system causes turbulence, resulting in an inconsistent and unsatisfactory performance. (These are much the same aberrations as effect poorly designed compression driver/horn combinations in public address systems, where turbulence and diffraction effects result in audible distortion.)

So far we haven't said much about mouthpieces for members of the bugle family, such as the euphonium, baritone and tuba. Actually, these three have remarkably similar, deep, C cup mouthpieces. The exception in the family is the tenor horn, which usually sits halfway between small brass and big brass in terms of its overall mouthpiece dimensions. However, the shank size is the same as a trumpet, which provides trumpet players with an opportunity to play a good party trick.

Placing a trumpet mouthpiece into a tenor horn enables the same sort of high-note gymnastics as on the trumpet itself. This is quite an impressive trick to a non-specialist audience, as

Mixing mouthpiece sizes

Traditional folklore used to have it that players shouldn't play instruments with mouthpieces of different diameters because it would mess up their embouchure. Modern thinking suggests that the opposite is true, and many a dedicated trumpet player will practise trombone in order to gain the benefits of using a larger mouthpiece from time to time. It seems that having more lip in the mouthpiece builds up the embouchure, rather than harming it. As an additional benefit, a trumpet player who's learned embouchure control on a trombone finds it easier to transition to a larger trumpet mouthpiece, gaining the benefits described in the main text.

Lately, there's also been a trend towards trombone players practising trumpet in order to gain better control of the trombone's upper register. It seems to be that there are some merits to this approach.

it creates the impression of unrivalled technique compared to 'normal' tenor horn players. Equally, trumpet players can get an interesting tonal effect by placing a tenor horn mouthpiece into their trumpet.

Throat

For any given instrument, there's a throat bore that can be considered 'standard'. On a trumpet, for instance, it's around the 3.7–3.8mm mark. (One thing that we learn from this is that anyone considering altering the throat of a mouthpiece is likely to need a set of drill bits graduated in far finer increments than the average set from the DIY store.)

Over the years the 'standard' bore size has increased somewhat, partly in response to the enhanced air delivery techniques modern players are taught. In simple terms, a bigger throat equates to more air and therefore more volume – but only if the player can deliver and control it. It's fair to say that the performance parameters of playing techniques and the instruments players use have grown hand in hand, not unlike sportsmen/women and sports equipment. As the performance level goes up, so do the expectations of the equipment.

One aspect of the throat's dimension that seems to attract little discussion is its length. This is probably because it has less affect on the feel of the mouthpiece than the throat's diameter. Nonetheless, the straight section plays an important role in steadying the airflow. While there is undoubtedly a range of measurements within which a workable length for the throat sits, we don't believe that this can be expressed as an absolute quantity. Practical experimentation shows that if the throat is too long, it strangles the notes, while if it's too short, the instrument produces some notes less well. It would appear to be the case that the former problem is primarily a question of impedance to the airflow, while the latter is because at different frequencies there's a variable in the minimum length of throat required for the air to become 'coherent' and free from the effects of turbulence.

We believe that the optimum throat length is actually a function of its diameter. While we don't consider throat length to be by any means the most critical parameter in mouthpiece design, we would advocate a 'holistic' approach to the subject, on the basis that the performance of any mouthpiece depends on its success as a complete system.

Stronger players, and particularly those in search of more volume, will often go for an increased throat size, but this is a strategy to be approached with caution. On a trumpet, for instance, a throat diameter bigger than 4mm will be exceptionally difficult to control due to the lack of back pressure within the cup. Although the instrument will deliver more volume, the constant need to deliver high velocity into the mouthpiece will be fatiguing, and quieter, subtler passages will be difficult to deliver. Because of this, great tone and high volume don't necessarily sit together very easily.

Louder and louder

It would be a mistake to think that brass players necessarily 'want' to get louder, but those playing in contemporary band settings are largely forced in this direction in order to be heard. This isn't just a brass-versus-guitars kind of issue either. Once you have louder trumpets next to you, you'll be wanting a louder trombone… and so it goes on.

Trumpets have definitely been at the forefront on the move towards louder instruments, but that's down to physics as much as egos. It's harder to make a larger brass instrument, such as a trombone, louder without making major sacrifices in the tone department. 'Loud' tends to be the enemy of 'subtle' on any instrument, but on a trombone there's a distinctly raspy quality that creeps in with an increase in volume.

In a modern band setting, part of the solution undoubtedly lies with appropriate use of sound-reinforcement technology – not just the sound balance the audience hears 'front of house', but the monitor mixes that go to the musicians. If players can't hear themselves properly, they're inclined to believe they aren't loud enough, even if they're popping the ears of the first five rows out front.

The standard throat size of a flugelhorn or cornet mouthpiece is bigger than that found on a trumpet, although the rim diameters aren't noticeably different. A flugelhorn isn't played with anything like the dynamic power of a trumpet – in fact the flugelhorn sounds considerably better when it isn't approached with athletic ambition. This is perhaps the opposite of what we would infer from the greater throat diameter, which tells us that the size of the throat has to be considered in relation to the instrument for which the mouthpiece is being designed.

Backbore

Continuing our journey through the mouthpiece, past the throat we come to the backbore. The backbore is shaped with a specialist cutter, and the first thing that becomes evident when looking at these cutters is that the rate of taper and length of backbore varies from one type of instrument to another. For instance, a trumpet backbore is longer than that of a flugelhorn but is narrower at the throat end and wider at the exit, compared to a flugelhorn. Controlling the size of the backbore on a custom mouthpiece is often down to how far the cutting tool is pushed in.

The backbore conforms to much the same rules as the throat, in that the bigger it is, the bigger the resultant tone will be, but the harder the mouthpiece is to control. The bigger backbore also delivers more dynamic range, meaning that louder passages can be, well, louder! This applies to all brass instruments but brings us neatly to the question of whether the taper of the backbore is straight, or concave. (When we say 'concave' we mean the profile of the backbore itself, which is the result of using a convex cutter.) This is a question of personal preference, rather than being associated with any particular type of instrument, but in either event the backbore taper is usually very close to, if not absolutely, straight.

An important factor on all mouthpieces, with the exception of those for the French horn and flugelhorn, is the size of the backbore as it exits the mouthpiece. This is because it affects the way it lines up with the venturi of the leader pipe. On most instruments these measurements are standardised to within a relatively small tolerance. However, players will often change mouthpiece when they change to a new instrument and a major factor here is a mismatch between the backbore of the mouthpiece and the venturi of the leader pipe. It is perhaps unsurprising, then, to discover that the general consensus between players is that a Bach instrument plays better with a Bach mouthpiece, a Yamaha instrument plays better with a Yamaha mouthpiece… which strongly suggests that an exact match is better than even a close match.

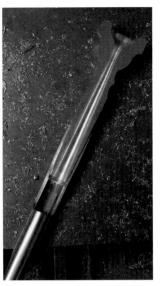

This cross-section clearly shows the gap between the end of the mouthpiece shank and the receiver.

You might be tempted to think that the objective is therefore to create an absolutely seamless transition between the mouthpiece and the venturi, but it's not quite as simple of that. This is because of a factor many players know simply as 'the gap'. This is the distance between the end of the mouthpiece shank and the onset of the leader pipe. (The gap will, of necessity, be the diameter of the external of the shank. It's the length of the gap that is the key variable.) The strange thing is, a small amount of gap has a beneficial effect through most of an instrument's range and only becomes a liability when attempting to play very loudly and very high. It seems to be that a small gaps acts as some kind of 'buffer'. Alas, too much gap and there's a vortex effect, which is detrimental.

So how much gap is optimum? There's probably no scientific answer to that but there are players who have discovered a gap size that seems to represent a 'sweet spot' for them and will go to great lengths (pardon the pun) to recreate that gap whenever possible. Generally speaking, the gap is 1.5–2mm on a trumpet, but in the world of custom building 'generally speaking' isn't really what you're aiming for. (On bigger instruments this gap increases – to about 10mm in the case of a tuba.) There's also a mundane, practical reason why there has to be 'some' gap, as the panel entitled 'The taper caper' explains.

External dimensions

As this picture shows, the external dimensions of trumpet mouthpieces in particular have changed over the years, with the trend being towards heavier, thicker walls that are less likely to allow any of the player's energy to be dissipated through them. The mouthpiece on the right is the older and appears almost flimsy by today's standards. The mouthpiece far right is contemporary and has added mass to the bowl.

Arguably, the most important feature of later mouthpiece functionally isn't so much the general increase in the wall thickness of the bowl, it's the abandonment of the purely decorative beading. Lathe-turned on the traditional design, this leads to a wall thickness between the beads that must be very little. The Vincent Bach Mega Tone mouthpiece, for instance, is a very practical design that's found favour with many trumpet players in the classical as well as contemporary music fields.

From left to right: classic Olds Mendez, King and Jupiter trumpet mouthpieces.

Many players today – especially in jazz – favour a much heavier mouthpiece construction, which in turn necessitates a heaver receiver construction. This creates a very distinctive look to the instrument, as there's no obvious end to the mouthpiece and start to the receiver (indeed, on some instruments, the two are actually fixed together).

There is no doubt that, in the hands of the right player, a mouthpiece of this kind of mass can deliver an exceptionally hefty payload into the instrument. However, unless the instrument is a good match for this type of mouthpiece, the energy is likely to be dissipated elsewhere in the overall system. This is one reason why instruments that are a good match for a mouthpiece of this type are so heavily braced – the object is to transfer as much energy as possible to the bell, with minimal inefficiencies along the way.

Similarly, these modern

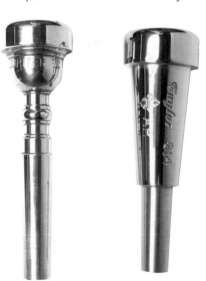

The ornamental beading and light construction of the traditional Jupiter 7C is in stark contrast to the much heavier Taylor S14.

mouthpieces are heavy, so it's important to think about balance in a very literal way. Couple one of these mouthpieces with a light trumpet and you'll have an instrument that handles very

The taper caper

Although we've explored the sonic implications of 'the gap' between the mouthpiece and the venturi, there's a very practical engineering reason it has to exist, at least to some extent. The shank of the mouthpiece is tapered and only secures the mouthpiece in the instrument's receiver when the two components are firmly touching. If the end of the shank were to hit the start of the venturi before the taper had fully bedded in, the mouthpiece would be loose. Given that the union between the two tapers will always be subject to wear over the years, leaving just a tiny gap between mouthpiece and venturi is likely to cause trouble, because the mouthpiece will sink lower into the receiver over time. This isn't uncommon, and the usual fix is to remove a little off the end of the mouthpiece. On older instruments that have a particularly thin receiver the issue isn't confined to wear, as the successive insertion of the mouthpiece will actually expand the receiver over time.

The situation is somewhat different on French horns because there's no 'receiver' as such. Instead, the end of the mouthpipe itself is flared outwards to form the taper that holds the mouthpiece. While this region of the pipe is covered by a nickel silver 'chemise', it isn't especially effective in preventing the expansion of the pipe under the force of the mouthpiece. This traditional arrangement also means that while there's no gap, there's a step between the mouthpiece end and the pipe. However, this has come to be regarded as part of the characteristics of the French horn, rather than an engineering defect to be addressed. (Whether the step in bore is actually a significant contributor to the tone of the French horn is a moot point – but any maker who invests in an 'improved' design is unlikely to get many takers in such a traditional market.)

On the subject of tradition, it must be said that the whole arrangement by which the mouthpiece is conventionally held in place is fatally flawed because it's based on a Morse taper. Invented by Stephen Morse in the 1860s, these tapers were specifically intended as a way of holding drills and the like in chucks using nothing more than a forceful push. Small wonder that so many mouthpieces end up jammed in instruments – that's what the Morse taper is designed to do!

Unfortunately, once the world has adopted a system – however flawed it may be – it's hard to drop it in favour of a better one. Let us not forget that the QWERTY keyboard was originally designed to slow down typists, so that they didn't jam the keys of early mechanical typewriters. Equally, the gauge of railway lines around the world is based on the width of tracks

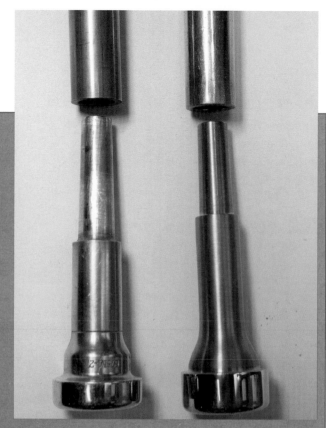

The mouthpiece on the left has a traditional Morse taper shank, the one on the right has a slightly different taper, favoured by Taylor Trumpets because it's less prone to jamming.

left by Roman chariots (hence the joke that the size of seat you get on a train today is dictated entirely by the width of a Roman horse's backside).

Because of this reluctance to abandon the 'installed base' of existing instruments and perhaps opt for an alternative that initially enjoys very little demand, very few manufacturers have dared to abandon the Morse taper. It should be said, however, that Taylor trumpets offers mouthpieces in a fit unique to its own instruments as well as in standard fit.

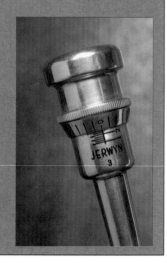

This unusual mouthpiece features an adjustable depth cup. A lock-ring at the back displays the cup-depth that the mouthpiece is set to. One use for this device is as an aid to 'fitting up' a customer, who may be reluctant to have a mouthpiece made to specification without evaluating it first. It's also a valuable aid for teachers, who can combine the mouthpiece with their experienced ear to help students select an appropriate model.

strangely indeed. As an analogy: if you're going to put a V8 engine in a Model T Ford, you'd better be prepared to beef up many other aspects of the design, from the suspension to the brakes and the engine mounts.

Again, this is why it's necessary to look at the whole picture – from player to bell – and not just think about mouthpieces in isolation.

Mouthpiece materials

Most mouthpieces are made from brass, then silver or gold plated – or even left raw for a more modern, oxidised look. Brass that machines easily, known as 'free machining brass', has a certain amount of lead added to it. Although we don't know of any instances where people have been made seriously ill as a result of contact with the small amount of lead involved, some people exhibit allergies to the metals commonly used in mouthpiece manufacture. However, this is highly unlikely to have anything to do with the tiny percentage of lead used in free machining brass.

Allergies to nickel and copper are far more common, and this can be a problem even when a mouthpiece is plated, for a number of reasons, including (a) the plating seldom provides a 100% barrier to the underlying metal, and (b) nickel is often found in other metals, including gold, unless it's of an exceptionally high grade. Unfortunately, nickel is one of the most likely alternatives to brass when making mouthpieces.

For players who are highly allergic to one or more of these metals, one solution is to fashion the rim from a non-metallic substance, typically Perspex (known as Plexiglas in North America). This material is easy to machine for anyone experienced in working with brass, although it has a tendency to tear if overheated by machining or polished too rapidly. The best way to connect the metal mouthpiece to the plastic rim is with a fine thread, which needs to be cut with some care if the two halves are to connect accurately. Unfortunately, the solution still leaves a metal cup, and the likelihood of intermittent contact with the player's lips.

An alternative is a mouthpiece fashioned from stainless steel, but there are more complications here. Firstly, not all stainless steel formulations are the same. Although all involve the addition of some amount of chromium to the steel in order to inhibit corrosion, some formulations also use nickel. Secondly, stainless steel is an exceptionally hard material that requires specialist tools to fashion. It will quickly blunt and destroy the cutting tools most brass instrument makers use. On the plus side, stainless steel mouthpieces generally have good tone, are highly resistant to wear and are easy to clean due to their corrosion-resistant properties.

These Taylor mouthpieces are striking visually but also ideal for players with metal allergies.

A more recent innovation is a mouthpiece where a substantial cup and rim are machined from a block of hard synthetic substance, which is then mated to a threaded brass shaft, which contains the complete backbore and throat. With the synthetic material available in a variety of marble, tortoiseshell and ivory-like finishes, the result is visually striking and, as a mouthpiece, it can be the best of all worlds for the player with a metal allergy. Because the whole shank is brass and the bowl so thick, no tone is lost through the substitution of hard plastic for metal. It's worth adding that the mock ivory finishes really look the part in early music ensembles!

At the opposite end of the price spectrum, plastics and nylons have the edge, because they can be moulded, rather than machined. They can also be made in clear plastic, as well as 'funky' colours, including ones that glow in the dark. Because of the lack of metal-to-metal contact at the shank, plastic mouthpieces aren't always major players when it comes to tone, but they're a lot of fun and bring new levels of affordability to

The Kelly synthetic mouthpieces are available in a range of fun colours. (*Kelly Mouthpieces*)

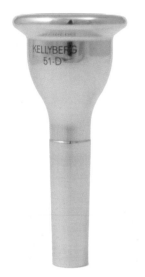

Kelly's stainless steel mouthpiece range includes the trombone model shown here. (*Kelly Mouthpieces*)

The Truing Tool from Kelly offers a cost-effective way of adjusting mouthpiece shanks. (*Kelly Mouthpieces*)

Mouthpiece manufacture by hand

1 The process starts with cutting a length of turning brass somewhat bigger than the final mouthpiece, using a bandsaw.

2 The raw material is inserted into the lathe chuck. Note that the collet chuck shown is capable of holding the blank with considerably greater accuracy than a standard three-jaw or even four-jaw chuck.
Equally, it's preferable to use a high-precision lathe, in this case a Harrison M300.

3 Next, the end of the blank is turned flat.

4 One end of the air hole is drilled, initially with a centring tool and then with the appropriate twist bit.

5 The blank is taken out of the chuck, turned round and steps 2, 3 and 4 repeated.

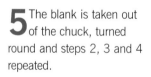

the student market. And, if a mouthpiece goes missing, it's a minimal financial burden to a school that's buying them in bulk.

The US company Kelly Mouthpieces produces a wide range of affordable designs to suit different instruments and styles, many made from a Lexan synthetic. Kelly also offers metal mouthpieces, including some stainless steel models, plus a number of useful accessories. These include 'sound sleeves', designed to give a darker tone to trumpet mouthpieces, and a low-cost mouthpiece truing tool that can remove dents and distortions from a range of mouthpiece shanks.

And so...

Without taking all the factors and variables above into account, the odds of creating a custom mouthpiece that performs as well as expected aren't much better than pure chance. That said, if your requirements as a player are different to most players', going to an experienced custom mouthpiece maker will get you to where you want to be. The maker should be creating a mouthpiece not just for you but for your instrument, so that, for instance, if you've already found 'the gap' for you then that's exactly what the new mouthpiece will match.

A custom mouthpiece will cost you more than a mass-produced one. But the alternative may be to spend a long time trawling through the stores before coming to the same conclusion as every really tall guy in a clothes shop: there's nothing on those racks that's going to fit properly.

6 It is the backbore reamer that determines the profile of the mouthpiece's backbore. Again, this is defined using a succession of passes to avoid overheating the reamer, or snagging the material.

7 The exit of the backbore has any burr removed using a hand-held triangular bearing scraper.

8 Callipers (also known as a vernier gauge, after the linear scales traditionally used for measurement on this type of device) are used to mark the extent of the shank.

9 The lathe carriage is set so that the turning tool cuts the shank to the required taper.

10 A mouthpiece receiver is used to check for correct fit.

11 Excess material is removed as an initial step in shaping the external profile of the cup.

12 The mouthpiece is removed, a smaller collet inserted in the chuck and the inverted mouthpiece shank inserted.

13 The external profile of the cup is turned to the exact diameter desired.

14 A purpose-made turning tool is used to shape the inside of the cup.

15 The external diameter of the rim is shaped with a file. (The lathe is in motion, so this is essentially a fine-turning process.)

16 Further shaping of the internal profile of the cup and the rim is achieved using small, hand-held cutting tools.

17 The profile can be checked against a mould, to ensure that the new mouthpiece is a precise match for an existing model.

18 A succession of emery cloths, of graduated fineness, are used to smooth the mouthpiece.

19 The mouthpiece is again inverted for final finessing of the external profile, again using hand-held tools and emery cloth.

20 The finished mouthpiece can now be buffed to a high shine using an electric polishing mop and mopping soap. The mouthpiece is now ready for use, or may be plated, usually in silver or gold.

Bell design

The function of the bell as converter from high pressure/small displacement to low pressure/high displacement is covered in the chapter *The Fundamentals...*, along with the role the bell plays in intonation.

There's no such thing as the 'correct' dimensions for a bell. Makers evolve a particular size and profile over a period of years, as best suits a particular tone, or style of playing. As a general rule of thumb, an instrument of bigger bore will be louder but will require more lung power and be harder to control. In addition to the overall bore of the instrument, these characteristics in a horn can be manipulated by adjusting the relative diameter of the throat. It's worth considering at this point that most horns have the bell facing the audience (the French horn being a notable exception), therefore designing a horn that disperses the sound in a more directional fashion is a strategy for creating an instrument that is, for all practical purposes, louder, without putting ever greater demands on the amount of sound pressure created by the player.

It must be stressed, however, that all musical instrument makers stand on the shoulders of giants. That is to say, they learn their craft by copying the efforts of others, and only when they can do that with success can they start to make small changes, thus subtly shifting the performance parameters in the desired direction.

Looking at the more fundamental issues of how a bell is constructed, the vast majority start life as sheet material of approximately 0.5mm or 20 thousandths of an inch, in the case of a trumpet, cornet, French horn or trombone. (Generally speaking, the bigger the brass instrument, the thicker the gauge of the brass sheet used.) This is then cut into a tapered strip, folded round and joined by a braising process. The resultant metal spout is then beaten into a symmetrical shape using a mallet against a metal former, before being smoothed on a lathe.

Because of the almost exponential nature of the taper, forming the complete spout and bell from a single sheet would be particularly wasteful and difficult to achieve on the larger brass instruments. There are two common design approaches to this problem. One is to inset a V-shaped gusset of additional sheet (Figure A). The alternative is to spin the flare from a flat disk of sheet material, which is joined to the spout with a seam around the throat (Figure B). Although there are adherents of both techniques the difference in the end result is almost entirely cosmetic. Anyone who claims that they can hear a difference between the two is almost undoubtedly detecting one of many other possible variations between instruments – typically bore, type of brass and so on.

Another variable between one instrument and another is the wall thickness of the material, which the maker needs to control with extreme care. Once a bell gets thinner than about 13

Figure A: Bell with gusset.

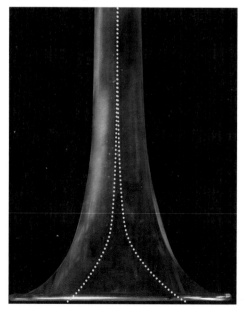

Figure B: Spun bell and spout.

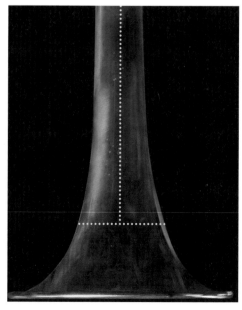

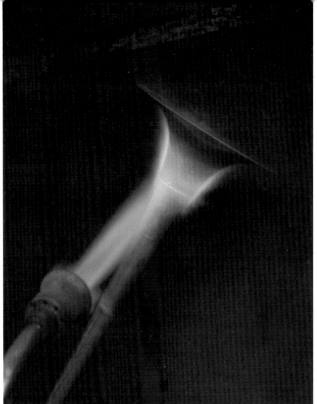

This ornate garland is on a natural horn belonging to Giles Whittome.

thousandths of an inch it will buckle. Conversely, a bell that's too thick will make for a heavy instrument, and some believe it will impair the tone. However, since the 1980s there's been a growing belief among a great many players that 'carefully used', thicker gauge materials can enhance instrument performance.

We would argue that a thin bell can impart a pleasant 'zing', but the throat area, where the air pressure is still relatively high, needs to be thicker. This helps to ensure that the sound is projected out of the front of the bell and doesn't dissipate through the wall of the throat. These are generalisations, however, and the appropriate wall thicknesses for a tuba will be considerably greater than those for a French horn.

Nearly all bells are finished off with a rim. This is put in while the bell is still on the former and involves turning the edge over into a soft U shape while it's spinning, into which is inserted a solid brass wire. This wire must be cut precisely to length, so that it's forced into the U and won't vibrate. With the lathe restarted, the bell material can be trimmed and the edge turned fully into the bell, completely concealing the wire inside.

On a few instruments – including the Vienna horn – it's traditional to add a 'cuff' or ring of nickel into the rim, often referred to as a 'garland', which may then be ornately engraved, or worked into a relief. Some players believe that the garland adds projection.

(A notable exception to the 'rim rule' is the Conn Vocabell. This has no wire, or fold, but is made from a thicker gauge material at the edge and is hardened to make it more resilient to damage. These were popular in the 1930s and '40s but fell out of favour and are now mostly in the hands of collectors.)

Key stages in bell manufacture

1 The spout is marked out on sheet metal using a template and a scribe.

2 The sheet is cut to shape using shears.

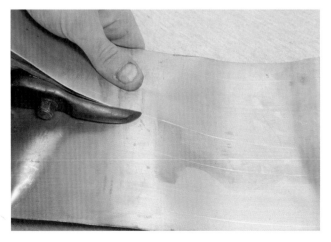

3 The material is softened with a gas torch, then cleaned with acid.

4 Next, the sheet is bent round a mandrel and the edges then smoothed with a burnisher, so that they can form a

tidy seam. An acid bath cleans all traces of oxide and grease from the metal, which will otherwise not braise correctly.

5 Teeth are put into the metal using special pliers. The teeth will hold the seam together while it's braised.

6 Braising is again accomplished with a gas torch. The melting point of the material and the braising metal are close, so care must be taken not to burn through the sheet.

7 Reducing the overlapping seam back to a single thickness requires a planishing hammer.

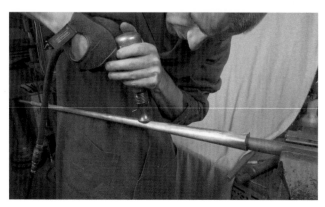

8 Once re-softened, the spout is beaten into shape by slamming it down repeatedly onto a metal former and hitting any high spots with a nylon mallet. A series of draw rings are applied manually to smooth and round the metal. (Some manufacturers draw the entire assembly through a thick ring of lead, which presents enough opposition to flatten the bell against the former.)

9 In a separate operation, the flare of the bell is spun from a flat disk of metal, by pressing the metal against a former while it's rotating on a lathe.

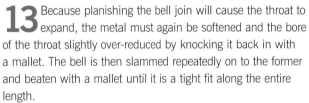

10 The throat end of the flare is cut off and the edge ground flat using a disk sander. The flare is then used to mark the reciprocal cutting point on the spout.

11 Joining the bell and spout is a similar process to seaming the spout. The spout is toothed, then a burnishing action is used to create a tight seam.

12 The seam is braised, then planished to a single thickness, again in a similar fashion to the seam along the spout.

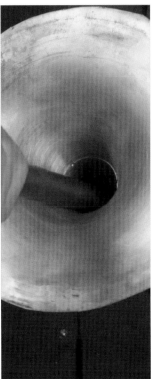

13 Because planishing the bell join will cause the throat to expand, the metal must again be softened and the bore of the throat slightly over-reduced by knocking it back in with a mallet. The bell is then slammed repeatedly on to the former and beaten with a mallet until it is a tight fit along the entire length.

14 After another softening the bell and former are attached to a lathe, where further smoothing is achieved using a large 'spoon' kept at the correct pressure by levering it against the hand-rest. (A more forgiving wooden spoon is often used before the metal one.)

15 Although spinning has created a smooth interior surface, the seam must be filed at this point to remove any exterior imperfections.

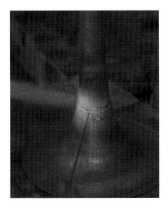
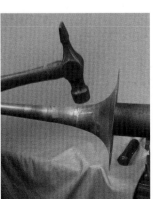

DESIGN AND MANUFACTURE

16 Smoothing the throat and flare involves cutting away the metal using a tool ground from a machine hacksaw blade, and a succession of emery cloths from 100 grit to 400 grit. (Prior to cutting it's advisable to remove any remaining oxide with coarse emery. Otherwise the cutting tool will blunt very quickly.)

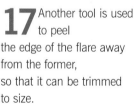

17 Another tool is used to peel the edge of the flare away from the former, so that it can be trimmed to size.

18 Trimming the bell is again achieved with a hand-held tool.

19 The diameter is checked using callipers, to ensure that the finished bell will be of the required dimensions.

20 A blunt chisel is used to fold the bell rim back on itself, forming a soft U shape that will hold the bell wire.

21 Once the wire is cut to length it will be held into the rim by its own pressure, and the end of the flare can be folded right over the wire, concealing it. (Some manufacturers chose to solder-in the wire.)

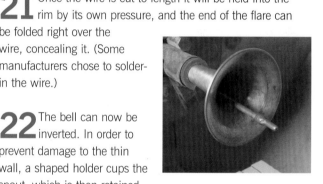

22 The bell can now be inverted. In order to prevent damage to the thin wall, a shaped holder cups the spout, which is then retained at the other end of the lathe by either a long bolt (shown here) or shaped wedges.

23 Depending on the precise manufacturing process and the type of bell, the flare may be thinned at this stage using a triangular bearing scraper. This introduces a number of hazards into the process, of which over-thinning is the greatest. As a result it's periodically necessary to measure the wall of the flare with a thickness gauge.

24 A succession of emery cloths is again used to smooth the surface and to ensure that there's no trace of irregularity at any joining seams.

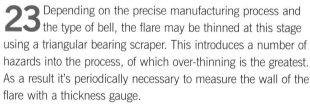

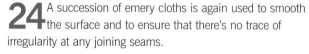

Tubing

Bending tubing

Brass instruments are a mass of curved tubing. In order to prevent a tube collapsing while it's being bent, it must be filled with a liquid, which will cool into a malleable solid. In the case of the spout it's filled with a premixed pitch/resin solution formulated for specific ambient temperatures. This enables trouble-free bending to be carried out in a range of climates.

Smaller diameter tubing is sometimes bent by first filling it with molten lead. However, we have chosen not to show this process because it's potentially hazardous, and we don't want anyone to gain the impression that working safely with hot lead can be learned from a book.

A safer alternative to lead is Wood's metal, also known as Lipowitz's alloy. Available under the brand names Cerrobend, Bendalloy, Pewtalloy and MCP 158, it's a lead alloy with a melting point low enough for it to be removed from tubing by boiling in water. But user beware – when hot this stuff still burns skin, and it hurts! Like any metal containing lead, it's also toxic, so contact with the skin is to be avoided.

Even working with hot pitch/resin could be injurious to anyone without the correct safety wear – thick safety gloves, overalls and goggles.

For small-bore tubing, such as that used to make the crooks for slides, there's a still safer alternative to lead – ice. The mix is water with a small amount of washing-up liquid (detergent), which provides enough elasticity to prevent the ice from cracking when the tubing is being bent. This isn't a technique we've used personally but we've seen it employed with success. Some experimentation with a domestic freezer and lengths of tubing should be all that's needed to finesse this approach.

A young 'Satch' Botwe bends a French horn spout at Paxman's, c1980. We think the longhaired lad behind the bells is none other than Andy Taylor.

This is how a bell is bent in detail:
- An end stop will prevent the hot mix from flowing out, and also provides a clamping point.
- The molten pitch must be poured in with great care to prevent excessive splashing, or air bubbles inside the tubing.
- A metal rod, held in position by the spacers attached to it, will form the bending handle once the pitch is set. Temperature is critical to the consistency of the set mix, so a temperature-controlled water tank or insulated cupboard is required during setting.

Providing the spout has bent without undue puckering, it can be sanded with the pitch in place.

- The bell is clamped against the former, with the braised seam facing inwards. A slow controlled bend – keeping the spout straight in the vertical plane – gives the best results (see left).
- Any puckering to the tube is best removed by taking down the high spots with a jeweller's hammer. (If the puckering is too severe the remedial work will need to be done after the bell is emptied, using normal de-denting techniques.) Once the surface is sufficiently smooth, a file, and then emery grades, are applied by hand.
- A gas torch on a gentle heat is used to ease the pitch out.
- Where a traditional high shine is required, the electric mop (buffing wheel polisher) is used. Great care is taken, as even momentarily snagging the end of the spout on the mop can cause the whole assembly to 'wrap' into the spindle of the machine, while exerting too much pressure can buckle the flare.

DESIGN AND MANUFACTURE

Leader pipe manufacture

Changing the leader pipe for one of slightly different profile is one of the more popular options among the customising community. Although choice of leader pipe is hardly as personal as that of a mouthpiece, the taper, thickness and overall rigidity of the assembly undoubtedly impacts on the performance of the instrument.

There are essentially three ways of making the tapered tubing required for a leader pipe. One is strictly for the largest manufacturers and involves the use of a hydraulic press to force oil into the tubing under great pressure. This should cause it to blow up like a balloon, but the tubing assumes exactly the right shape because it's constrained by the two halves of a solid steel mould, which has been machined to match the profile required.

The second method employs a lead doughnut and a drawbench. Here, the tube is pulled through an undersized hole in the doughnut and thereby forced down on to a tapered mandrel inside the tube. This is a good technique for medium-scale production.

The hand-builder's alternative is the exact opposite but produces results that are every bit as good. A tapered steel mandrel is made on a lathe and this is used to define the internal dimensions of the leader pipe.

1 Having selected a length of tubing that matches the larger diameter of the tapered pipe, it needs to be softened using a torch.

2 With the tubing over the tapered mandrel, it is pushed through a steel draw-ring slightly larger than the tube itself, with the operator maintaining constant pressure by twisting the plate slightly out of square with the mandrel.

3 There's a tendency for the tube to reduce in a series of steps initially, rather than a smooth taper. These steps can be gradually eliminated by swaging the tube – essentially an ironing movement.

4 Once the tube has been made as smooth as possible – and is a good fit for the mandrel along its length – the outer surface can be lightly filed.

5 A strap of emery can then be used to remove the file marks and prepare the piece for polishing, if desired.

Note: A similar technique can be used to produce parallel tubing of a specific diameter, although a powered draw press is preferred if significant quantities of tubing are required. This technique is very important to the small-scale builder, as the ability to produce tubing on demand greatly reduces the amount of raw material that must be kept in stock.

Valves

Valve design

While it would probably be possible to write a book about nothing other than the design and manufacture of valves, it's a highly specialised topic, even in the small world that is brass instrument making. For the purposes of this book, we've distilled the subject down to the points that are most useful to an understanding of how best to repair and maintain these essential devices.

In theory, you might say that 'all' a valve does on an instrument is to introduce an additional length of tubing, thus permitting a new selection of notes to be played. But for the valves to work as the heart of a workable musical instrument they have to work with speed and reliability, and they have to be light enough to allow the player to operate the keys with dexterity.

Perhaps that list of requirements doesn't sound too demanding – but there are more. Even a non-player will appreciate that it's important for the valves not to leak unduly. However, players will add that valves also mustn't impede airflow when they're open, closed or in motion. Meeting these requirements requires ingenuity on behalf of the designer and has a massive effect on the fluidity with which the instrument can be played.

In the chapter *The Fundamentals...* we touched upon the fact that most valves can be considered to be piston or rotary in nature. At this point, therefore, it might be an interesting diversion to look at two of the less common variations on this theme.

The Vienna horn is very similar to a French horn but has a distinctive valve section based on double piston valves, which are linked to finger levers via long rods. This is known as a 'pumpenvalve' system and dates back to the 1840s, but remains in use. Its advantage is that it presents reduced air resistance to the player when the valve is depressed, as each valve in the pair redirects the air by 90°, allowing for a more fluid legato. However, it must be said that the system is mechanically somewhat cumbersome, making it difficult to play passages of fast notes.

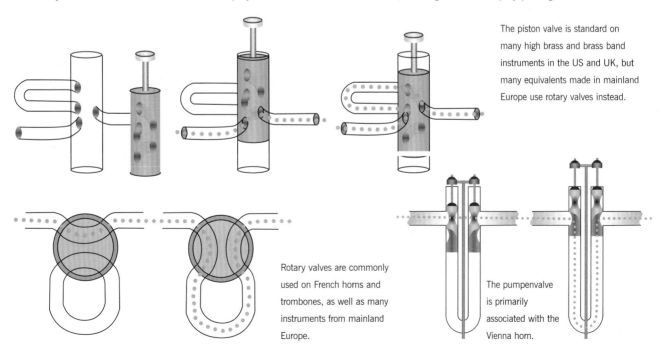

The piston valve is standard on many high brass and brass band instruments in the US and UK, but many equivalents made in mainland Europe use rotary valves instead.

Rotary valves are commonly used on French horns and trombones, as well as many instruments from mainland Europe.

The pumpenvalve is primarily associated with the Vienna horn.

The disk valve is a relative rarity that works in a way a bit like the chamber in a revolver; but instead of bringing a new bullet to the barrel, the rotating disk marries up two alternative lengths of tubing.

It must be acknowledged that many repair technicians go from one year to the next without encountering either a pumpenvalve or a disk valve, whereas anyone who works with trombones is likely to encounter on a regular basis the newer valves from Hagmann, Rotax and Thayer. The merits of these are discussed in the chapter *Modern innovations*, while the specific advice on maintenance appears in the next chapter.

Equally, any discussion of valves would be of limited practical value if the interface between them and the player's fingers were not also examined. This is especially true of rotary valves, which have quite a complicated linkage system between the vertical motion of the finger levers and the rotary motion of the collar that connects to the valve itself. All of this is looked at in detail in the 'Professional repairs' section of the chapter *Maintenance and repair techniques*.

Valve manufacture (piston)

1 The casing parts have their exteriors turned to shape and threaded for the end caps.

2 The interiors of the casing parts are machined to a preliminary diameter.

(Hoxon Gakki Corp)

3 The casing parts have their air holes drilled using a turret lathe. In large-scale manufacture, where speed is important and high machinery costs can be justified by high production, the knuckles (connection tubing) are usually passed through a high-temperature oven. This even heat helps to minimise any distortion to the metal. At smaller production levels a skilled operator will silver solder these joints while the components are held firmly in place (as shown above).

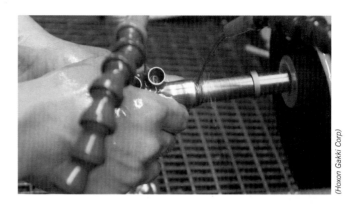

(Hoxon Gakki Corp)

4 Now the insides of the casings can be machined to a finer tolerance.

(Hoxon Gakki Corp)

5 The airways through the valve are inserted and their ends flared out slightly to hold them in place while they're hard soldered.

(Hoxon Gakki Corp)

6 Flux is applied to the body of the valve in preparation for soldering.

7 The airways are hard soldered.(Hoxon Gakki Corp)

8 Any excess material is removed in a precision grinding process, designed to make the valve pistons as close a match for the casings as they can be without becoming a 'force fit' (*ie* locked solid).

(Hoxon Gakki Corp)

9 The slotted column that holds the valve pin and spring assembly is soldered into the valve casing.

10 'Lapping' is the process by which each individual valve and its specific casing are adjusted for the best possible fit. Lapping paste is made from a fine pumice powder. Contrary to what might be expected, the powder tends to embed in the softer of the two metals and abrade the harder. Hand lapping is an art: too little lapping will result in a valve that sticks, but too much will result in a valve that leaks unduly.

Hand lapping: this procedure is covered in more detail in the section on 'Professional repairs' in the next chapter.

11 An experienced lapper can substitute a cordless drill, which speeds up the process but increases the chance of making a mistake.

Valve manufacture (rotary)

Some rotary valves are machined from solid metal. While there's nothing wrong with this approach per se, it can have a noticeable effect of the weight on the instrument, especially in the case of double or triple horns, which have larger valves. As the valve becomes heavier, there's more mass to move. This in turn means stronger springs and more effort on the part of the player.

Until recently, the main way of mitigating this problem was to make hollow halves, which involves techniques that are similar to those used in piston valve making, as described above. A more recent innovation is the use of much lighter metals than turning brass, notably titanium.

Traditionally, much of the rotary valve manufacturing process has relied on a combination of a turret lathe to cut the airways and a flat-bed lathe to cut the cylinders, followed by careful hand lapping to match each casing and valve. Today's computer-controlled machines can complete all the stages with great speed and precision. However, the process leaves little to see in action, because there's no need for manual intervention.

This valve has just been machined, as evidenced by traces of soluble oil and the fact that the valve is still attached to the blank rod that will be used to make subsequent valves. (*Chris Huning, Paxman Musical Instruments*)

Modern valves can be machined to very close tolerances, reducing the significance of the lapping process. However it's achieved, the optimum gap between valve casing and body is in the order of 0.025mm. Note also the hole through the valve body, designed to reduce its weight. (*Chris Huning, Paxman Musical Instruments*)

Ferrule manufacture, fitting and finishing

Anyone who wants to customise horns, or is taking a serious interest in brass instrument repair, would do well to master the art of making ferrules, those short sections of nickel silver tube that hold the main tubes together. For one thing, if you know how ferrules are made you'll be able to copy the ferrule styles of other makers. Details like that make the difference between a professional custom instrument and a 'Frankenhorn'.

1 Appropriate diameter tubing is selected and secured in the lathe chuck. (**NB:** don't leave long lengths of narrow tubing sticking out of the back of the lathe because it will whip from side to side in ever-increasing circles.)

2 The end of the tubing is cut true using a cutting tool set in the lathe tool post.

3 De-burring the interior of the tubing will ensure a tidy fit further down the line.

4 Callipers are used to set the length of the ferrule – 12mm in this case – and rotating the chuck slightly with the callipers in contact with the tubing will leave a visible mark to align the cutting tool to.

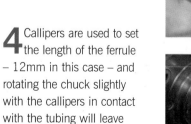

5 The ferrule can now be cut to length. **NB:** It's very important that you insert a drill or similar metal object into the tube before it's cut all the way through, ideally held by the tail chuck, so that when you cut off the ferrule it's retained and cannot fly off in an uncontrolled fashion.

6 You may choose to add a decorative bead to one end of the ferrule, or both. The classic rounded beads are best created by grinding a cutting tool that matches the desired profile. (Mild steel is a good material for this, providing the cutting tip is then hardened by getting it red hot and then plunging it into cold water.) The bead in our example uses only a simple triangular cutter.

Any further finishing is best accomplished once the ferrule is soldered on to the instrument.

An alternative approach is to leave the cut end plain, for a more modern, 'clean' look. Although this eliminates step 6, it's actually a harder look to achieve to a high standard, as the cuts and subsequent soldering have to be very neat.

Soft and hard soldering

The main materials required for soft and hard soldering are listed at the back of *An illustrated list of tools and materials*, which also explains the difference between the various types of solder. This section deals with the techniques used to achieve successful soldering, as they're key to instrument repair and manufacture.

Any kind of soldering relies on certain key points in order to work:

- The two surfaces to be joined must be free from oxide and grease, whether achieved by abrasion, acid cleaning or both.
- The surfaces must remain oxide-free despite heating, which is the purpose of flux.
- A viable solder joint can only be achieved when both the work surfaces are hot enough to melt the solder.

Places where soft solder is used on a brass instrument are:

- Where ferrules connect to tubing.
- Where the flanges of stays connect to tubing.
- Where receivers connect to leader pipes.

In contrast, hard solder is used where mechanical strength is more important than ease of disassembly:

- Where flanges connect to bracing stays.
- Where knuckles attach to valve casings.
- Where finger lever pads attach to the pivot and lever parts of the assembly used with rotary valves.

The lists above aren't exhaustive, so a rule of thumb is that if it looks like a join – particularly between dissimilar metals – it's probably soft soldered. Conversely, if it looks like one piece of metal – but logic says it would be difficult to fashion it from solid material – it's probably hard soldered.

A typical soft soldering process

Connecting a ferrule

1 The tubing is introduced to the ferrule and the assembly, supported mechanically by clamping or binding with wire if necessary.

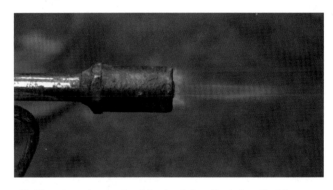

2 The air and gas mix of the torch is adjusted so that the flame burns blue and forms a distinct point.

3 The metal components are heated a little to help the flux to 'bite'.

4 Liquid flux is most easily applied with a small brush – but expect it to splash somewhat.

5 The torch is used to bring the components up to temperature.

6 Once the metal is hot enough, the solder is introduced to the work. Providing the join is tight enough, capillary action will draw the solder into the joint. Careful use of the flame helps to ensure that the solder runs all the way round the join, with little going where it isn't wanted.

7 Where the solder runs is dictated by which parts of the metal are hot enough to melt it. With practice, a small amount of solder can be made to run all the way round a join using the flame. If the joint is tight, capillary action alone will draw the solder.

8 If necessary, excess solder is best wiped away with a cloth while it's still molten.

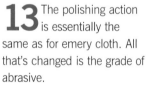

9 Once the join has cooled any temporary supports can be taken away and unwanted flux wiped off with a wet cloth. Running the join under a hot-water tap is also very effective for this.

10 A sharp scraper can be used to remove any remaining excess solder.

11 A strip of abrasive cloth will remove any remaining traces of solder.

12 The assembly can now be polished, using a strip of cloth that's been primed with mopping soap. In addition to removing any scratches this process will also remove any discolouration caused by the flux.

13 The polishing action is essentially the same as for emery cloth. All that's changed is the grade of abrasive.

14 A pleasant decorative contrast can be obtained by giving the tubing a satin finish using a Scotch-Brite cloth.

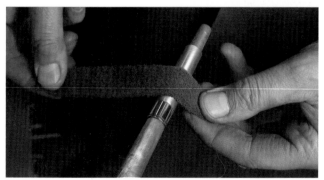

A typical hard soldering process

Making a brace

1 The simplest brace is two flanges back to back. A file, or a belt sander, are two possible tools for fashioning the flatwork.

2 A mandrel of appropriate diameter and a mallet are all that's required to curve the flanges.

3 A belt sander will smooth the outer surfaces of the flanges, remove burrs and take off any oxide.

4 You need a much hotter flame for hard soldering than for soft soldering, because the material has to become red hot.

5 An adapted pair of pliers will hold the work while minimising their surface contact with the work. This will make it easier to bring the work up to temperature.

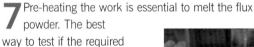

6 The solder rod is warmed until it's hot enough for the flux powder to stick to it. The rod will serve as an applicator.

7 Pre-heating the work is essential to melt the flux powder. The best way to test if the required temperature has been reached is to dab the flux on the work periodically. This will help to ensure that the flux is applied before a significant level of oxidisation has occurred to the work.

8 The work will be red hot before hard solder will melt! Failure to grasp this will result in a joint that's merely held together by the melted flux and will fall apart when it's cleaned. It's also worth bearing in mind that hard solder doesn't fill gaps very well, so a tight mechanical fit between the parts is important.

9 Cooling the flange is important before undertaking the next step.

10 Because the flux is so tough when cold, acid dipping is required to start the cleaning process.

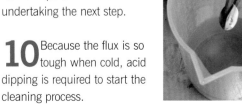

99

Slide manufacture

Any reader who's grasped the basics of bending and drawing tubing, making ferrules, and hard and soft soldering is armed with almost enough theory to make a slide, an activity that brings together all those skills.

There are two important aspects to making a successful slide. One is the quality of the fit between the slide leg and the outer sleeve, while the other is the related issue of how parallel the whole assembly is. Both these factors will impact on how well the slide works.

On most brass instruments many of the slides need only work reasonably well in order to fulfil their function as a means to correct pitch and intonation. This is because the slide will typically be adjusted only periodically, or once before a performance, in the case of the main slide. So if the slide is a little sticky in action, it's hardly the end of the world.

The two notable exceptions to this are the first and third valve slides on a trumpet, or the compensating slide on larger brass – notably euphoniums, the length of which an experienced player will adjust for intonation during performance using the finger rings; and the main slide on a trombone, which is, of course, in constant use. More specifically, it's a vital part of the way the instrument is played, which is why trombone players, quite rightly, care passionately about how smoothly the slide works on their instrument.

Uniquely, on a trombone slide not only is there considerable scope for the two legs to drift out of parallel, but they're also long enough to get bent out of true. Either of these conditions will materially affect the playability of the instrument and the remedies will be looked at in detail throughout the chapter *Maintenance and repair techniques*.

From a design perspective, it's useful to note that the last 100mm to 120mm or so of a trombone's slide legs are the only section at the full diameter of the sleeve. This 'stocking' is achieved on the tube drawing machine (drawbench) and greatly reduces the friction between the two parts.

Assembling a trombone outer slide

The legs (or 'rails') of a trombone slide start life on a draw bench, where a huge amount of pressure pulls pre-made tubing between a mandrel and a die, or drawplate. This allows the maker to fashion slide legs to very exacting tolerances and to a diameter specifically suited to a particular model. In addition, by employing two dies of different diameters the maker can draw the 'stocking' part of the inner slide.

A jig placed on the 'surface plate' (known to some makers as the 'stone'), holds the slide legs in parallel while the assembler solders first the bottom bow and then the hand brace.

Despite the rigidity of the jig, the assembler works quickly, in order to minimise any distortion to the tubing caused by heat from the soldering torch. Note the use of clamps to secure the tubing and wire clips to hold the flanges in place. Once a part has been soft soldered it can be cooled with water.

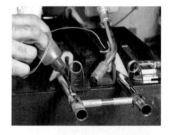

After all but one joint of the hand brace is soldered on, the assembler checks the width of the two slide legs with callipers to ensure

that everything is parallel, before soldering the remaining joint to make the whole slide rigid. If small adjustments are required before soldering, a series of gentle taps will move the slide legs in a controlled way.

Polishing

There are two main techniques for polishing brass instruments in the final stages of the manufacturing process. As with other finishing techniques, they're both highly relevant in addition to the repairer.

Polishing by hand

1 The instrument is held securely using a bell stick at one end, plus a string from the ceiling attached to the receiver in the case of larger instruments. This is the standard method for holding a brass instrument when access to both sides is required.

2 Mopping soap applied to the cloth, as shown in the section on soft soldering. (An alternative is Brasso liquid, but it has a tendency to splash during the procedure that follows.)

3 The strap is hooked over the tubing to be polished and a rapid, two-handed, up-and-down motion is applied to the cloth.

4 Any residual polishing material can be wiped off at the end using a soft, clean, lint-free cloth.

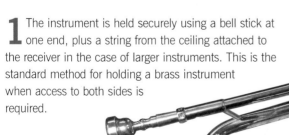

Polishing with an electric mop

1 The appropriate cloth mop is selected, according to the firmness and size required. (Final polishing is more effective with a soft mop, while a harder mop will take out scratches more effectively but can inflict dents in areas such as a bell if too much pressure is applied. Similarly, the optimum diameter of mop depends on the size of the area to be polished versus the radius into which it has to fit. Put simply, it's big mops for bells and small mops for crooks.)

2 The tapered thread on the mopping machine engages the mop as it rotates.

3 With the machine running, mopping soap is applied to the face of the mop.

4 The work is advanced with care to the face of the mop. (Complex shapes, such as instrument bells that have already been bent to shape, need particular attention as it's all too easy to be polishing one end but fail to notice that the other end is about to snag the mop.)

5 A smooth, ironing-like action will give an even polish and prevent the build-up of soap in one spot.

For the very highest polish, jeweller's rouge is used for the final finish. Not all manufacturers use – or even like the look of – this extremely high gloss.

Lacquering and plating

The variety of finishes offered to brass players has never been wider. For some purchasers, lacquering or plating are simply ways of making the instrument more durable, therefore easier to maintain. For others, they're techniques to achieve a decorative effect. Because both lacquering and plating require specialist techniques and equipment that might be used only occasionally by musical instrument makers, it's generally only the largest manufacturers that perform these processes in-house.

Lacquering is applied using a spray process, not unlike that used to paint cars. One of the problems for the small-scale manufacturer is the need for a dedicated booth with an air filtration system to ensure that the particles found in everyday air don't end up spoiling the lacquer finish. As many processes used in musical instrument making – such as sanding – actually increase the number of particles in the air, the conflict in the two requirements is clear.

The term 'lacquer' covers a wide range of formulations, some of which are considerably hardier than others. The lacquers that harden chemically, rather than air dry, are generally the most resistant to attack from chemicals such as the naturally occurring acids in the body, but care has to be taken in choosing a formulation that's not so brittle that it will fragment if the instrument becomes dented.

Repairing lacquer damage and relacquering small components is certainly within the grasp of the repair shop, or even the keen amateur. These possibilities are discussed in the chapter *Maintenance and repair techniques*.

Electroplating is a process whereby metal ions in a solution are moved by an electric field to coat an electrode – in this case a musical instrument made of metal. By far the most popular plating for bass instruments is silver, hence the term 'silver band' for a brass band playing only plated instruments. Silver resists oxidisation better than brass, making it a hardier option for bands that often perform in the open air.

Other finish options available from the plating process include frosted silver and gold. The latter finish is likely to be plated in addition as it isn't as hardy a metal as silver.

(Osprey Metal Finishers)

It's equally important to stop lacquer entering areas where it isn't wanted, such as the inside of slide legs and valve casings.

Thorough degreasing in a solvent tank is essential if the lacquer is to adhere to the surface of the metal.

(Osprey Metal Finishers)

Working out how to hold an instrument so that it can be lacquered from all sides takes a certain amount of ingenuity.

(Osprey Metal Finishers)

Applying the lacquer is a real skill. Any sags or runs will ruin the result, and require the entire finish to be stripped before starting again.

(Osprey Metal Finishers)

Great care must be taken when hanging up the instrument to cure, because the finish will be ruined if it touches anything else before it hardens.

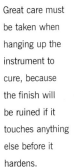

(Osprey Metal Finishers)

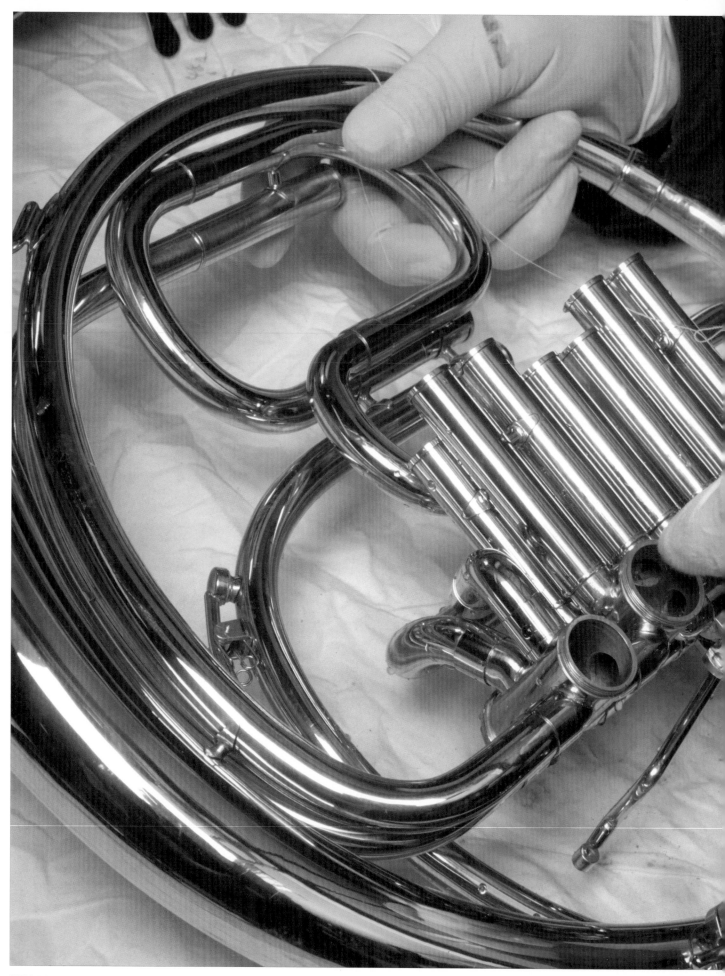

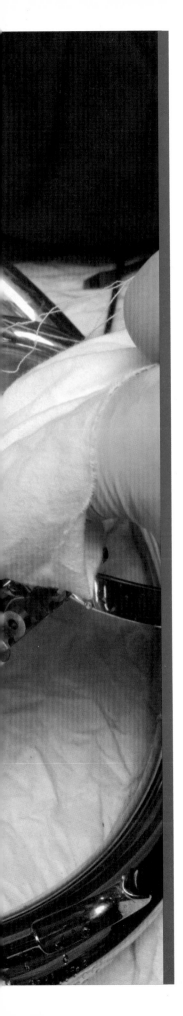

Maintenance and repair techniques

This chapter is broken down into three sections, each with progressively more challenging techniques. The first of these, 'Section A: Routine maintenance', is suitable for all abilities and carries very low risk of causing accidental damage.

Section A: Routine maintenance

When they're new most musical instruments come with an upbeat little leaflet that starts something like this: 'Congratulations on your purchase of a Fabbybrass horn! Providing you handle this instruments with care and follow our simple maintenance routine, it should give you years of trouble-free playing pleasure.'

You know what? That leaflet might be irritatingly cheerful but what it's saying is basically right. Unless you damage a brass musical instrument, simple routine maintenance can keep you from the repair shop's door for a very long time. Not only that, but an instrument that's clean inside and out – with correctly lubricated slides and valves – will play better as well as last longer.

We've listed these procedures in order of frequency, so if they're at the top of our list they really should really be top of your list too.

1 Lubricate the valves

It's worth checking the valves before every playing session because dry valves don't only feel rough but will also wear out faster. (See the separate boxouts for instructions on lubricating the different types of valve.) Use an oil designed for the purpose, rather than anything from a DIY store! Even dedicated brass valve oils aren't all equal, as the ones with a high solvent content evaporate quite quickly. Also, some of the more volatile oils can make you feel unwell if you over-lubricate the valve immediately before playing, as you end up breathing in the fumes. 'Sparingly' is a word often used to describe how much oil to put on.

Now and again it does no harm to add a little oil to the pivot point of the water key(s) as well – doubly so if the instrument has push-type water keys. These newer keys are essentially mini-piston valves and need to be treated as such for reliable operation. Third valve slide oil from a pipette is ideal. Twist the top of the key a little as you apply the oil and it will cover the entire valve.

Note: For trombone players, top maintenance task on the list is, of course, 'lubricate the slide'. Although any valves on the instrument should also be maintained, when it comes to playing action the slide IS the trombone.

2 Wipe down your instrument

Always wipe down your instrument with a duster or other absorbent cloth before you put it back in the case. Removing excess moisture will help to prevent discolouration of the finish, as well as more severe corrosion in the longer term. So it's worth keeping a cloth in the instrument case for this purpose.

3 Clean out the leader pipe and mouthpiece

Cleaning the leader pipe is most safely achieved using a flexible 'snake' brush that can be fed into the pipe and pulled through from the main slide. How often this needs to be done varies widely from player to player and is also dependent on how often the instrument gets used.

Once you've performed this operation and seen what comes out of the tube, you'll soon come to your own conclusions about when to brush it through again. Cleaning the mouthpiece's throat and backbore is easily achieved with small brushes sold for this purpose. The remainder of the mouthpiece only needs wiping over with a cloth.

Leader pipe brush.
(JHS/Gary Barlow)

Mouthpiece brush.
(JHS/Gary Barlow)

Avoiding damage

Just because they're made of metal, don't make the mistake of thinking that brass instruments are even close to being indestructible. In reality, even seemingly trivial events can lead to costly repairs. Fortunately the causes of many accidents can easily be avoided once you're aware of them.

DIY DISASTERS

By far the most common self-inflicted wound stems from attempting to remove a stuck mouthpiece with pliers. But there are also seemingly innocent ways an instrument can be damaged.

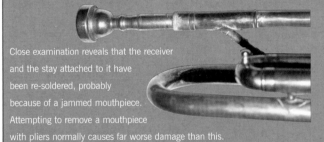

Close examination reveals that the receiver and the stay attached to it have been re-soldered, probably because of a jammed mouthpiece. Attempting to remove a mouthpiece with pliers normally causes far worse damage than this.

LOOSE MOUTHPIECE INSIDE THE CASE

Not only can this damage the tubing of the instrument, if it impacts with the thin walls of a piston valve casing it can push the casing into the valve itself, causing it to stick.

CRAMMING SHEET MUSIC INTO THE CASE

The case was designed to be a snug fit for your instrument, to protect it from damage. Cram music on top and you'll put the instrument under pressure when the lid is shut, potentially bending the instrument out of shape and straining the hinges and latches on the case.

SITTING ON THE CASE

Never a good idea, because the case wasn't designed to withstand this kind of abuse.

'PROTECTIVE' COVERINGS

Some players wrap a plastic material – such as electrical tape or a length of tubing that's been split open – round the leader pipe. Or they get a leather cover for some part of their instrument in the belief that they're 'protecting the metal'. Sadly, the opposite is true. No matter how impervious the covering appears to be, moisture from the hands will eventually get behind it, where it becomes trapped. Over time this acidic damp eats into the metal. Often this continues undetected until a repair requires the removal of the cover and the truth is exposed. In extreme cases it's been known for the acid to eat right through the wall of the instrument.

STICKY SWEETS AND DRINKS

It's best to avoid eating sweets, snacks or fizzy drinks before you play. If there's any left in your mouth, it will probably end up inside the instrument, where it can cause problems – especially if it finds its way into the valves.

FALLING OFF A CHAIR

The classic 'tea break at band practice' accident. You leave your instrument bell-down on the chair, someone else tips the chair, or brushes the instrument as they walk past. The rest is history.

How does a horn get a bell like this...?
...Getting knocked off a chair is one very likely answer.

FREEING A JAMMED VALVE/SLIDE

The use of force on a brass instrument should always be a last resort. Even then, it has to be applied in a very controlled way by someone who knows exactly what they're doing, otherwise the cost of the eventual repair can be a lot more than it would have been to cure the original problem.

DROPPING MARCHING BAND INSTRUMENTS

The clue to this one lies in the two words 'marching' and 'band'. Not all accidents are avoidable.

LEAVING THE INSTRUMENT ON THE BED

This is especially common with trumpets. Typically, the player puts the instrument 'safely' on the bed, then sits down next to it, tipping the trumpet on to the floor. Depending how it falls, the damage can range from a stuck mouthpiece to a detached stay or a mangled bell. (The second valve slide often takes the impact as well. That can actually damage the valve casing.) If the instrument happens to be lacquered, making it 'like new' can be a painfully expensive process.

SLAPPING THE MOUTHPIECE

We know the instrument will make a satisfying 'pop' if you slap the back of the mouthpiece, but please don't. It may cause it to get stuck.

Oiling piston valves

Lubricating a piston valve requires its removal from the casing so that oil can be applied directly to the body of the valve. This is accomplished by unscrewing the top cap, pulling the valve out and applying a small amount of oil (four or five drops is about right). If you put a few drops on the lower part of the valve body you can then rotate the valve, as well as moving it gently up and down, to spread the oil around. When you put the valve back in, you'll need to rotate it until the plastic or metal valve guide sits in the reciprocal slot in the casing before you can push it all the way down and do the top cap back up again.

The alternative is to remove both the top and bottom cap, then remove the valve and apply four to five drops of oil to the lower part of the valve. Gently place it into the casing upside down from the bottom. This allows you to turn the valve to ensure the whole valve has an even amount of oil without the valve guide getting caught in its slot. Remove the valve then immediately place it back in from the top the right way round. Don't use this technique unless the inside of the valve casing looks clean and has been well maintained. Of course, this can only be done on instruments that have adequate access to the bottom of the valve casings.

Most valves are numbered for position but it's best to only remove them one at a time if you're not sure where they go.

Note that piston valves aren't interchangeable – they must only go back into the casing from which they were removed. For this reason we suggest that you only remove one valve at a time whenever possible. (Most – but not all – valves are marked for position, though.)

4 Remove, clean and lubricate slide legs

For trombone players this will be item number one on the list!

Whenever removing a valve slide from an instrument, press down on the appropriate valve to relieve the back pressure. Otherwise you'll have to pull too hard and might damage the slide as it comes out.

Some players use valve oil to lubricate slides. It's much better to use lubricants formulated especially for the job. This particularly applies to trombones but also the first and third valve slides of trumpets, because smooth operation is crucial if the slide rings are to be operated with speed and accuracy.

For slides that aren't operated as part of the playing technique, proprietary slide grease is a better bet, as it will be the right consistency

It's best to lubricate slides with a dedicated product.

to lubricate the slide legs without clogging them up. An old towel provides a forgiving surface for taking the slides out of an instrument. Generally speaking it's better to remove, treat and return one slide at a time, rather than create an untidy pile of slides before turning your attention to the instrument itself. When you have the slide out you can wipe off any residue on the legs of the slide with a lint-free cloth, before cleaning out the inside of the instrument's slide tubes with a brush. Try to avoid brushing dirt into the valves, though, because you'll probably end up having to take the valve out for cleaning. This task is best performed around once a month – unless you're a trombone player, in which case you'll probably be constantly cleaning and lubricating the slide to get the smoothest action.

Note that the instructions above assume the slide legs came out freely. If the slide is jammed you'll require more difficult techniques, which may result in damage to the instrument. These are covered in Section B and again in Section C.

5 Periodic piston valve maintenance

The aluminium used on modern trumpets and other piston-valve stems can be a problem once spit has got in and corroded the thread. Unscrewing the stem and putting a little Vaseline on the thread helps to prevent the pillar fusing with the valve and shearing when it's removed at some time in the future.

While you're taking the valves out you can clean the valve

Oiling rotary valves

The rotary valve found on French horns – as well as other horns of Continental design and some trombones – sits on two bearings. The bottom one of these is located at the fixed end of the valve casing, where the linkage to the valve levers is located. In common with the body of the valve, the bottom bearing is slightly tapered, allowing the valve to wear into the casing over time rather than simply wearing out. The bottom bearing can be oiled without removing anything from the instrument – simply put a couple of drops of bearing oil into the gap between the bearing casing and the collar of the linkage assembly.

To prevent the rotor from drying out and to help to sluice any debris out of the valve, it's a good idea to lubricate it slightly by applying a couple of drops of rotor oil to the valve itself. This is done by removing the associated slide(s) and applying the oil down the outer slide sleeves. Holding the valve lever halfway down as you do this will ensure that the oil is applied to the body of the valve, rather than simply running into the airway through the valve.

What you don't want is for the oil to run down the inside of the slide sleeve, dragging slide grease into the valve. Some rotor

Oiling the bottom bearing.

Oiling the top bearing.

Oiling the valve body.

The other bearing is located under the valve cap, which needs to be unscrewed to reveal it. Again, one or two drops of oil accompanied by a couple of depressions of the valve lever should be all that's required to lubricate it. It's also worth applying a small amount of the same oil to the shaft bearing and spring of each valve, to help the parts to remain free running.

In an ideal world, that would be all the lubrication a conventional rotary valve requires. In reality, however, the clearance between the body of the valve and the casing is very small. This is a necessity because a larger clearance would result in an overly leaky valve, which would degrade the performance of the instrument.

As a result it only takes a small amount of foreign material to get between the valve body and the casing for the valve to become sluggish. And if the instrument is left for long enough for the valve to dry out, it's quite common for a valve to seize up completely.

oil bottles have an extended applicator nozzle to help you to aim the oil at the valve. You can also help the situation by oiling the valve *after* you've cleaned the associated slide but *before* you've regreased it.

Rotor oil and bearing oil aren't interchangeable. Rotor oil is the lighter of the two, and substituting bearing oil will result in a very sluggish valve. In addition, some players find significant difference between different brands of rotor oil, typically switching to a lighter formulation when moving to an instrument with more finely engineered valves.

Valves that are seized – or even partially seized – are best removed, thoroughly cleaned, relubricated and reassembled. The procedure is detailed in Section C of this chapter. As professional repairs go, it doesn't require very high-level skills but it does need specialist tools.

The slide will always come out more easily if you hold the valve lever down, so that the air can move freely.

The valve stem, held here in the right hand, can become difficult to remove if not kept lubricated.

casings with some lint-free cloth, such as cotton, on a cleaning rod. Although a lot of these rods have an eye on the end you can put the cloth through, it's important to wrap the cloth right over the end, so that there is no exposed metal when the rod goes into the valve casing. That way the valve casing isn't going to get scratched. As a cleaning agent, you often need nothing more

Some repair pros prefer to remove the eye from the end of the cleaning rod.

Stringing a rotary valve

Mechanical linkage systems have the advantage of being more robust than string linkage but also tend to be noisier, so string linkage is a popular option. Periodic replacement of the strings will help to minimise the chance of one of the strings breaking at an inconvenient moment. It's best to do this one valve at a time if you don't have a lot of experience.

- Lay the horn on a soft, clean surface such as a towel or blanket, with the valve collars upwards.

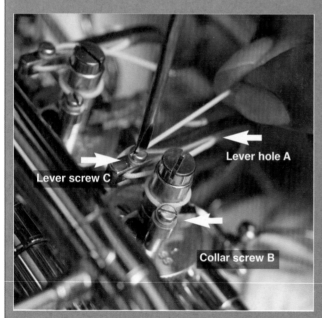

Lever hole A

Lever screw C

Collar screw B

- Carefully unscrew lever screw C, then collar screw B to release the existing cord. (On most instruments the fact that

it's sitting on a flat surface should be enough to restrain the finger levers at this point, so that they don't fly backwards and dent the tubing. Otherwise, use some cloth to protect the instrument, and use your hand to slow the travel of the levers as they're released, if you can.)

- Unthread the existing cord and pull it through lever hole A.
- Take a new length of valve cord and form a double knot at one end, then fuse the other end in a flame to prevent it fraying. (A gas lighter generally works well, but it's best to use this well away from the instrument.)
- Thread the cord through hole A. Then, following the picture, wrap it round the collar, round collar screw B and round the rest of the collar. Before you tighten screw B it's a good idea to set the finger lever to the same height as the others. Then, with the collar in the correct position and the cord under tension, tighten the screw. (This isn't easy to illustrate, but don't worry – you can adjust the height of the levers at the end if you don't get it exactly right first time.)
- Thread through point C in the lever, wrap around screw C as shown and tighten, while keeping the cord under tension. (Many upmarket lever assemblies now have a slot or 'bird beak', rather than a hole, which makes the process a little faster.)
- Once you've restrung all your valves, you may find the finger levers are at different heights. You can adjust this by slackening off collar screw B, holding the collar in the correct position, then depressing the finger lever to where you want the 'up' position to be – and hold. Now release the collar and retighten screw B, holding the finger lever in position until the cord is again secured.

complicated than a tiny amount of washing-up liquid dissolved in warm water. However, if the valve casings are noticeably sticky you can use cellulose thinners on the cloth instead. This can be obtained from the sort of automotive accessory shops that also sell touch-up paints.

A word of caution: cellulose thinners are *highly* flammable. If using this substance, make sure you work in a well-ventilated area, away from naked flames or danger of sparking. Be sure to leave the instrument for 30 minutes – so that the thinners evaporate completely – before relubricating and returning the valves.

6 Polish the bell, tubing and valve casings

... or not? Providing you wipe down your instrument every time after use, there's no functional requirement to ever polish it. Seriously, you can live a long and happy life without ever having bought one of those cleaning kits they sell in musical instrument shops. However, if you're determined to have the shiniest brass in your band, it's important to determine whether it has a lacquered or natural finish. Lacquered instruments should only be cleaned with a soft cloth and maybe a little furniture spray polish – never anything abrasive. Uncoated metal, on the other hand, can be cleaned with good old-fashioned Brasso, which should then be buffed off with a soft cloth to remove the outer layer of oxide. Be careful not to apply too much physical pressure. The bells of French horns in particular are often thin and relatively easy to bend out of shape.

Axial flow valves

No discussion of axial flow valves should begin without acknowledging that the term is a cover-all for a number of different valve designs – all with the common aim of improving the airflow in trombones. For the purposes of discussing routine maintenance we'll confine ourselves to the Hagmann and Thayer designs, both of which are currently popular choices.

Invented by René Hagmann and made by Servette Music, the Hagmann valve has a recommended weekly maintenance routine. This requires piston-type valve oil.

- Remove the A cap: no tool is required – just rotate while pulling.
- Spray about ten drops of oil inside the D section.
- Lubricate the stem underneath the C spring (three drops).
- Put the cap back over the valve.
- Action the valve several times while pressing on the B part, with it facing towards the ground.

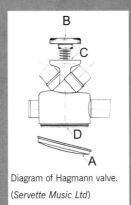

Diagram of Hagmann valve. (*Servette Music Ltd*)

In order to ensure long-term high performance, Servette Music recommend professional maintenance every two years. This service routine is detailed in Section C of this chapter.

Invented in 1976 by Orla Ed Thayer – apparently with assistance from Zig Kanstul – the Thayer valve was the first to challenge the orthodox cylindrical rotary valve, and it is frankly the more complex of the two designs, and therefore demands more rigorous maintenance.

Thayer-type valves are no longer unique to one manufacturer, as the original patent has expired and a number of variations have emerged. Therefore the steps below are only a guide. Where possible refer to the manufacturer's instructions as well.

- At intervals of approximately twice a week, oil the rotor through whichever slide leg gives the most direct access. There's some debate about which oil is the most suitable, but piston valve oil is of an appropriate weight, while formulations that include Teflon (PTFE) seem to be especially beneficial.
- At intervals of approximately once a week, apply a drop of spindle oil to the valve's spindle.

Note that these suggested intervals depend on the amount the instrument is used but also vary considerably from one manufacturer to another.

Taking a Thayer valve assembly apart and putting it back together again is covered in Section C. It's a procedure best avoided unless routine lubrication isn't enough to keep the valve working properly. Again, some manufacturers consider their valves to be easy to take apart, but some definitely are not. Hence we've lumped them together in Section C, 'Professional repairs'.

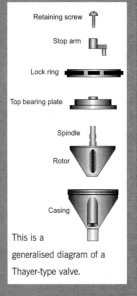

Retaining screw
Stop arm
Lock ring
Top bearing plate
Spindle
Rotor
Casing

This is a generalised diagram of a Thayer-type valve.

Giving your trumpet a bath

Although this technique also works well for other high brass, there comes a point where the size of container needed probably means you'd also need a diving suit! On a more serious note, it also requires you disassembling the instrument. So if you're not comfortable with taking all the valves and slides out – and, more importantly, putting them back correctly – then this isn't the maintenance routine for you.

The disassembly instructions that follow assume your instrument is fitted with piston valves. Taking rotary valves apart is more complicated and usually requires specialist tools. An alternative technique is to pump water into the mouthpipe of the assembled instrument through a hose connected to the hot tap, then direct it though the various sections of tubing by operating the valves.

Professionals often use a machine to pump soapy water through the instrument at high pressure. While this is a very effective way of cleaning the inside of the instrument, it requires all the slides to be tied in place so that they don't shoot out. If you're cleaning your instrument through from a domestic tap we suggest that you keep the water pressure low, so that there's no risk of the slides coming out. Afterwards, be sure to go through your normal cleaning and lubricating routine.

Assuming the above hasn't completely put you off, you'll need the following before you get started:

- A large bowl of warm water. A soft, rectangular plastic container is best. These are sold as plant troughs in garden centres and are perfect, providing you pick one that hasn't had the drain holes pushed out. For larger instruments you'll need a full-sized dustbin, bath or water tub.
- Domestic washing-up liquid.
- Bottle/slide brushes. In addition to purpose-made brushes and 'snakes' there are a number of economical sources for these, including baby-care stores and discount household outlets.
- Non-abrasive pan cleaner.
- Washing-up cloth.
- Lint-free drying cloth (a tea towel is a good choice).
- Oil.
- Grease.

Disassembly of the instrument is best performed on an old bath towel or similar soft surface. (Carpet should be avoided, though – you'll probably end up with bits from the pile all over your instrument.) A bath towel is good because it's large enough for you to lay out safely all the parts you've removed.

Laying out the parts logically helps to keep them safe and makes putting everything back easier.

1 Remove the slides, remembering to first remove any retaining nuts fitted to slides with rings (this especially applies to the third slide).

2 Unscrew the bottom caps from the valves.

3 Unscrew the top caps from each valve in turn, removing the valve.

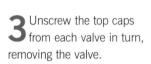

4 Remove the valve stem from the valve, along with the spring and valve guide, as it's best not to wash them. Place these parts on the towel, along with the valve itself.

5 Be sure to group each valve and its associated parts so that it's obvious which position they're to be returned to.

6 Fill up your container with warm water and a normal amount of washing-up liquid.

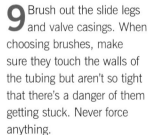

7 Gently submerge your trumpet.

8 Thoroughly clean the outside of the instrument with the non-abrasive pan cleaner, or a washing-up cloth – not a scourer!

9 Brush out the slide legs and valve casings. When choosing brushes, make sure they touch the walls of the tubing but aren't so tight that there's a danger of them getting stuck. Never force anything.

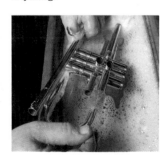

10 Pay attention to the leader pipe, because a lot of any unwanted material will be here. Again make sure the head of the brush will go through the receiver.

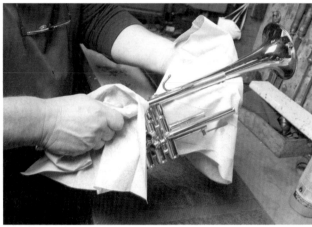

11 Once you've finished the main body of the instrument, remove it. Rinse it off with clean water, inside and out, then carefully tip the instrument to remove any trapped water. Dry it off with a soft, lint-free cloth.

12 Place the main body of the instrument on a soft towel for safety. Now turn your attention to cleaning each slide individually, both inside and out.

13 Next clean each valve in turn, using a brush to clean out the airways. Before placing them back on the towel it's a good idea to dry the casings with a soft, clean, lint-free cloth. (If used very carefully, rolling them on paper kitchen towel is a reasonable substitute.)

14 Once all the parts are clean, leave them to dry thoroughly. (About an hour should do it.)

15 Put a little grease on the thread of each valve pillar to prevent long-term corrosion.

16 To reassemble each valve, start by inserting the valve guide, twisting it into the correct position.

17 Put the spring back in.

18 Now reintroduce the valve pillar assembly. Push down on to the spring and screw it finger-tight.

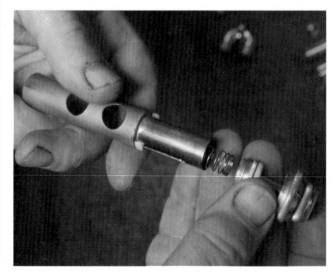

19 Oil each valve body, then reinsert the valve. If you rotate the valve a little as you push it down it will help to distribute the oil. Take care in locating the correct position for the pin and don't force anything. Repeat for the remaining valves.

20 Put the bottom caps back on to the valves.

21 Oil the slide legs on the third valve and put the slide on. Don't forget to screw the stop nut back on.

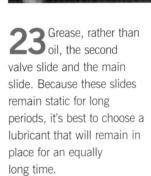

22 Oil legs of first slide, then put the slide on the trumpet.

23 Grease, rather than oil, the second valve slide and the main slide. Because these slides remain static for long periods, it's best to choose a lubricant that will remain in place for an equally long time.

24 A final rub over with a clean, soft cloth and our trumpet is good to go.

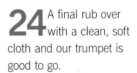

Section B: Running repairs and quick fixes

What's a 'running repair'? It's one you make because something unexpectedly happens to your instrument and you need to get it in playing order immediately. As such, a running repair isn't a long-term fix – it's just a way to keep you in business until you can get to a repair shop.

Just like Douglas Adams' *Hitchhiker's Guide to the Galaxy*, our book should have the words 'Don't Panic!' splashed across the cover. This is doubly true of a running repair, because it's a solution to a problem that's occurred without warning. When that happens mere minutes before you're due to take to the stage it's all too easy to make the wrong decision.

For that reason we'd advise you to forget about any ideas that involve soldering irons, hammers or glue in places you wouldn't normally find it. There's very little chance of you fixing anything by going down that route, but there's a big chance of making things worse.

The first question to ask yourself before performing a running repair is whether the problem impacts on the playability or stability of the instrument. If it doesn't, it's best to leave well alone until a proper repair can be performed.

For instance, a jammed mouthpiece is an inconvenience because it often means the instrument no longer fits the case. But if it's your own mouthpiece jammed in your own instrument, it's hardly a showstopper is it? Depending on its size, wrapping the instrument in a blanket, putting it in a carry bag and taking it to a repair shop is a much better solution than attempting to un-jam the mouthpiece yourself.

A note to well-meaning Dads everywhere: when one of your family comes to you with a stuck mouthpiece it's very tempting to reach for the pliers. However, attempting to twist a mouthpiece free can easily rip the leader pipe off the instrument, and the repair bill won't be small. Seriously. Don't do it. Please.

Sticking valves

However tempting it may be, we urge you not use brute force to free valves that are locked solid, or to disassemble a rotary valve unless you have all the tools detailed in Section C. Similarly, general-purpose lubricants such as WD40 and 3-In-One oil shouldn't be applied to instrument valves.

In general terms there are three reasons for a valve to stick, or become sluggish:

This valve is extremely dry, as evidenced by the almost powdery appearance of the surface. The extent of the scoring on the body of the valve also suggests it's been used in an under-oiled state for some time. Ideally, the whole trumpet should be given a bath, as shown in Section A, but even a few drops of valve oil will work wonders.

■ It's dried out due to lack of lubrication (common when an instrument hasn't been played for weeks or months… so check the valves in the days before your gig and you won't have an emergency!).

■ Unwanted material in the valve (sticky residue from sweets, wrong type of oil, build-up in the leader pipe due to lack of cleaning…)

■ Physical damage (typically, distortion to the valve casing caused by dropping).

Reasons 1 and 2 can be addressed using the cleaning and lubricating routines explained in Section A, 'Routine maintenance'. As the title implies, prevention is better than cure.

As for problem 3, there's one routine in Section C that can

be carried out without specialist tools (see 'Freeing sticky middle valve when horn is dropped'). However, we've categorised it as a professional repair due to the risk of causing further damage. For the most part, though, valve problems caused by mechanical shock require expert attention – and it's better not to use the instrument in the meantime.

Sticking slides

As with valves, slides that are merely sticky in action – as opposed to locked solid – are best treated to routine

This slide is very dry and will have to be worked repeatedly before it'll go in fully.

maintenance. Assuming that the instrument hasn't been damaged in the meantime, all that's likely to have happened is that the sleeves have suffered a build-up of dirt and the slide grease has either hardened or worn off. Providing that not too much time has elapsed, the normal cleaning and lubrication procedures will soon sort that out.

However, it's sometimes the case that a tuning slide has been left in one position for so long without routine care that it's either impossible to move in, or move at all, using normal hand pressure.

When a slide cannot be moved in (ie sharpened in pitch), it's usually because of a build-up of muck in the section of the sleeve beyond the end of the slide leg. This becomes especially problematic if the instrument then lies unused, because the deposit within the tubing dries out and hardens over time. Assuming it's still possible to remove the slide, the best procedure for clearing the deposit is as follows:

1 Remove the slide, clean the slide legs and re-grease it (or oil it, in the case of trumpet first and third slides).

This is how the pros clean slide legs.

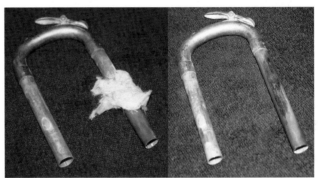

If you have nothing else to hand you can clean slide legs with Brasso cloth, although it's a slightly inefficient technique. Just be careful not to pull the legs out of true.

2 Using a cleaning brush and warm soapy water, dislodge as much of the deposit within the sleeves as possible. (This also has the benefit of making the deposit wet, which helps the procedure that follows.)

3 Orientate the slide to an angle of 90° and insert the lower leg of the slide into one of the slide sleeves.

Ideally slide legs should look this clean before greasing, but don't worry too much about a little oxidisation, as long as the legs are free from dirt.

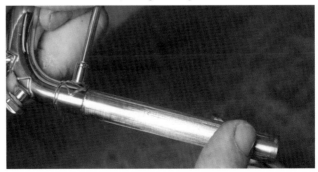

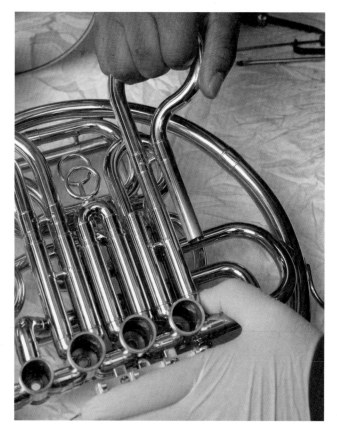

A French horn gets its slide legs cleaned out.

4 Move the slide in and out, swivelling the slide to rotate the leg as you do so.

5 Once the slide can be inserted fully, repeat the procedure to clear the other sleeve.

A slide that cannot be moved at all is potentially a more serious problem, as the procedures to free it carry a risk of damage. In addition, the time they take to execute makes them of limited value to the 'running repairer'. However, the two main strategies are described in Section C.

Emergency de-denting

Professional repairers spend a great deal of their time removing dents from brass instruments, for the simple reason that the instruments are prone to this kind of damage. While many dents have little or no effect on the instrument's playability, severe crushing may need immediate attention before the instrument can be used. This can happen to trumpets, and brass of similar size, if they're dropped or sat on. Fortunately it's possible to perform an emergency repair to the spout of the instrument using a broom handle if the damage is to the straight section.

1 Make sure the end of the broom handle is rounded and doesn't have any attachments, such as a hook, that might damage the instrument.

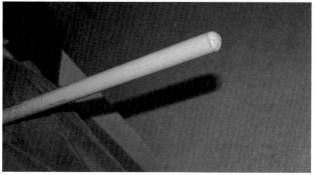

2 Secure the broom handle in a horizontal position. The ideal way to do this is with a bench-mounted vice, but if none is available lay it across a table and ask an accomplice to secure it by sitting on the broom and holding it as firmly as they can. (It's probably best not to refer to your accomplice as either 'Harry Potter' or 'an old witch' at this point.)

3 To avoid unnecessary 'give' in the broom, make sure that that there's no more unsecured handle than is needed to ensure the bell of the instrument cannot strike the mounting point (*ie* vice or edge of table).

4 Hold the instrument by the bell and spout, rather than other parts, as this will avoid unnecessary stress on the bracing.

5 Push the instrument over the broom handle using a slow, controlled force. Try to restore the roundness of the spout by using an ironing action to create a series of small improvements.

6 Avoid pushing the broom handle so far down the spout that it becomes jammed, or pushes a ridge into the spout wall.

7 Remember, your objective is to make the instrument playable, not cosmetically perfect. Once you've achieved your objective it's best to stop and leave the rest of the job to someone with the right tools.

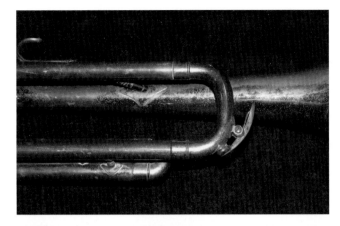

As this is only intended to be a temporary measure you may want to simply rely on the force of the key's spring to keep the rubber in place. While this has the disadvantage that the rubber may fall out when the key is activated, it will save you time, and keeps glue away from you and the instrument. Just pop the eraser slice under the key and release. Job done!

Missing corks – water key

Quite how the cork from a water key can go missing is one of life's little mysteries. After all, if it came off while the instrument was being played the effect would be immediately noticeable, and if it fell off when the instrument was in the case, well, it should still be in the case. For all that, water key corks go missing from time to time.

Before fitting a replacement, it's a good idea to remove any trace of the old cork and the glue that held it in place, using a screwdriver.

One ready source for a suitable substitute is the eraser found on the end of many pencils. Simply cut 4mm or so from the ends with a sharp craft knife, then whittle down the diameter if necessary to get a reasonable fit with the key and hole. (You'll probably find it fits quite well as-is.)

If the eraser has already been worn down through use it's a good idea to cut the end flat, then cut off a 4mm slice.

On the other hand, you may be sufficiently pleased with your handiwork that you want to convert it to a more permanent solution. (And if it does the job and looks neat, why not?) All you have to do is pop the eraser out again, now you've checked that it fits, hold the key open and put a dab of Superglue in the cap. We recommend the gel-type Superglue, as it's less likely to run where it isn't wanted.

Pop the eraser back in, release the key and the key spring will clamp everything together for the few seconds it takes for the Superglue to go hard.

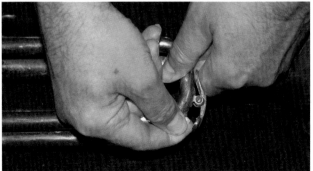

A note to teachers and bandleaders

The procedures in this section are designed primarily to help musicians who find themselves faced with unexpected problems, hence our emphasis on using materials that are likely to be at hand.

Anyone used to dealing with brass players on a regular basis has probably encountered these situations often enough to know the value of being prepared. The following is a selection of items you may find useful to keep in your 'first aid' kit:

- Cleaning brushes.
- Electrical insulating tape or masking tape.
- Blu Tack, as a stopgap seal for leaks.
- A gas lighter.
- A variety of screwdrivers.
- Valve and slide lubricants.
- Valve string.
- Rubber bands.

Where you have many instruments of the same brand in your care you'll also have a commonality of parts. Keeping holding screws for lyres and linkages, valve felts, valve guides, a few springs, some water key parts etc can go a long way

to keeping the instruments in working order. The Amado push-button water keys have particularly small parts that are as good as impossible to find should they unexpectedly make a bid for freedom on the parade ground, or even on to a carpet. Spare circlips are therefore a small but wise investment.

There are in addition further small repairs that we've included in Section C that some teachers and bandleaders may care to undertake themselves. These include changing water key springs and corks, and adjusting the weakness or strength of various valve springs. In order to do these, you'll need:

- Neoprene 'corks' for water keys and rotary valves.
- A craft knife.
- Gel Superglue (not the more watery formulation).
- A small pair of round-nosed pliers.
- A small pair of flat-nose pliers.

Although professional repairers traditionally secured corks with shellac, it has to be heated, and the risk of accidental burning to the skin is high. Consequently Superglue is the weapon of choice for many repair pros today.

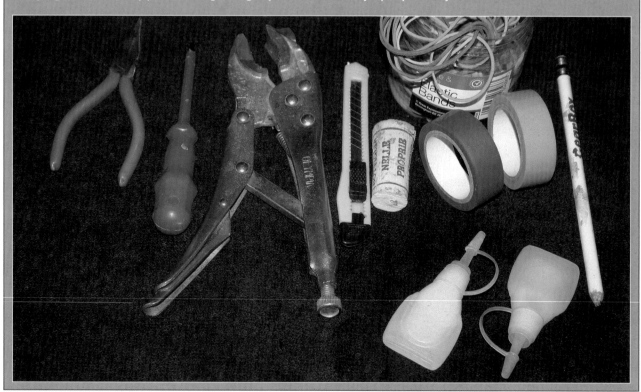

If you need to perform this repair without a spring to help you (*ie* it has broken), a small piece of wood or card makes a useful barrier between you and the key while the glue sets. Alternatively, consult Section C for details on removing the water key assembly and replacing the spring as well as the cork.

Missing corks – rotary valve

Instruments fitted with rotary valves have more corks to go missing, as there are two in each bumper plate, which perform the task of preventing the valve from rotating past its intended position. Again, the eraser from a pencil makes a suitable substitute – in fact most instruments are fitted with neoprene rubber 'corks' from new.

Although traditional corks are usually inserted into the bumper plate by first compressing the material with a pair of small flat-nosed pliers, for a running repair you may notice that (a) you don't have any flat-nosed pliers and (b) come to think of it, you haven't got any 'corks', neoprene, ends of pencil or otherwise. Fear not, you can still get that horn up and running if you're prepared to improvise.

You'll probably find these tasks easier to perform having first removed the bumper plate from the valve, which normally only requires a screwdriver with a fairly narrow blade. An electrical screwdriver has about the right blade size, but one with a good-sized handle will give you a better grip.

Put the screws somewhere safe, like an eggcup or a bottle cap. They can be very difficult to find if they're knocked on the floor.

The plate should slide off without you having to remove more complex parts of the instrument, such as the linkage.

You'll then need something to hold the plate firmly. If no vice is available, a pair of Mole grips, or locking pliers, make quite a good substitute, especially if you can persuade someone to steady them while you work. Whatever you use, it's best to line the jaws with soft plastic, wood or leather to avoid bruising the metal of the bumper plate. We've lined the jaws of the grips in the picture with electrical tape.

If you've cut yourself a slice of pencil eraser, as detailed in the water key repair, previous page, you may find it easier to cut a slight figure-of-eight before easing it into the bumper plate, especially as it's likely to be somewhat over-diameter.

But another substitute for the missing cork is... cork! The corks – real or synthetic – used in wine bottles are a perfectly fine source of material, but the amount of work involved in trimming it to size will be a little more than using an eraser, so it

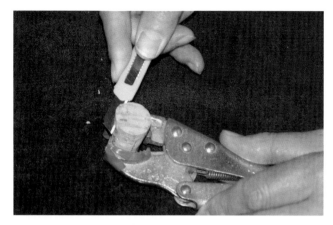

depends how much time you have. Draw a reasonable diameter for a bumper on the top of a wine cork, and then cut round it with a craft knife. Holding the cork in grips is important, because it keeps fingers away from a very sharp blade.

Once you've cut round the shape you need to a depth of 4mm or more, you can slice across the wine cork and the bumper you need should pop out.

If you don't have a pair of flat-nosed pliers, almost any pliers will do the job now that the bumper plate is free of the instrument. Simply compress the cork a little and push it into the bumper plate socket.

Any excess height in the cork is easy to trim off at this stage. Once you've done that put the bumper plate back and replace the two screws.

For the valve to be lined up absolutely correctly in both the open and closed positions it may be necessary to trim the replacement bumper cork you've just inserted. The correct positions can be seen by removing the valve cap, which will reveal two alignment marks.

In this section of the book we're dealing with running repairs, remember, so we'll assume that the alignment of the valve is good enough to get you through the performance.

You'll find a detailed look at aligning rotary valves in Section C.

Broken springs

The traditional water key is especially prone to broken springs. Fortunately a temporary substitute can be made by winding a few rubber bands around the slide tubing and water key, on the cork side of the pivot. This looks somewhat inelegant, but, if done with care, permits the key to be opened and closed as usual.

Rubber bands can also be used as a short-term replacement for a broken spring on a rotary valve lever, although a certain amount of ingenuity is required. Essentially, the bands have to be anchored on the lever at the point where it hinges to the

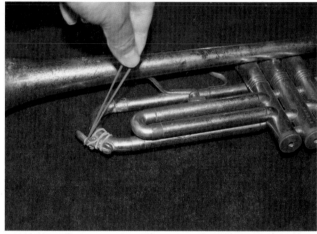

linkage and then attached to the instrument itself somewhere behind the pivot point. This will enable the bands to pull the lever plate back up and close the valve.

A little experimentation will soon show how many bands it takes to give the right finger lever tension.

Broken brace

A broken brace or stay can be a serious problem if it leaves, for instance, the leader pipe unsupported, because of the obvious potential for further and substantial damage. When performing an emergency fix it's best to avoid glues, as these will leave residues that must be removed before a professional repair can be attempted. (Two-part epoxy resins are the repair shop's least favourite amateur repair, as the chemically hardened glue is difficult to remove.)

If you must use tape, masking tape is the best choice because it's 'low tack'. Although it sticks quite well to itself, it's designed for easy removal, providing it's not left on for so long that it starts to harden. Try to get the instrument to a professional repair person within a week, while the tape is still soft and can be removed without problem. PVC electrical tape is also effective and is easy to remove afterwards. If you stretch it a little as you put it on, it will bind the parts more tightly.

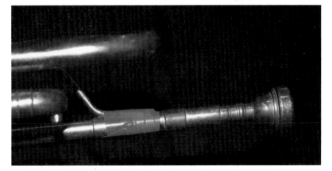

But what if you don't have any tape to hand? The kind of string used to truss joints of meat before putting them in the oven is another good candidate.

It must be stressed that these are all temporary measures. Until the stay is re-soldered the instrument remains vulnerable to further damage, and the longer it's held together by tape or string the more likely it is that the temporary repair will fall apart unexpectedly.

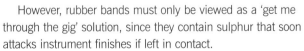

However, rubber bands must only be viewed as a 'get me through the gig' solution, since they contain sulphur that soon attacks instrument finishes if left in contact.

There's no instant fix for a broken spring on a piston valve. However, it's highly likely that a spring from, say, one tuba will work well enough in another. As a result it may be possible to cannibalise an instrument that's otherwise deemed not as good, in order to rescue the instrument required for the performance.

Section C: Professional repairs

As a general rule we've categorised the repair techniques in this section as 'professional' on the basis of three criteria: (a) the skill level required is generally higher, compared to the routines described in the first two sections of this chapter; (b) some of the equipment required is often uneconomical to own unless it will be in regular use; and (c) many of these procedures carry a level of risk and shouldn't be undertaken by anyone who doesn't have the ability to repair any attendant damage that may also occur.

With such a cautionary start to this section, the reader is entitled to wonder why we've even written it. Although we fully accept that many readers will not – indeed, should not – attempt the procedures described here, we believe it's helpful to all brass players to know what happens to their precious instrument once it goes the other side of the workshop door.

Also, not all of the procedures in this section are the sole province of the repair pro. As noted in Section B, teachers and bandleaders are likely to have sufficient instruments in their care to become proficient in replacing broken water key springs, swapping valve felts and other tasks for which the lone player may not keep spares.

We also acknowledge that there's a community within the brass world that wants to roll up their sleeves and have a go at repairing and customising instruments (or 'Frankenhorns', as

Paxman's main repair guy, Satch, is wearing latex gloves because he's about to handle acid. He's also wearing overalls – not just to keep dirt at bay, but because 'day clothes' often contain buckles and loops that can get caught in machinery.

the results are sometimes disparagingly described). We wouldn't criticise that: after all, if we weren't gripped by the very same passions we'd be in no position to write this book!

For those ready to learn professional repair skills, we urge you to consider four important factors first:

1 Safety
Knowing how to operate machinery safely – and what safety gear you should be wearing – is important. If you've had no training in this, we suggest you enrol in a short metalwork course before you operate any power tools found in this section.

NB: Never operate power tools without tying back long hair under a cap so that it cannot connect with any moving parts, and always remove any jewellery that could get caught on machinery. Do not wear a scarf, necktie or necklace. Always wear safety goggles when there's a chance of flying debris.

2 Environmental factors
Some liquids, particularly solvents, may only be used in workshops that have specialist container systems to prevent escape into the environment. Other liquids, including acids, can be purchased easily but aren't so easy to dispose of safely. Please take the time before obtaining solvents or acids to learn not just how to use them safely, but how to dispose of them correctly afterwards.

3 Practice
No one makes their best repair first time, because skills build with repetition. The world is full of brass musical instruments that are now so worn they're beyond economic repair. Those are the ones to hone your skills on.

4 Plan ahead

Before you start a repair, make sure you've taken on board all the procedures involved, and also made sure you have the tools and materials to get from start to finish. This includes the procedures you may have to go through if things don't go to plan – such as a stay breaking when you're trying to free a mouthpiece.

To help you assess the risks, we've included a little evaluation headed 'What can go wrong?' at the end of each procedure. (There's also a scary boxout called 'Baptism of fire'…)

The working environment

While the kitchen table with a protective blanket on top is a good enough environment for light or occasional repairs, its limitations as a working environment will become apparent as more advanced techniques are employed. In addition, you'll soon realise that you don't want your kitchen to smell of hot flux, or the table to be covered in dents, scorch marks and the remains of various chemical compounds!

Ideally, the professional repairer needs a metal-framed bench (angle iron is a good material for a self build) secured to a solid floor using expansion bolts. This needs a substantial top made from a wooden material such as blockboard, which is then best covered with zinc or aluminium sheet.

The reason the top needs to be substantial isn't just the weight of larger brass instruments, but also because it has to provide secure mounting for a vice, which in itself will need to hold metal formers, mandrels and the like. The vice needs to be mounted at a sufficient angle that the bell of any brass instrument mounted on a stick will clear the edge of the bench. (Alternatively, some vices have a swivel mount.)

Time is money when you're running a business, so the best place for the most frequently used small hand-tools is a series of clips mounted on a board at the back of the bench. That way you'll know where they are when you need them next. Getting into the habit of returning tools to their correct location after use also has the benefit of minimising the chance of accidental damage to any instrument that may be in your care.

A pad made of foam, or a similar soft material, is needed to protect instruments from scratching or denting when they're being repaired on the bench top. It's important to ensure that whatever material you use, it isn't flammable and won't give off toxic fumes if a flame is applied to it.

The other useful device for securing instruments is a length of string, attached somewhere above the bench. (How useful you find this largely depends on the type of instrument you're working on. For a French horn it's virtually essential, but for a trumpet isn't especially necessary.) When an instrument is

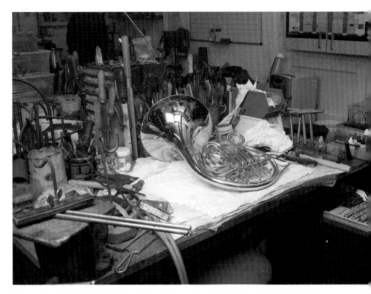

A bench isn't just a surface to work on, it's a workspace, where efficiency comes from knowing exactly where each tool is.

Before you take it apart…

You probably think we're going to say '…make sure you know how to put it back together'. Well, that's important. You should certainly make sure you've noted identifying marks on components such as valves, so you know which casing they go in. But there's a bit more to it than that.

In any professional repair shop, someone has to look at every incoming instrument and estimate the cost of repair. That doesn't simply mean working out how long it's going to take. There's also the question of whether it will require parts and, if so, whether they need to be ordered. In a larger shop, the estimator often has to consider who's qualified to perform the repair, because the most senior people will be on a higher rate than the trainees.

Of course, if you're performing your own repairs the time taken is less important, but the thinking process is still essential. What's wrong with the instrument? More precisely, what's changed since the instrument was working (damage, wear, lack of lubrication)? What procedures, materials and tools will be necessary to fix it? Do you have them all? Just as importantly, how confident are you that you have the skills to carry out the job?

These are all questions you should ask yourself before you start, along with: are you prepared to take the risk? If the answer is yes, we wish you luck with it. If the answer is no, make it someone else's problem and take your instrument to a pro!

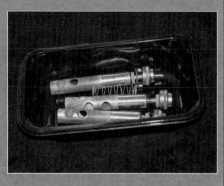
mounted on a bell stick, the string forms the second anchor point and allows processes that need unimpeded access to the underside of the instrument. (For instance, polishing using a strip of cloth hooked over the tubing.) Natural materials are preferable to synthetics because the string is likely to be caught by the gas torch quite frequently, at which point you don't want blobs of molten plastic dripping off.

A mounting point for the gas torch is important, as it's likely you'll have the torch alight for most of the day, and therefore the head of it will become hot. Pipes for gas and air are best run under the bench top and fitted with taps at the attachment points for the flexible hoses. Not every workshop merits a compressor, and a portable gas torch with a butane canister is an acceptable substitute.

NOTE: For your convenience we've placed these repairs in approximate order of difficulty, starting with the easiest. However, the precise difficulty will vary from instrument to instrument. For instance, removing a moderate amount of denting is considerably easier than removing severe denting, while working on instruments that are old and thin requires a much lighter touch than working on a modern instrument.

Replacing a water key spring

This procedure has elements in common with the one in Section B, which you may find useful to read first if you haven't already. In the professional version here, we'll take the water key assembly apart and replace the spring, as well as fitting a purpose-made synthetic water key cork.

1 Unscrew and partially remove the pivot pin from the carriage. The key itself is under tension and should therefore be restrained with one hand, while the pin is removed with the other. (The essence of this is shown in step 8, when the process is reversed.)

2 Prise the spring apart, so that it slides off the water key. Be aware that the two legs found on many springs are sharp and can easily puncture the skin.

3 If the cork is still in place, prise it out with a screwdriver and scrape any residual material out of the water key cap.

4 You should now have a number of separate components, as shown here.

5 Offer up the new cork to the water key cap to make sure it's a good fit. If it's too small, find a larger one. If it's too big, file and/or cut it to the correct diameter.

6 Fit new spring and, if necessary, squeeze the back of the spring with a small pair of pliers, so that the coils sit snugly against the sides of the key.

7 The spring should be fitted as shown here, with the enclosed end pressed up against the underside of the water key lever.

8 Introduce the key back to the instrument, ensuring as you do so that the legs of the spring are compressed against the instrument.

9 Keep holding the key in place with the thumb of one hand while you push the pivot pin through the assembly.

10 Once the pin is around halfway in it can safely be released and the pin tightened.

11 Open up the water key, put the new cork in position and release. Look at the fit between the components. If the cork appears too high to make a good fit with the key and the drain hole, remove it and cut some off. Repeat until the fit is satisfactory.

12 Open the water key and put a drop of Superglue inside the cap. Insert the cork and gently release. At this point the cork should self-seat and become firmly glued within about ten seconds.

13 Put a drop of brown engine oil on each coil of the spring.

What can go wrong?
Not a lot. However, the ends of the springs are pin-sharp and it's easy to draw blood from fingertips when your attention is concentrated on the tricky job of reassembling the key. Also, if the pin won't unscrew, easing oil and low heat is to be preferred to brute force.

When a screw breaks

Screws and bolts that unexpectedly shear, or cannot be removed by conventional means because the head is damaged, are a fact of life in the repair shop. There are a number of strategies for dealing with the problem, and it's always best to start with the easiest option and only move on to the more drastic solutions if it fails.

■ *Snapped screw with exposed shaft.* If there's still part of the screw above the surface, you're lucky, because it's relatively easy to score a new slot across the top using a needle file or a fine saw blade. (If you don't have a fine saw blade, you can make one by tapping a Junior hacksaw blade flat and reducing its width on a grindstone.)

■ *'Chewed' head, no bite.* Crosshead screws normally have enough metal left in the head to treat it like case 1 above and cut a slot. Otherwise, it's better to file flat what remains of the head and treat it like case 3 below.

■ *No head or exposed shaft.* This one's trickier but you can often cut enough of a slot across the shaft by scratching across it repeatedly with a jeweller's screwdriver until there's enough of a slot to get a flat-blade screwdriver to bite. This works a lot better on soft metals like brass than on hardened steel.

■ *Still not winning?* There are reverse thread taps, which will enable you to drill a hole into the screw, thread it and screw in a reverse thread bolt. As the bolt drives home, it will start to unscrew the broken bolt.

■ *Drill it.* It may be that you don't have a reverse thread tap and bolt – in which case about the last resort is to drill out the existing screw/bolt. This leaves you with two options: (a) tap the enlarged hole to accommodate a new bolt of larger diameter, or (b) fill the hole with hard solder, re-drill and tap to the original size (the better option in most cases).

With all of these approaches, heating the material into which the screw/bolt is threaded and adding easing oil is highly recommended before attempting the extraction. This will minimise the pressure you need to apply.

Aligning piston valves vertically

Many players are passionate about the accuracy with which the valves in their instrument line up with the holes in the casings. There's nothing wrong with such attention to detail, especially as the materials required to achieve it are inexpensive and relatively easy to use.

One question that crops up again and again is: 'At what point does increased accuracy cease to make a noticeable difference to the performance of the instrument?' This is a question for which there can be no absolute answer, because it will vary from instrument to instrument and – more importantly – from player to player. To further muddy the waters, it's undoubtedly the case that many players will experience enhanced performance from an instrument if they believe it to have been improved in some way.

It should also be acknowledged that valve alignment is only one aspect of the instrument as a whole. A clean mouthpiece and leader pipe are good instances of factors that can greatly help in getting the best from an instrument. These are key areas over which every player has direct control, but you'll seldom see a thread on a forum where someone asks 'How much better did your horn play when you cleaned out last year's collection of cheese and pizza crumbs?'

For simplicity, we'll refer to the washers that stop the vertical travel of a piston valve as 'felts', regardless of whether they're actually made from cork, a synthetic material or even cardboard. Regardless of the material, they're all performing the same task and the options are much the same: shim, trim or replace.

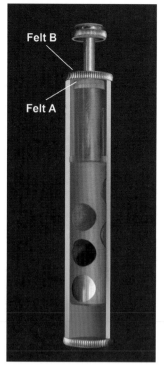

Fig 1: A correctly aligned valve in the up position. Felt A is of appropriate thickness.

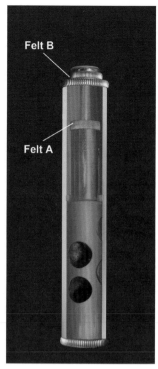

Fig 2: A correctly aligned valve in the down position. Felt B is of appropriate thickness.

(A 'shim' is a piece of material, typically used to make two components fit or align when they otherwise would not.)

Felts are cheap items and are readily available in different sizes. However, brass and marching bands often prefer to keep a set of cutting tools, and to cut their own felts from sheet material. Because the diameters don't have to be cut with surgical precision, a paper hole punch and a pair of scissors are all you need to cut shims, which can be made from the soft plastic used for the wallets that sets of guitar strings are sold

Baptism of fire: a true-life disaster story

Before we get started, let us be very clear: this is a true story and it happened to Simon Croft. For reasons that will become apparent, Andy Taylor wishes it to be known that this incident did not occur on the premises of Taylor Trumpets, nor was he anywhere near the trumpet in this story when the unfortunate events started to unravel.

Simon Croft explains: 'Many years ago, back in the days when people bought their music on a vinyl format referred to as an LP, a player came into the shop with the seemingly simple job of getting the jammed mouthpiece out of his otherwise immaculate trumpet. As I'd just finished another job, the task fell to me.

'The customer wanted to wait, and we'd just moved into new premises, where we had yet to build a customer waiting area. So I asked the customer if he'd like to help himself to some coffee from our staff room while I set about tapping round the receiver

to free the mouthpiece. At that point, the leader pipe stay popped off. It happens.

'I wired the stay in place and started to re-solder it. What I didn't realise was that not only was the trumpet lacquered, but the lacquer was highly flammable. At the point the customer walked back into the room I was throwing a bowl of water over his trumpet. That's because there were 2m high flames coming from it.

'As the steam cleared it became apparent that about a third of the instrument was now a dark brown colour, in stark contract to the shiny nickel of the rest of the instrument. Obviously, the owner of the instrument was furious and I was extremely embarrassed, but there was no way to put it back to new, short of stripping the lacquer completely and refinishing the entire trumpet – normally one of the most expensive jobs on a repair shop's price list.'

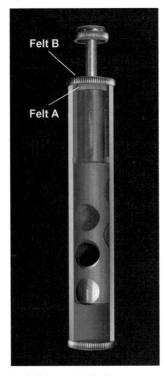

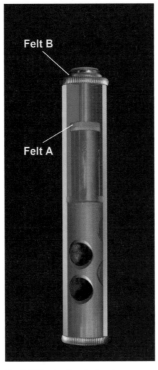

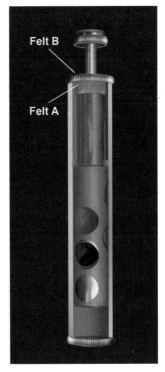

Fig 3: Valve too high in the up position. Felt A is too thin.

Fig 4: Valve too low in the down position. Felt B is too thin.

Fig 5: Valve too low in the up position. Felt A is too thick.

Fig 6: Valve too high in the down position. Felt B is too thick.

in. (Many types of sheet material are suitable for this task, but it helps if they aren't unduly affected by moisture.) Again, the procedures detailed below aren't affected by whether the felts are self-made or bought.

Alignment basics

There's a raft of material about piston valve alignment on the Internet, and it must be said that much of it is confusing, even if it was written with the best of intentions. Part of the problem is an almost total lack of diagrams, leaving the reader to imagine procedures they've never seen – and the positions of valves that can be remarkably tricky to observe.

Hopefully we can put all that right, because the basics are remarkably simple – as is achieving 'real life' accurate alignment in the majority of cases. For the six figures above, let us imagine that the casing is made of tinted glass, rather than metal, and that there are simply two holes where the slide legs would normally be.

What we can see from Figures 1 and 2 is that Felt A controls the alignment of the valve in the up position and Felt B controls alignment in the down position. This state of affairs is easy to verify in a trumpet's second valve because removing the slide gives direct sight of the airways. However, if the felts have compressed with age you're likely to see something slightly different.

Figure 3 shows a valve that's sitting too high in the up position, meaning that Felt A is too thin. Figure 4 shows a valve that's sitting too low in the down position, meaning that Felt

B is too thin. Both these conditions are very typical of a horn with old felts that have compacted over time. Confirmation of this comes from noisy operation, due to the lack of 'give' in the hardened felts. Again, both of these are clearly visible down the second slide as 'crescents' of silvery metal where the valve has travelled past its optimum resting point.

Figure 5 shows a valve that sits too low in the up position, which is caused by Felt A being too thick. This will cause a distinctive crescent of valve casing at the top of the airway when the valve is up. Figure 6 shows a valve that sits too high in the down position, a condition caused by Felt B being too thick. This time the crescents will appear at the bottom of the airways.

At this point, you may be thinking: 'Yes, yes, this is blindingly obvious!' If you are, we're delighted, because you now know all that there is to the theory of vertical alignment in piston valves. You've also learned the practical way to check for alignment in the up and down positions of the second valve (ie look down the slide legs).

The first and third valves are considerably more difficult to check, but here's the truth: unless the valves were manufactured in a really approximate fashion, the correct thickness of felts for the second valve will also be correct for the other two. As a result, the 'simple alignment procedure' over the page may be all you ever need.

For those of you who suspect your horn's valves may not be made to the finest of tolerances – or who are simply curious to find out the truth – we'll then tackle the thorny topic of how to get sight of the other two valves.

Believe it or not, the degree of misalignment on the valve of this old Melody Maker trumpet was for real. The felt was about double the thickness it needed to be.

The white line shows where the valve pillar should be marked.

The two marks indicate the difference between the current felt thickness and the correct thickness.

Simple valve alignment procedure

1 Put your horn on a bench with a clear light source (such as an LED or Halogen desk lamp).

2 Depress valve and remove second valve slide. Release valve.

3 Observe the alignment of the valve in the up position, as explained in previous section. Assuming the up position requires remedial action, go to step 4 or 5 as appropriate. But first, mark the current position of the valve relative to the top cap using a sharp pencil on the valve pillar.

4 If the valve is too high in the up position, depress the valve until it's in the correct position and make a second mark. The correct thickness for the new felt is the thickness of the existing felt, *plus* the gap between the two marks. (Some instruments have the correct up position permanently marked on the valve pillar.)

5 If the valve is too low in the up position, remove the finger button, top valve cap and Felt A. Replace the top valve cap and finger button and put the valve back into the casing. Depress the finger button until the valve is in the correct position and make a second mark. The correct thickness for the new felt is the thickness of the existing felt *minus* the gap between the two marks.

Note: One way of establishing the thickness of the new felt, or felt plus shims, is to use callipers to measure the distance between the two marks on the valve pillar. Then measure the thickness of the existing felt and add/subtract as appropriate. At the other extreme, you can simply look at the size of the crescent down the slide leg and guess. You can always try again if you get it wrong.

6 Observe the alignment of the valve in the down position. Depending on what you see, go to either step 7 or 8 if necessary.

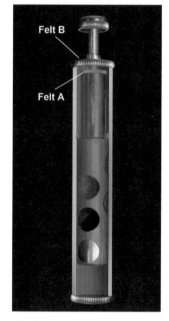

With Felt A removed, the valve won't be forced too low, so the correct position can be marked.

The Taylor woe

Andy Taylor will admit to having once worked on the wrong trumpet, albeit greatly to the customer's benefit.

'I had two older trumpets in for repair at the same time, and they happened to belong to people with very similar names. One was in for a minor repair, the other for a full restoration.

'I mixed them up and fully restored the trumpet that was in for the minor repair: dents, new parts, re-lacquer, the works. The guy hadn't given a time limit, as this was only his back-up horn, so was not surprised it took three weeks. He came in to collect it expecting the broken braces to be fixed. Instead he got a gleaming, like-new trumpet presented to him. Guess who had to swallow the bill?

'Then, to add insult to injury, I had to restore the other trumpet, knowing what had happened. Gutted? Yeah, but you have to see the funny side of these situations.'

Pretty though these finger buttons are, it's the felts in the top caps we're interested in here.

7 If the valve is going too low, reduce pressure on the finger button until the valve rests in the optimum position.

8 If the valve is sitting too high, unscrew the finger button to achieve the right position for the valve.

Note: There are a number of ways to calculate the difference between the two positions but the most obvious is to remove the bottom cap and use callipers, or even a rule if the graduations are fine enough. Again, just guessing will get you there eventually.

9 Make a note of the felts/shims you've fitted to valve two and apply the same to the other two valves.

What can go wrong?
Realistically, no more than any procedure that involves removing the valves. Even if you make a complete mess of the actual alignment, there's no permanent damage to the instrument. However, there's an outside chance that the alignment of valves one and three could be different to valve two, which brings us to the next section.

Checking valves one and three
There are no additional alignment procedures in this section, as we've already covered these in the section above. But, for those of you who fear your 1957 Shinemaster Dogsbreath isn't the miracle of engineering the marketing guys originally claimed, this is how to sight the other two valves in their own right.

The most common way is to use a small mirror set at 45° on the end of a rod or stick, sighting from the second valve casing into the first and third. These are often described as 'dental mirrors', but many of those are too big for anything but the larger diameter valve casings of low brass. Purpose-built valve

inspection mirrors aren't expensive and can be bought from specialist brass repair tool suppliers.

The alternative is a fibre optic scope, but this is a big investment for a tool that might make the job a little easier but isn't necessarily going to make the end result any better. It's worth bearing in mind that any minor disparity in alignment will be constant through the instrument's life. So providing those differences are accurately recorded, it should only be necessary to perform this observation once.

1 With the instrument securely seated, either on a bell-stick or lying on a towel, remove the second valve and bottom cap. Put these safely to one side.

2 From the top of the casing, insert the inspection mirror. Shine the torch on to the mirror and position the mirror so that it's possible to see into the upper port of the first valve. This allows you to check whether the up position is correct. Take any remedial action required.

3 Put the mirror into the bottom of the second valve casing and get sight of the lower airway through the first valve, while depressing the valve, so that you can assess its down position. Take any remedial action required.

4 Repeat steps 2 and 3 but with the mirror pointing into the third valve.

Note: Some accounts of alignment procedures based on sighting each valve individually suggest that the first and third valves should now be removed, in order to take a look at the second valve. While there might be some curiosity value in seeing how well the airways line up on one side of the valve compared to the other, there seems little point in terms of remedial action.

After all, once we're considering minute tolerances we need to look at all the factors. These include the fact that felts can be compressed beyond the nominal down position by applying additional force, and also the efficiency of the player in fully depressing/releasing the valve. In addition, it may be that the bore of the airway through the valve is slightly greater than it is through the casing (this as a result of a deliberate decision by the maker to create a freer-blowing horn).

What can go wrong?
We would caution against putting anything into the instrument that could scratch the valve casing, or get stuck in the tubing. Other than that, no real problems.

Attention to detail

If there's one thing that makes us bite our lips until we can find something nice to say, it's when a customer produces a horn that screams REPAIRED and announces: 'The repair guy suggested we go for a sympathetic repair...' We feel that's just spinning

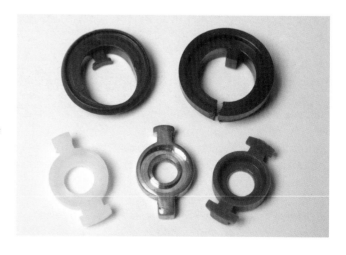

Clear evidence of previous repair work is not 'sympathetic restoration', it's sloppy workmanship in our opinion!

the customer a line to excuse sloppy workmanship. No repair pro looks at an instrument and thinks: 'You know, I might just make the repair on this one totally unsympathetic.'

But unfortunately there are a few around who think it's acceptable to leave scratches that are the obvious result of de-denting, then send the instrument to the lacquer shop. We cannot agree that there's any sense in which such work can be described as 'sympathetic'.

On the contrary, unless the customer requests otherwise we think it's the absolute duty of any repair shop undertaking a restoration to get the instrument as close to looking new again as is possible. If it isn't a full restoration we feel that at least the repair should be as close to invisible as possible. (Just because the instrument still has slightly noisy valves, it doesn't follow that the owner should be forced to face burnisher marks, or clear evidence of where a brace was re-soldered, every time the case is opened.)

Equally, not every repair can return an instrument to exactly the way it was when it left the factory, but patches can often be made to look like an original design feature with a little ingenuity.

We accept that schools have limited budgets and that the priority has to be on making student instruments functional, but when an instrument is someone's 'pride and joy' it's a different story. For that we reason we would urge any player seeking the services of a repair shop to be guided by the testimonies of other players – and to discuss the work required with the repairer – rather than going for 'the best quote'.

Piston valves – horizontal play

Any valve that's permanently misaligned in the horizontal plane is unlikely to be found on an instrument of great quality (if it's found at all).

Far more common – and easier to fix on modern instruments – is rotary 'play' caused by wear to the valve guide pins. This usually manifests itself in excessively noisy operation long before it has any appreciable affect on the playability of the instrument. Gently rotating the fingerplate will soon establish if there's excessive play.

1 Purchase a new set of valve guides. Most are made of nylon but they come in a variety of shapes and sizes, so it's important to establish that the replacement guides are actually correct for the make and model of instrument. Any good repair shop should be able to help with this.

2 Unscrew the first valve top cap and remove the valve. Unscrew the finger button and slide off the cap. Store safely.

3 Unscrew the valve pillar, remove the spring, then twist and remove the guide pin. Put these to one side.

4 Place the new guide into the valve, place the spring on top, and screw the valve pillar back on. Place the valve cap back over the valve pillar and screw the finger button back on.

5 Ensure that the valve is clean and well lubricated before replacing it.

6 Repeat this procedure for remaining valves.

What can go wrong?
Not a lot, but beware of forcing any part that doesn't unscrew freely. Also, springs and small parts find it hard to resist the call of the wild, so make sure none of them escape.

Older piston valves use a very different guide pin system that's a lot harder to repair, because the pin isn't a removable part but a semi-permanent fixture screwed/soldered to the side of the valve casing. Because most readers may never have to repair one of these valves we won't provide a detailed, step-by-step account of the repair procedure, but the diagram shows the bare bones of the problem.

The solution is essentially in two parts:

■ The walls of the slot are made straight again with a small flat file (with the 'blind' edge against the floor of the slot, so as not to make it any deeper).
■ The original pin is removed from the valve and an oversized nickel bolt put in its place. This is then filed until it's a good fit for the enlarged slot.

Achieving a smooth running valve after this requires a fair amount of polishing and lapping. It's important that the player's expectations regarding performance aren't unrealistic. Just as even upmarket vehicles of yesteryear rarely outperform a modern equivalent, a vintage instrument offers charm and character but cannot compete with its contemporary counterpart when it comes to speed and consistency.

What can go wrong?
Make no mistake, working on vintage valves requires expertise and experience. Overheating the valve, dropping it while trying to get the pin out, or sloppy file work to the casing, could easily leave you with a write-off. (The only reason we haven't put this procedure near the end of the chapter with the other really difficult stuff is that it made more sense to keep all the piston valve material together.)

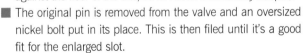

Visible only on the inside of the casing, the old system relies on a slot cut into the wall of the valve casing. Over time the slot becomes larger, as shown by the valve on the right

Removing stuck mouthpieces

This job is often presented as risk-free if a purpose-built puller is used, and there are those who encourage musicians to carry their own puller so that they can deal with a stuck mouthpiece immediately. For a student this isn't an option, as the cost of the puller is likely to be about the same as the value of the instrument. (Discouraging students from producing a satisfying 'pop' by slapping the back of the mouthpiece will greatly reduce the number of jams at no cost at all.)

Actually, using a puller isn't risk-free, hence we've included it in professional repairs on the basis that you should only undertake a procedure if you're confident that you can also repair any collateral damage that may arise.

(Conn-Selmer)

1 Place the two halves that make up the puller over the mouthpiece shank and pressed up against the receiver.

2 Tighten the two bolts that lengthen the puller until the mouthpiece starts to come free.

3 Put both hands round the puller and mouthpiece and move them clear of the instrument.

What can go wrong?
If it isn't very well engineered, the puller can often permanently scar the mouthpiece and may do an equal amount of damage to the instrument's receiver. In extreme cases the receiver may need to be replaced, as it has become so distorted by the force exerted by this well-intentioned device.

The alternative technique involves gently beating the receiver with a jeweller's hammer to free the mouthpiece:

1 Soak a little penetrating oil in the stuck area (not essential, but it can help).

2 Place a sandbag on a cleared section of bench, raised slightly by a wooden block.

3 Lay the receiver flat on the sandbag then gently tap the receiver near the mouthpiece end while turning the instrument. (Bear in mind that this is only possible on an instrument with enough access.) Always hit square to the receiver lying on the sandbag. Tap all the way round, or as far as you can. Don't pull or twist the mouthpiece.

4 The mouthpiece should simply drop out after a few attempts. This is because the receiver has expanded very slightly, breaking the seal of the taper.

What can go wrong?
Excessive force, or just bad luck, can cause the solder joint around the receiver, or a brace, to break. Most of the time this isn't a big deal, because re-soldering these components is relatively easy.

Repairing a mouthpiece shank

Damage to mouthpiece shanks is a common problem that can happen all too easily – if the mouthpiece gets trodden on, for instance. Fortunately it's an area of repair that bandmasters and music teachers can tackle with some confidence.

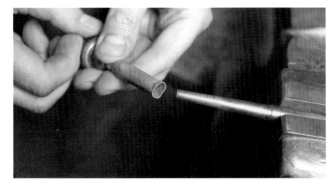

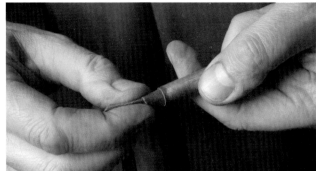

1 Push the shank of the mouthpiece over a mandrel that matches, or at least approximates, its backbore.

2 Iron out as much damage as possible using hand pressure against the mandrel.

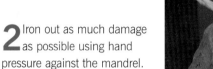

3 Apply further pressure if necessary by forcing the mouthpiece on to the mandrel using a mallet (not a hammer).

4 Use light, glancing blows with a jeweller's hammer to round the shank of the mandrel.

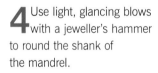

5 Clean out the backbore using emery cloth.

6 Use a strap of cloth with mopping soap on it to polish the shank, then clean up with a soft cloth.

7 The mouthpiece should be good to use again.

What can go wrong?
There will come a point where the metal becomes too thin and brittle to manipulate, and the shank will split while it's being worked.

Note: Kelly Mouthpieces offer a handy Truing Tool that can be used to fix less extreme cases.

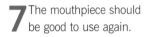

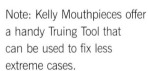

Increasing piston valve string tension

Hand adjustment of strings is increasingly uncommon now that replacing the springs is the preferred option. However, these techniques can still be useful if one replacement spring exhibits a different tension, or a player has a preference for a playing action lighter than the manufactured springs can offer.

1 Disassemble the valve, as described earlier in this chapter, and take the spring out.

2 Grasp each end of the spring with a small pair of round-nose pliers and stretch.

3 Reassemble valve and test for playing action

What can go wrong?
Pulling too hard can ruin the spring, so it's best to have some spares to hand. (In fact, replacing the springs is often the more effective way to go.) Achieving equal playing action across the valves takes practice.

Increasing rotary valve spring tension

1 Grasp one leg of the spring with a small pair of round-nose pliers and pull, so that the leg lengthens as the coil of the spring tightens.

2 Release and repeat for the other leg of the spring.

What can go wrong?
It takes a little practice to gauge how much the lever tension will increase, and using too much pressure also increases the chance of slipping and damaging the instrument with the pliers. If you're really unlucky, or heavy-handed, the solder joints can snap and the entire lever carriage will come away.

Decreasing rotary valve string tension

1 Grasp one leg of the spring with a small pair of round-nose pliers and pull it back on itself, so the spring over-compresses.

2 Release and repeat for the other leg of the spring.

What can go wrong?
As with increasing spring tension, you can slip and dent the instrument.

Freeing sticky middle valve when horn is dropped

This one almost made it into the 'Running repairs' section, because it can literally get you out of a jam in an emergency. But it's risky enough to merit inclusion under 'Professional repairs'.

This repair is necessary when a horn has been dropped and the second valve then goes sticky because the second slide has taken the brunt, forcing it backwards. This deforms the valve casing slightly.

1 Mount the horn on a bell stick to hold it steady. (In emergencies it's possible to hold the horn's valve section firmly in your left hand instead.)

2 While holding on tight to the valve casings, use your right hand to gently pull the second slide upwards.

3 As you do so, operate the valve to see if it runs more freely.

4 If it does you need to pull the slide upwards further still, so that when you release it it stays in the corrected position.

What can go wrong?
If you push too hard there's a fair chance of breaking the slide legs off the valve casing, which turns it into a soldering job, assuming you've now fixed the original problem. If it doesn't fix the problem it'll probably be necessary to use an adjustable reamer to skim the inside of the casing to remove the high spot – or an expandable valve casing mandrel to push it out – then lap the valve and casing lightly to restore smoothness.

This is definitely a procedure best practised initially on instruments of little or no value.

Power pump-through

Although you can perform this procedure to some extent using a hose connected to the normal mains hot tap, it's more effective using a purpose-built machine because the pressure achieved will be higher. Also, you can introduce cleaning chemicals to the water. (At Paxman Musical Instruments, shown here, the preference is for a mix of detergent and disinfectant.)

The most basic pump-through machine is less complicated than a fishpond with a filtration system. In fact, a centrifugal pump designed for a fishpond or a shower pump would make a good starting point for a self-build. (Just remember to use a jubilee clamp on every hose, because the instrument will present a lot of back-pressure when connected.) Whether you introduce a heating element or simply pour in pre-heated water is another design choice. Whatever your design, it's vital that the switch is genuinely waterproof, because your hands will get wet.

Note: For smaller brass, it's questionable how beneficial this procedure is, due to the ease with which the tubing can be cleaned with soapy water and a brush. It's only when you get to larger instruments, with lengths of inaccessible tubing, that the effort really pays off.

1 Tie up all slides so that they won't jump out under pressure.

2 Hang on tight to the pump hose unless you like wearing a mix of water, detergent, disinfectant and horn player goo! (There's a cloth over the top of the machine to sieve out the worst of this, however.) Then, pump through with tap water to rinse thoroughly.

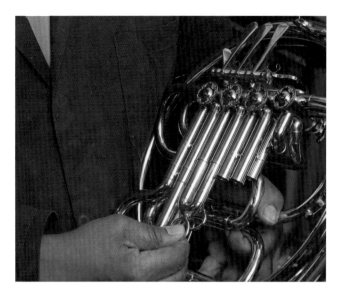

3 Get the water out by a combination of removing slides and rotating the horn.

4 Re-lubricate the upper and lower bearings.

5 Re-oil the valve bodies through the slide legs. (One of the virtues of pumping through is that it's effective in cleaning the inside of the instrument without having to dismantle and service the valve section.)

6 Put all the slides back.

What can go wrong?
Although pumping through isn't fundamentally a risky process, sooner or later there's a fair chance you'll forget to tie one of the slides in, meaning it will get dented and/or cause a dent to the main body of the instrument at the point of impact. When this happens, expect that you – and anyone standing near you – will get extremely wet!

Easing a slide

1 Apply a graphite-based easing oil (such as WD40) to the slide legs.

2 Warm the outer sleeves of the slides to help the oil to penetrate the full length of the slide legs. (Professionals will use a gas torch set to a gentle flame, but the two most obvious risks are the inflammable nature of the penetrating oil and the possibility of burning the finish, if the instrument is lacquered. Placing the instrument over a plastic bowl and pouring hot water over the sleeves of the slide is a less risky alternative, albeit also less effective.)

3 While wearing a protective glove, attempt to remove the slide using a combination of normal hand pressure and a slight twisting action.

4 Repeat steps 1 and 2 if the slide cannot be removed.

5 The above procedure can be made more effective by also gently tapping round the sleeves of the slide assembly with a jeweller's hammer.

What can go wrong?
The biggest risk comes from the use of excessive force, especially when applying a twisting action. Although you're unlikely to do too much damage to a tuba, warping a trumpet is a real possibility. In addition, when a main slide frees unexpectedly, striking the bell is all too easy.

Pulling a slide

This procedure is best performed only if easing has been attempted first.

1 Wrap cloth around the bow of the crook to minimise the chance of impact damage.

2 Wrap a nylon cord around the stay of the bow and secure the ends in a vice.

3 Grasp the instrument tightly, at secure points as close to the slide as possible.

4 Pull the instrument smartly but evenly away from the vice in a direction parallel to the slide legs.

If the slide is some way out of the sleeves, an alternative strategy is to grasp the leg behind the ferrule with smooth-jawed pliers and gently tap them, repeating the procedure on each leg until the slide frees.

What can go wrong?
It's possible to twist the entire instrument out of shape, even to the point of being beyond economic repair. (The danger of this varies, in that a trumpet is considerably more vulnerable than, say, a euphonium, due to its basic geometry and bracing arrangement.) There's also a real risk of damaging or detaching the stay, as well as causing dents in the slide or elsewhere on the instrument. (See below.)

Re-soldering slide legs

This information appears directly after instructions on easing and pulling slides – and it's no coincidence. In fact, it's probably best that you *expect* a solder join to break when you

perform physically aggressive procedures on an instrument.

Note: The steps required to complete this procedure are explained in the chapter *Design and manufacture*, especially the section on soldering a ferrule. In fact, at this level it's probably appropriate to think of the repair as being manufacture, albeit with components that have been assembled before.

1 Clean solder out of the inside of the detached ferrule using a triangular scraper and from the outside of the detached tubing with a small strap of emery cloth. (If necessary, remove excess solder by heating and wiping off first.)

2 Having ensured that both legs are clean and move freely in their sleeves, place the legs in their correct position on the instrument, and with the crook in the ferrules.

3 Move the slide out of the fully-closed position to ensure that it won't become soldered into the sleeves. Check both legs are extended by the same amount by measuring the gap with callipers.

4 Heat the join slightly and apply flux.

5 Bring the join up to temperature with the torch and apply solder, using the flame to encourage the solder to run all the way round.

6 Wipe off any excess solder with a rag while it's still molten.

7 Once solder has set, use water to cool the joint and remove flux.

8 Remove traces of solder with scraper.

9 Use a small strap of emery cloth to move any scraper marks, then remove emery marks using strap impregnated with polishing soap. Alternatively, an electric buffing wheel can be used if access permits.

You may find it more convenient to complete steps 8 and 9 with the slide in a jig or clamp.

What can go wrong?
If you aren't quick and tidy at soldering you can make quite a mess, especially if you apply heat for too long and start unsoldering ferrules or braces that weren't part of the original problem!

Re-soldering stays/braces

The following is generally valid for all stays/braces, regardless of their location on the instrument.

1 Clean area of instrument under the stay flange with a small strap of emery cloth. Ensure that any lacquer is removed to a least a couple of millimetres from the solder join.

2 Reverse emery cloth and repeat, this time cleaning the underside of the flange. (This assumes that only one of the two flanges has become detached, which is generally the case. If the stay is completely detached, heat each flange in turn and remove excess solder with a cotton rag.)

3 If the stay and the tubing aren't held together tightly (*ie* by the legs of a slide), wrap binding wire around the flange and the tube, then twist the end with pliers until the stay is held tightly in place. Alternatively, it's often possible to use brass repair technician's wire clips. These inexpensive aids are quick to use and are a must for any professional repair shop.

4 Follow steps 4–9 in previous instructions on the left.

What can go wrong?
Generally speaking, the biggest failing in soldering by inexperienced repairers is that the finished result looks somewhat messy. This is partly due to lack of attention at the scraping and polishing stages, but it must be said that an experienced hand with a torch leaves a lot less surplus to remove in the first place! The newer lead-free formulations are harder to work with in this respect. Other than that, try not to dent the tubing by excessive force with the scraper or by over-tightening the binding wire. Sometimes, when one solder join is very close to another, the heat will travel and unsolder the other join.

De-denting

This topic merits a section of its own because a variety of techniques are used – and which is the most appropriate is often a judgement call by the repairer. For instance, a component may be repaired in situ, or unsoldered in order to get better access to the damaged area. Sometimes the component will be so damaged that it makes more sense to replace it completely (either with a stock item or, as is often the case, by fabricating a new piece.)

A significant complication in many de-denting jobs comes from the fact that the instrument is lacquered, plated, or both. This means that extra care must be taken to minimise scratches or hammer marks on the surface. Polishing them out may either mean a complete refinish, or an instrument that looks like it has obviously undergone repair.* Again, this is something of a judgement call, as well as a question of budget. A good repair shop should discuss the options with the customer before starting work.

Note: This section isn't graded from easy to hard, but from leader to flare. All de-denting procedures require specialist tools and skills that are learned through practice, so it's fair to say they all belong at the 'hard' end of this section to at least some extent.

De-denting leader pipes

Most brass instruments have leader pipes that are at least partially accessible through the receiver, or the main slide sleeve. (Although our pictures imply that the leader pipe is easily accessible from both directions, it has been detached. When the leader pipe is still on the instrument only a flexible rod will reach the inside of the tubing from the slide end.)

This is good news from a repair perspective, because it means that dents can either be tapped out against a tapered

Typical leader pipe damage.

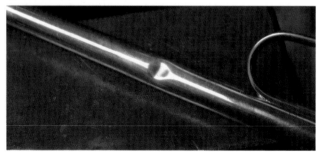

---

*There is some scope for small-scale refinishing using lacquers sold by automotive accessory shops. Compared to an entire instrument, valve caps and small slides are fairly easy to lacquer. Equally, taking the old lacquer off up to a natural break point – such as a ferrule – is less obtrusive than leaving half the tubing lacquered and the other half of that section stripped.

mandrel using a jeweller's hammer, or pushed and tapped out using a metal ball on a rod. A typical trumpet leader pipe repair goes like this:

1 Select and secure a mandrel or rod horizontally in a vice, making sure to choose one with a diameter no greater than the internal diameter of the tube you're working on. (Measure external tubing with callipers, then deduct 0.5mm.)

2 It's useful to get the measure of where the dent is relative to the rod, so you'll know at what point to start ironing the dent out.

3 Slide the instrument's leader pipe over the mandrel or rod and start working the dent, with the objective of removing it as far as possible. (Look carefully and you can still see where the dent is, although it's already a vast improvement.)

4 To remove the last of the dent, manoeuvre the instrument while gently tapping on the area to be worked until it can be heard that there's solid metal underneath (a 'clink', rather than a softer 'thud').

5 Using controlled, glancing blows, tap the dented area until it rises to the level of the surrounding metal. (It's very important not to use a hammer, or blows, that are too heavy, because any thinning to the metal cannot be reversed.)

6 Burnish the tubing to make it as round and flat as possible. In this example a straight burnisher has been employed, but a swage or a curved burnishing tool are also possibilities.

7 File the worked area lightly. This is to remove the slight hammer marks, not the last of the dent!

8 Remove the file marks with a strap of emery cloth, holding the two ends at an angle to reduce the chance of it 'sawing' ridges into the metal.

9 Remove the emery marks with a finer grade, working along the pipe. This will enable the polishing stage to work across these fine marks, producing a better finish.

10 Using a similar technique to step 8, remove the scratches using a strap of cloth covered in mopping soap.

11 When performed with skill and care the result is truly an invisible mend.

Instruments that have curving leader pipes may need plugging or pulling to reach the required area. These techniques are explained in the notes below on de-denting slides and other tubing. When working on low brass, pulling may be preferred to plugging, because the weight of the instrument makes plugging virtually impossible without removing the leader pipe. This in turn requires soldering on a temporary brace to prevent the tubing from straightening somewhat during de-denting – quite a lot of work if there's only one dent to remove.

What can go wrong?
Often, one or more stays detaches while the metal is tapped. Excessive hammering may bruise and over-thin, or even split the leader pipe if it's already thin. Trying to tap out a dent without solid metal (whether mandrel, ball or plug) underneath is likely to make the dent worse.

De-denting slides and other tubing

As with leader pipes, removing dents from slides is easier if it's possible to access the inside of the affected area with a mandrel or rod inserted in the slide leg. When there's denting in the non-accessible part of the slide's crook it's a judgement call whether it's best to:

- Push a plug through the tubing into the affected section.
- Remove a slide leg to get better access.
- Pull, rather than push, the dent out.
- Replace the crook/bow entirely.

Each approach has its plus and minus points. An experienced repairer will weigh these up before deciding the strategy that will lead to the most satisfactory repair in the least time. We'll look at each procedure in turn.

Plugging

This requires a ball/plug set. In many repair shops the plugs are threaded and can be used in one of two ways. One is mounted on a rod, which frequently has a flexible section at the end. This technique is explained step-by-step below.

The other technique is illustrated above. Here, a plug is propelled through the tubing with a chaser plug known as a 'driver'. This repeatedly strikes the plug through a swinging motion set up by the repairer. Most easily understood when seen in action – and best learned through practice – the motion isn't unlike that of a traditional Hawaiian oarsman. Fluidity of movement and a constant rhythm are the important factors, though. Brute force and speed are not required.

Plug and driver: in this dent removal technique, the plug (shown here in grey metal) is chased through the tubing using a driver (shown here in yellow metal). By using a swinging motion something like that shown by the black arrows, a technician can drive the plug with a series of impacts to the desired location, as suggested by the red arrow. Driving a plug back out requires the driver to be the other side of the plug, so it's a good idea to have established an 'exit strategy' before inserting the plug in the first place! Often you'll need to put the driver through a knuckle in one of the valve casings if you're working on the main body of an instrument. When you're working on a slide the exit strategy is somewhat more obvious, but it's important to ensure that the driver will negotiate all the bends in the tubing when working on, for instance, the third valve crooks of a French horn.

Note: The amount of dent repairs that can be carried out using plugs on a rod, rather than propelled around the tubing by a 'driver', varies greatly, depending on the type of instrument. For example, the tubing on a trumpet is relatively accessible, particularly if components are unsoldered for dent removal, so a flexible rod and ball is a useful approach much of the time. Conversely, considerable sections of a French horn are quite inaccessible, so driving plugs round the tubing is a necessity.

In theory driving a plug of the exact internal diameter of the tubing would remove any dents, but the reality is more complicated. The plug doesn't 'know' what you're trying to achieve, so will tend to push out the wall on the opposite side to the dent if you attempt to drive it all the way through without tapping out the dent as you go. In addition, the edges of the dent will remain as creases.

When working on a tapered section it's necessary to drive in a succession of plugs, each smaller than the last.

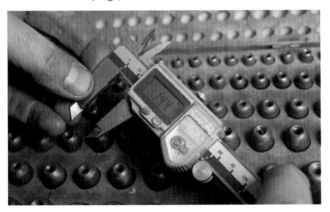

1 Use callipers to measure the external diameter of the tubing at the point where it's to be plugged. Rotate the callipers to determine whether the tubing is round or slightly oval. If you get differing measurements, take the widest and narrowest and settle on halfway between the two.

2 Subtract 20thou/0.5mm, as this is the average wall thickness of the tubing times two. Obviously, this is only an approximation of the internal diameter but it's good enough as a starting point. (Go 0.2mm smaller still if the dent is deep, so the tube will distort less, then go up to size.)

3 Using the callipers locked to this reduced diameter, select the appropriate plug from the tray and insert or slide it into the tubing (a little oil on the plug can help). Note: If you're inserting the plug into a slide leg and it seems a tight fit, choose a smaller plug. There's no point in taking a dent out only to end up with a slide that no longer fits!

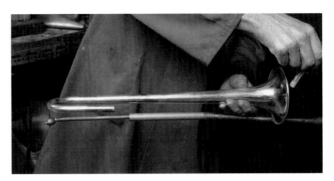

4 As the end of the ball rod is flexible this will only be an estimate, but marking on the rod approximately how far in it will be when it reaches the dent is a useful aid to locating the plug when it's no longer visible.

5 Get the plug to the desired location with care and patience. The taper of the trumpet is gradual at the point to be worked on, so the plug will start to bind some distance from its intended location. In addition, the flexible section at the end is moving in a different direction to the applied energy, so its progress needs to be eased rather than forced. It's also worth remembering that the plug size has been estimated. As a result, it's best to stop and find its location as soon as significant resistance is encountered.

6 Use a combination of your initial mark on the rod, evidence of the plug starting to remove the dent and tapping with a hammer, to establish exactly where it is.

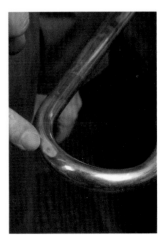

7 Once the plug is in position, tap out the dents as necessary using a jeweller's hammer for external curves, and an appropriate radius of de-denting hammer for internals in the case of tight curves.

8 In parallel-sided tubing the plug can be repositioned as required, but in tapered tubing it should be removed as soon as work on a specific spot has been completed, and a plug of appropriate dimension selected for the next section if necessary.

9 Restore the roundness of the tubing, which is usually compromised somewhat by the dent-removal procedure. On tight bends like this a draw ring is an appropriate tool, but on tubing where there's no 'open end' to access a U-shaped swage is the tool to use. The radius of the draw ring must be slightly greater than the tapered tubing going through it. Therefore it's necessary to push the tuning through at a slight angle to maintain contact, and to rotate the tubing somewhat to achieve roundness.

10 Decide how you want to finish the repair. The photograph tells you two things. One is that the marks left by the hammer are slight but visible. The other is that the instrument is silver plated. As the plating has already been polished through by previous repairs, this bell will be repolished where the repair has been done. If the plate was intact, it would probably make more sense to tolerate the slightly matted area left by the hammer work.

11 If desired, lightly file the affected area to remove any hammer marks (not the remaining dent!).

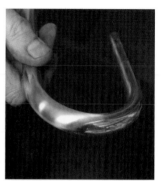

12 Emery out the file marks. At this point, the repair should look almost perfect.

13 Either polish by hand, using a cloth strap and mopping soap, or use an electric mop. With a high shine, the missing silver plate is a lot harder to spot.

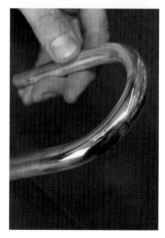

What can go wrong?
Driving a plug further than it should go into tapered tubing will cause the tubing to expand, until it looks like a snake that has just eaten! Although it is possible to reverse this with some deft hammer work, it is much better to avoid the situation by using your eyes and ears. The slightest sign of a bulge in the tubing is a signal to take the plug out. A plug that has been driven too far takes on a sharper tone as the driver strikes it and the resistance to further movement can be felt through the whole instrument. (It's not easy to describe the latter phenomenon but imagine the difference in feel between striking a golf ball with a club and then striking a metal stake that has been driven into the ground.)

The potential for damaging thin metal tubing when hitting it with a hammer should not be ignored either.

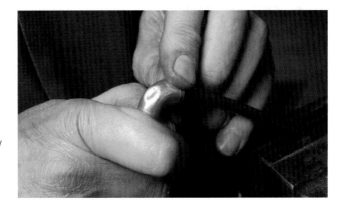

Removing a slide leg

Removing a slide leg to make it easier to iron out dents is relatively easy but shouldn't be undertaken unless you're confident of reassembling the slide when you've finished. (The procedure for re-soldering a slide leg appears earlier in this section.)

On low brass such as a tuba taking off the bottom bow is an attractive option, because it not only increases access but also sheds a considerable amount of weight. In addition, this part of the instrument is always constructed like a battleship, so there's a fair chance you'll want to remove the protective guard and de-dent this separately.

(As the section on patches and guards points out, specialists in low brass often use a rolling system designed for making and repairing guards. Without this equipment the hammer technique required becomes less a question of 'tapping' and more like the panel-beating required to repair cars.)

1 Place one leg of the slide into its sleeve, but don't push it all the way in. Leave the other leg free so that you can hold it.

2 Apply a torch to the bow side of the ferrule on the slide in the sleeve.

3 Move the other slide leg backwards and forwards gently until the bow comes free. Wipe off any surplus solder with a cloth.

4 Cool using water. (An earthenware bowl and a brush from a cookery shop are handy for this.)

5 Place the other leg into its sleeve but don't push it all the way in. Unsolder the other ferrule and wipe off any surplus solder.

6 Place detached slide legs into a parts container for later use.

7 If the denting is substantial, solder a length of brass rod across the bow as a temporary stay so that the width will remain unaltered during the de-denting process.

8 Select a ball tool small enough to go into the bow and mount it in the vice.

9 Use the same techniques as in the previous procedure to remove the dents – ironing, tapping out with a hammer and refinishing as necessary.

10 Remove temporary stay if one was attached.

11 Place slide legs back into their sleeves. Leave each one, say, 10mm out of the sleeve to prevent any danger of soldering the slide legs in accidentally. Place bow in ferrules and re-solder.

What can go wrong?

Depending on the size of the ferrule, unsoldering one side without affecting the other can be difficult. Therefore the joint between the ferrule and the leg may be disturbed. If this knocks the ferrule out of true, it may be necessary to disassemble the two parts and re-solder in correct alignment.

Pulling a dent

This technique first requires the making of a puller, which is best made from nickel silver rod, as it's more durable than brass. This is how to make it:

- Take a length of rod. (Any length more than about 200mm will be fine at this stage.)
- Soften the first 20mm by making it red hot, then beat it with a hammer over a mandrel to form a hook.

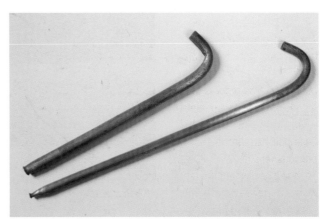

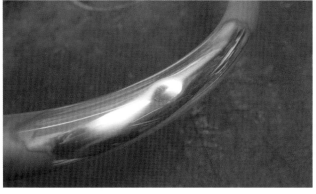

In reality it would be easier to plug this dent than pull it, but it's a good example because the dent is easy to see.

■ Cut the rod with hook to a length of about 170mm.
■ File the straight end of the rod so that it forms a dull (not sharp) point.

Once you've made a puller it should survive being used many times. Pulling is a more attractive option than plugging when access to the internal of the tubing is difficult and removing the tubing would be problematic. This is how pulling is achieved:

3 Cool the work, using your water bowl.

4 Grasping the instrument firmly with one hand, strike the hook of the puller so that it pulls away from the dent. (A large file is usually a good choice of striker.)

5 Repeat until the dent is raised slightly about the surface of the surrounding metal.

1 Heat the end of the puller, flux it and apply solder.

2 Soft-solder the rod to the dent. How much solder to use is a judgement call because too little will result in a bond that won't withstand the mechanical shock, while filling the dent with solder will prevent the puller from working properly.

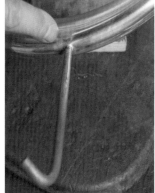

6 Unsolder the puller and clean off any surplus solder.

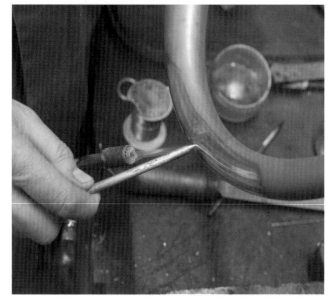

7 Tap the affected area of the tube smooth with a jeweller's hammer. (If access is limited you may need to tap it down by using the hammer on an appropriately sized swage instead.)

It's usually necessary on bigger dents to repeat sections 1–5 a number of times, strategically repositioning the puller for maximum effectiveness.

What can go wrong?
This is a difficult technique to master and the potential for damage ranges from accidentally hitting the instrument with the file, or the puller if it breaks free, to ripping a hole in the tube if it's thin and brittle.

Replacing the crook/bow

This sounds like the easy option, which it is if you happen to have exactly the same part to replace it with. But unless you happen to be the manufacturer of the instrument, the chances are you won't have a replacement part available. This is one of those times when the line between repair and manufacture is blurred, because replacing the part is likely to entail a whole list of processes (which we've only described in brief below – see the chapter *Design and manufacture* for more about tube bending).

- Locate or make a bending block to match the shape of the existing crook/bow.
- Measure the diameter of the existing tubing and either find it from stock, or draw it down from tubing of slightly larger diameter.
- Soften it, plug one end, then fill it with your chosen material – be it pitch, lead, or one of the safer alternatives mentioned in *Design and manufacture* – to resist buckling.
- Bend around block.
- Empty tubing of filler.
- Repair any puckering.
- Emery and polish.
- Cut to exact length.
- Solder in place.

Although the process is considerably more protracted than the short-form description above implies, it's sometimes the best option. More than that, it's sometimes the *only* option when the metal is worn through, as may happen on a vintage instrument. An alternative approach is a guard or patch, as described elsewhere in this section.

De-denting a trumpet bell

Despite some variations in technique, successfully de-denting a bell requires the thin metal of the instrument to be pressed against a solid metal former using some kind of burnishing tool to restore the original shape using an ironing action.

As a general rule, smaller instruments such as trumpets are de-dented against a former that follows the shape of the flare, while larger instruments are de-dented against a stake, which is more like a bicycle saddle in contour.

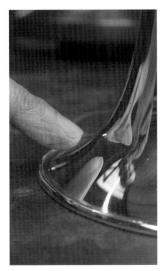

1 Observe the damage to the bell and decide on the remedial action. These dents are relatively straightforward, because they're simply deformations to the sheet.

Note: No two damaged bells are the same and the repair technician won't always use the techniques shown here in the same order. Please regard this as an example, rather than a sequence to be followed in all instances.

2 Pay particular attention to creases, as they're often caused by a bash to the bell which has bent the rim – as is the case here.

3 Straighten the rim with a mallet if necessary.

Note: The surface used here is wood covered in leather, which is hard enough to beat the rim flat but no so hard as to risk bruising the metal.

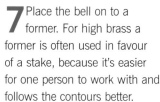

7 Place the bell on to a former. For high brass a former is often used in favour of a stake, because it's easier for one person to work with and follows the contours better.

8 Use the former to iron out any remaining creases. As with a stake, a former can be used as an ironing tool in its own right.

4 Check your results until the rim is flat.

5 Iron as much of the crease out as possible using a metal stake. The stake is a particularly important tool for removing dents and creases from larger brass instruments.

9 Burnish against the former. This is particularly useful for dealing with tight creases, or sharp dents, because the sheet material is sandwiched between the two tools and therefore has to take the shape of the former when placed under sustained pressure.

6 Smooth the contours with a burnisher. Again, this is a very important technique where a bell or flare has been ironed with a burnisher from the outside, as this has a tendency to produce steps, or ridges, which must then be smoothed from the inside.

10 Iron out dents from the throat of the bell using the former.

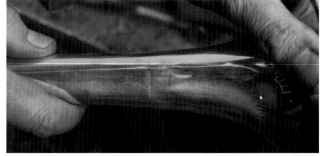

11 Swage the throat on to the former. This has the advantage of helping to restore roundness to the tubing, as well as taking out dents. Note: Be careful not to swage beyond the end of the former, as this will press an unwanted step into the throat metal.

12 Apply mopping soap to the polishing wheel and mop the bell inside and out.

De-denting a French horn flare

The stake bears no direct relationship to the shape of the instrument but is simply formed to allow maximum surface contact to a wide variety of bells. To an extent, whether a former or a stake is chosen is down to personal preference.

Similarly, some repairers use a burnisher to iron the metal while others prefer to use a dent roller (particularly popular when working on low brass, the bells of which are thick). Although a roller has the advantage of minimising scratches, some find it unwieldy to use, especially on smaller instruments.

Whichever tools are employed, it should be acknowledged that there's considerable scope for deforming and thereby damaging the flare. This is especially true of the French horn, as most have flares that are just thousandths of an inch thick, meaning that excessive pressure and/or inadequate support from the mandrel can stretch the metal so much that it can never be restored to its original shape. Although not as difficult to manoeuvre as a tuba, the French horn is also inherently unwieldy when held in anything other than its playing position.

For these reasons, repairers often prefer to work in a team of two when using a stake and burnisher for de-denting. This spares the person burnishing the physical strain of supporting the instrument for prolonged periods and allows them to concentrate on the task of dent removal.

As we will show, working in this way allows for a very structured approach that's particularly suitable for flares that are dented or creased more or less all over.

1 Ensure that the instrument, burnisher and stake are free from any dirt or corrosion that might scratch the instrument. Wipe them over with a cloth. If the instrument is lacquered or plated, apply a little petroleum jelly to the stake and burnisher.

2 Stand behind the instrument, facing the stake. Rest the bell on the stake so that a portion of the flare closest to the rim is resting on it.

3 Place the flat of the burnisher on the portion of the flare in contact with the stake and apply a consistent ironing motion, working to and from the rim over no more of the flare than is actually in contact with the stake.

4 Slowly rotate the instrument so that the person burnishing can cover a new area of the flare without significant adjustment to their working position. Eventually the flare will have been rotated 360° and a complete band of the flare will be burnished smooth.

5 Change the angle of the instrument so that a new band of the flare is in contact with the stake and continue rotating as before.

6 When creating each new burnished band, be careful not to work over too great an area, or to apply too much pressure at the point where the new band overlaps the previous band. Otherwise there's likely to be a pronounced step between each band.

7 Continue the process until the throat of the instrument is reached and it isn't realistic to continue working with the stake, as it won't reach any further.

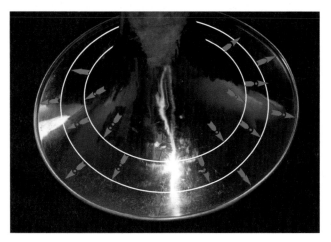

8 Turn the instrument over so that the person burnishing can work on the inside of the flare. (Whether you need one or two people at this stage is partly down to personal preference, but also to the size of the instrument. When working on a tuba you'll probably prefer to rest it on a sandbag on the floor.)

9 Observe the contour of the inside of the bell. No matter how careful you've been, it's likely that at least some of the bands of burnishing have slight steps between them.

10 Use the flat of the burnisher to iron out any stepping, using a smooth, even motion. Be careful not to dig the tip of the burnisher into the throat of the bell.

11 Polish out scratch marks using an electric mop.

Note: In contrast, working with a former is simpler because it can be mounted vertically, making the instrument self-

supporting. In addition the contour of the former is much closer to that of the flare. Together, those two factors make it easier to keep the flare in contact with the former while burnishing.

What can go wrong?
Until a repairer has developed an even burnishing technique, thin flares are particularly likely to be left with an unsightly corrugated effect, as well as pronounced stepping between bands. Student grade instruments tend to be thicker and a little more forgiving, although the physical effort required to iron out the dents is that much greater. It's worth remembering that anyone panel-beating a car can hide their handiwork under a layer of filler and paint. On a brass instrument you don't have that luxury! This is doubly true on a bell, where both sides are visible, and taking out marks with emery cloth isn't usually a good idea.

De-denting brass band instrument bells
Although there's considerable overlap in the techniques used on all brass musical instruments, the size and thicker construction of the instruments found in brass and marching bands calls for a more robust approach.

A dent roller is an alternative to using a burnisher and has the advantage of reducing scratching, which becomes especially significant on plated and lacquered instruments. (*Böhm*)

Double-handed burnishers are available in graduated sizes and allow greater pressure to be exerted, which is an advantage when working on thick-walled instruments. (*Böhm*)

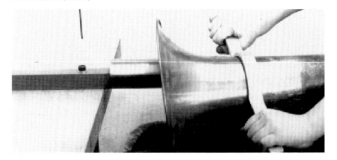

Repairing valves

Measuring air-tightness

There's a lot to know about valves, but at the very simplest level there are just three performance characteristics that matter to the player:

(a) How free-flowing is the air in the open, closed and transitional positions?
(b) How good is the playing action from a mechanical perspective?
(c) How airtight are the valves?

Characteristic (a) is one we can't do much about at the repair stage – it's really down to the way the instrument is designed and made.

Characteristic (b) is one we can do a lot with, which is why so much space in this section is devoted to the topic.

Characteristic (c) is complicated and expensive to adjust once the valves have become overly leaky – to the extent that it's a major factor in putting instruments beyond economic repair. However, measuring how airtight the valves are provides a valuable way of accessing the overall 'health' of an instrument.

A subjective impression of the overall air-tightness of an instrument can be formed by placing a rubber ball in the bell, removing the slides and blowing hard down the leader pipe. It will soon be apparent if there's significant leakage. However, this won't provide any definitive measurements. Fortunately it's easy to construct a tool to do this – a 'manometer'.

At its simplest, a manometer is like a trombone slide standing vertically and partly filled with liquid. However, we need to see what's happening to the liquid inside, so the legs need to be glass tubes, while the bow at the bottom can be nothing more complicated than a rubber tube of an appropriate diameter. (Readers with access to a school's science department have probably realised that everything they need is already in the physics lab.)

So far, the liquid in the tube will be subject to an equal amount of atmospheric pressure in both legs and they will therefore be level. But if we were to pump air into one leg it would start to displace the liquid, and the degree of displacement would indicate how much greater than atmospheric pressure the pressure was in the other leg.

It would, of course, be helpful if we put some sort of rule along the 'other leg' so that we could compare degrees of displacement and give them a numerical value. Assuming the pump is adjustable, we can set it so that the liquid reaches a point at the upper end of the scale that we'll call '100% airtight'. In other

words, all the pressure created by the pump is transferred to the manometer. Similarly, if we detach the hose from the pump the liquid will subside to equal levels on both sides, and we can mark that as '0% airtight'. In other words, none of the pressure created by the pump is transferred to the manometer.

Now let's introduce a trumpet into the test system. If we attach the pump to the leader pipe, we can take a hose from the instrument and – depending exactly what point that hose comes from – measure the efficiency of each valve. For instance, if we want to measure the efficiency of the first valve, we need to remove the first slide from that valve and connect the tube to the manometer from the 'outlet' side of the valve.

With the valve at rest, we'd expect almost all the air to be going straight through the trumpet and the measurement to be close to 0%. But with the valve depressed all the air should be fed to the manometer, leading to a score of 100%. It won't

A manometer is easy to make.

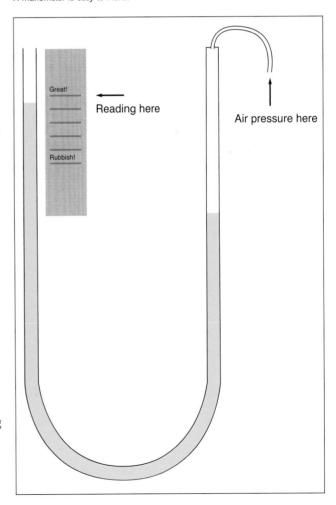

Great!

Rubbish!

Reading here

Air pressure here

be, of course, because the valve isn't 100% airtight. (With other valve positions there's also the possibility that some of the leakage is coming from earlier valves in the sequence.)

Following the same logic, you can test all three valves on our example trumpet. Perhaps more importantly, you can mark the relative performances of various instruments and start to mark zones for 'top professional', 'acceptable student model', 'almost unplayable', or whatever categories are meaningful to you.

Note: A certain amount of ingenuity is required when testing for leaks between layers in a double French horn. So called 'jug handle leaks' mean that air blown through the B flat side can end up in the F tubing, and vice versa. Detecting these leaks requires a series of tests, with various slide sleeves connected to the manometer.

What can go wrong?
We're pleased to report that this is a low risk exercise that's very informative. We recommend it not only to repairers but also to schools as an interesting co-operative project between the science and music faculties.

Lapping
The term lapping refers to a process whereby the gap between the body of a valve and its casing is fine-tuned by using a paste containing an abrasive pumice powder. Most manufacturers use lapping to achieve a point where the valves run freely but still achieve a good seal. Repairers use lapping mainly when encountering two conditions:

■ Heavy corrosion to the valve/casing.
■ Mechanical shock to the instrument has distorted, or dented, the valve casing (which may need to be reamed, or restored to shape with an expandable mandrel, prior to lapping).

As noted elsewhere in this section, lapping is best learned face-to-face from someone who can teach you by example how far is 'far enough'. Excessive lapping causes unnecessarily leaky valves – a difficult condition to treat.

Because the basic principle is the same for all valves, we've shown piston valves only in the procedure below:

1 Disassemble the valve, stripping it of finger key, valve pillar, spring, cork etc. Repair pros usually keep a range of valve pillars they've made up for no other purpose than fitting for lapping. If you don't have these you'll need to put the 'everyday' valve pillars back.

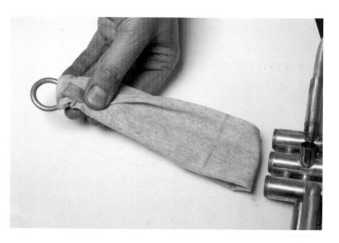

2 Use a clean rag and a swab to ensure that the valve and casing are free from unwanted material.

3 Apply lapping paste evenly to the body of the valve (1,000 grit/8 micron is a common choice).

4 Mount the valve pillar in a hand chuck. (The very experienced can use a high-torque cordless drill, but this demands considerable control.)

5 Rotate the valve in the casing using circular up-and-down motions in a random pattern to avoid excessive wear in one spot. Continue until it runs freely.

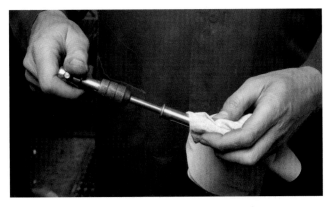

6 Withdraw the valve, then clean valve and casing thoroughly, paying particular attention to the air passages, which are likely to contain residual amounts of lapping paste.

Note: There are players who claim to have obtained good results lapping piston valves using Brasso, or even toothpaste. As both these products contain abrasive powder, we can certainly see how this would work. While a lapping paste of a specified abrasive grade is to be preferred, the two commonly available substitutes could be useful for an emergency repair.

What can go wrong?
It's hard to overstate the potential for creating a leaky valve by over lapping. It's often better to start with the assumption that the valve is already correctly lapped and that the appropriate remedy is thorough cleaning to remove any build-up of scale or corrosion.

The neoprenes on this Paxman horn are specifically manufactured to fit the bumper plate. The alternative is to use slightly oversized plugs of neoprene, which need to be compressed slightly as they're inserted.

Fitting new corks on rotary valves

The corks on a rotary valve don't simply minimise the operating noise – they're also the means by which the extent of travel is controlled. As a result, accurate cutting of the corks and periodic replacement play an important role in ensuring that the airflow through the instrument is unimpeded.

As with other uses for cork – such as sealing wine bottles – synthetic materials have largely replaced the original. Materials such as neoprene offer a number of advantages, including total consistency from one 'cork' to another and the ability to perform well over time, with no tendency to harden due to drying out.

1 Unscrew and remove the buffer plates. Place the screws in a container for safekeeping.

2 Clamp the plates into a vice fitted with soft protective covers. (Or clamp them individually, if you find it easier.)

3 Use your thumb, or a blunt pencil, to push out the existing corks.

4 Place approximately half the diameter of a new cork into a pair of smooth-jaw pliers, compress and insert. (Alternatively, if they're pre-shaped simply press the neoprenes into position with your fingers.)

5 Slice surplus cork from the bottom of the plate with a craft knife so that it's flush. Repeat for the top of the plate if necessary.

6 Reattach the plates to the valves.

7 Turn the instrument over and remove the valve caps. Note the small notches on the valve bearing spindles and the bearing cases. These should indicate the correct open and closed positions for the valves. (There should also be a notch on the plate to indicate the position in which it should be seated. If you have any doubt whether the marks are correct, take out a slide and check by eye the fully opened and closed positions of the valve.)

8 Using a craft knife, cut away the front edge of each cork until the valves align precisely with the notches on the bearings, or your own observations.

Note: You may want to make a protective shield for the valve casings from a small, L-shaped piece of sheet metal. Slide this under each cork before you cut it to the correct position and you'll avoid marking the valve casing by accident.

What can go wrong?
Providing you take your time and don't scratch the instrument when you cut the corks, or lose any of the screws, this is a relatively low risk procedure.

Servicing rotary valve and slide systems

When a valve seizes, or all the valves have become particularly sluggish, there comes a point where it's time to stop squirting oils down slide legs and take the valves out for a thorough clean. However, we don't recommend the non-professional to attempt this unless they have all the required tools and materials. As with many of the riskier procedures, removing and replacing rotary valves is best attempted on instruments of low value until a certain amount of knowledge and skill has been acquired.

For a professional repairer, any time a valve has seized is also a good time to review the functional efficiency of the overall valve/linkage system, as detailed in the next section. It may be that the problem isn't a dirty valve at all. It may be that the valve is being pushed into the wall of the casing when it's operated, meaning the bearings need tightening. It's important to remember the gap between the two is very small – especially in a valve with an efficient seal.

Equally, if a valve has started to lock up it's worth looking at the interior condition of the tubing. Without wishing to sound judgemental, every repair pro comes across instruments that look as if they're mostly played during wine and cheese parties! Pulling a cloth or brush through the leader pipe will soon reveal whether a complete clean is needed. Because all the valves are on the same instrument and have been subject to the same environment, they're likely to be in similar condition, so we suggest cleaning all the valves, rather than just the one that has stuck.

Similarly, once we accept that the some of the tubing is unclean, we can examine the possibility that there's a build-up of deposits in the slide sleeves. In short, the instrument needs a service (and possibly a pump through – see elsewhere in this section.)

The following is not the only possible sequence but it works and is the one followed by David 'Satch' Botwe at Paxman Musical Instruments much of the time.

1 Unscrew the valve caps and line them up in order in a clean, safe part of the bench. (Most caps are marked for the valve they belong to, but placing them in order is a good idea because the other parts can be lined up with them as they're detached, hence every component will go back in the place it came from.)

2 Turn the horn over and unscrew the linkage, whether string or mechanical.

3 Once you've removed the linkage you'll need to turn the horn over again, in order to remove the finger levers. Note: With the linkage removed there's nothing to prevent the levers hitting and denting the spout. Be sure to restrain the levers with your hand.

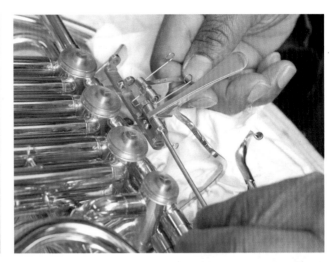

5 Unscrew the nut from the end, then start to withdraw the carriage rod. As the pin moves along, remove each lever in turn. As with other components the levers are usually numbered, but it's a good idea to lay them down in order.

6 Once the levers have been removed, return the three main valve levers to the carriage rod in the order they were removed, and add the retaining nut to keep these components together. Note: Repair professionals will at this stage normally add a series of useful but unobtrusive score marks to the underside of the levers if there's no pre-existing numbering scheme. While it's not strictly necessary, it helps to avoid mistakes, both this time round and on future repairs.

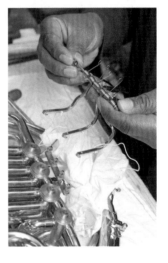

7 As every design of French horn is a little different, the degree to which the fourth valve on a double needs to be taken apart will vary. Unless there's a specific problem with the linkage, remove only the parts that prevent you from removing the valve (as described below), or might cause damage to the horn once the linkage is detached from the valve.

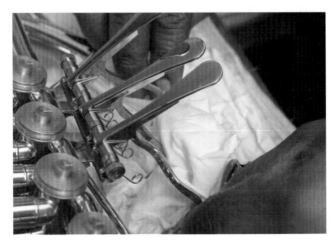

4 Having turned the instrument over, inserting a cloth between the levers and tubing will help to avoid minor damage to the instrument's finish.

8 Remove the screws that hold the valve collars on to the valve stems. Although a wide range of flat-blade screwdrivers can perform this job, the better the fit between

the driver and the slot in the screw, the less the head of the screw will get 'chewed'.
Note: An experienced brass tech can operate a screwdriver with one hand. This means the other hand can be placed over the blade of the screwdriver to prevent it slipping off the screw head. This is a useful skill, because an instrument can easily be dented or scratched by a screwdriver. For clarity, we haven't shown the 'other' hand in many of the pictures.

9 If you follow Satch from Paxman's advice, you'll lay even small items, such as screws, against the valves they came from. In theory a lot of these components should be the same, but some might have been swapped out in the past. Also, items that were identical on the day they were made will often wear differently over time, and will work best in their current location, so it's best to put everything back where you found it.

11 Gently tap each valve in turn with a mallet (not a hammer) to remove it. As you 'tap out' the valve, place your other hand underneath to prevent the valve and its plate from falling out in an uncontrolled way.

Note: You may want to wear a protective latex glove during the process. A horn that's been played for long enough to slow up the valves can be host to a surprising amount of offensive sludge.

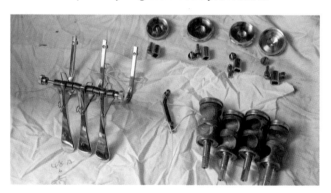

12 Examine the valves to get an idea of the amount of corrosion and deposits in the instrument. Also, make sure that the valves are numbered and that you understand the numbering scheme. (Some Eastern European horns feature a numbering scheme that runs in reverse to the norm.) If there's no numbering scheme present, it's best to make a series of small score marks on the indented part of the top of the valve that doesn't contact the casing, and again on the top of the plate. Either a scraper or an engraving tool are ideal for this purpose.

10 Use a collar lifter to remove the collars from the valve spindles, and place the collars with the other parts.

13 Clean the slides. If there are visible deposits on the valves, the same is probably true of the slides. Players often leave slides in the same position for protracted periods, allowing a build-up of scale in the gap between the end of the slide leg and the valve casing. The technique for removing this is to use one leg only of the slide to 'bottom out', or scrape the interior of the outer leg.

Rotating the slide slightly, while maintaining a backwards-and-forwards motion, is the most efficient way to do this. (On a double or triple horn the lower slides are somewhat inaccessible, so it's often necessary to make a tool based on the correct diameter of slide leg, attached to a simple right-angle grip.)

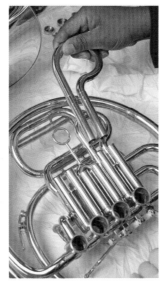

14 Assess each slide as you go. If the slide has been 'bottomed out' fully, the slide will go all the way in.

15 Safe storage of the removed slides is easily achieved using a rack, made from a piece of board with screws in it.

16 Clean the valves. At Paxman, a mix of sulphuric and nitric acid is used. For the purposes of cleaning valves, nitric alone would be effective; the sulphuric acid is added because of its ability to remove the flux used in hard soldering. The strength of the acid is partly down to personal preference. Satch prefers quite a strong mix due to its ability to produce bright, shiny valves in seconds. Other brass techs prefer a relatively dilute solution, sometimes referred to as 'pickle'. As noted elsewhere in this chapter, Michael Rath Trombones uses an industrial descaler in preference to acid, so there is no single 'right' method. However, protective gloves and adequate ventilation are essential if you use acid.

17 Remove all traces of acid from the valves by thoroughly rinsing in tap water, then dry.

18 Clean the valve casings, using a rag dipped in acid.

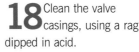

19 Use a piece of tubing for any valve too small to get your finger into.

20 Again, rinse valve casings and slide legs thoroughly.

22 Clean and dry the slide legs, using a cleaning-out rod, cloth and a degreasing agent. (Isopropyl alcohol is a commonly available alternative to the more industrial solvent employed at Paxman.) Repack the rod frequently, so that you aren't simply transferring grease and dirt from one slide to another.

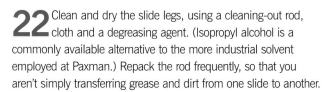

21 Dry the valve casings.

23 It's also important to clean and dry the main slide legs and the bottom bearing of the valves.

24 At some point before reassembly you'll probably want to polish the legs of the slides themselves. This is best achieved by mounting each one in a slide rack, and polishing using a strap of cloth covered in mopping soap. (Brasso is an alternative, but is messier.)

25 Whatever you use, you'll need to wipe it off again using a soft cloth and degreasing fluid.

26 Replace the slides. Whether you put the slides or the valves back first is down to personal preference. In this instance, Satch is putting the slides back first, lubricating each leg with slide grease as he goes along.

27 Put the valves back. Whether you start with the first or the fourth doesn't matter, but it's best to employ the following sequence for each valve. First, oil the spindle.

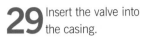
28 Change oils and oil the body.

29 Insert the valve into the casing.

30 Oil the top bearing on the plate and the reciprocal bearing pin on the valve itself.

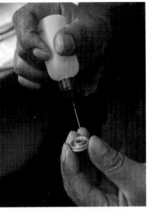

31 Put the valve plate back, being sure to align the notch on the plate with the one on the casing.

32 Seat the valve plate using a light tap on the valve seater, not directly to the plate itself. Note: Check that the valve rotates freely once the plate is seated. If it doesn't a very light tap to the spindle will shift the plate upwards slightly, which should fix the problem. This is similar in appearance to step 11

but needs a lighter touch and is best performed with the plate upwards, so that the valve won't fall out if the plate comes free.

33 Replace the valve cap. Now that the bearing has oil on it, it will attract dirt very readily.

34 Repeat sequence 26–32 for the other valves.

35 Replace the collars.

36 Screw the collars back on.

37 Replace the string on the fourth valve (this procedure is detailed in Section A, 'Routine maintenance').

38 Replace the levers, one at a time, pushing the carriage rod through as you go.

39 Restring the three remaining valves.

What can go wrong?
There's a lot to learn here and any procedure involving the valves goes right to the heart of the way the instrument plays. All of the procedures above need to be done with care and method – and certainly never in a hurry. Some of the substances used – notably the acids – are for the professionally equipped workshop only.

Tightening linkage and bearings in rotary valves

Note: Many of the steps below relate to the old-style mechanical linkage that's seldom found these days. When working on instruments with string or 'mini ball' linkage it's safe to simply ignore steps that relate to components not found on that instrument, and move on. Once the valves themselves are in good order it's often only necessary to follow the procedure for restringing the linkage, found in Section A 'Routine maintenance'.

A rotary valve – and the linkage attached to it – has to be viewed as a total system. As each linkage, pivot point and bearing from the lever plate to the valve itself wears, the system becomes increasingly inefficient. Although this makes the system increasingly sluggish and noisy in operation, the extent of the wear can be considerable before it stops working entirely.

Tightening only one link in the chain (normally because it's identified as the source of undue noise) can cause a valve system that was functional to seize up completely. This is usually because the linkage is now more efficient and is pushing the valve body straight into the wall of the casing – this is because the valve bearings are also worn.

Below is the complete tightening procedure, starting with evaluating the extent of the problem. Before taking the valve assemblies apart, please observe the notes in the previous section about storing all parts safely, and in a way that allows you to place each part back on to the correct location on the instrument:

1 Operate each lever in turn, while holding the valve collar still. Note how much unwanted play there is in the system – and where. Similarly, attempt to move each lever from side to side so see how loose they've become. Rock the valve collars from side to side to determine how worn the bearings are. This should tell you where remedial action is most appropriate.

2 Remove the linkage retaining screws from the valve collars and place in parts bin/marked-up sheet of paper.

3 Unscrew the retaining screw from the end of the valve carriage and store it.

4 Withdraw the carriage pin slowly, holding each valve lever in place so that it moves out of position in a controlled manner. Store it.

5 Take the spring off each lever to be adjusted, by bending the two coiled sections away from each other, and save the springs.

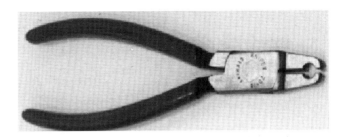

6 Use a pair of linkage pliers to grip either side of the barrel on the first lever, then grip and twist. This will reduce the internal diameter of the barrel. Repeat the procedure at several points along the barrel.

7 Test progress as you go along by inserting the carriage pin to see how tight it is.

8 Use the pliers to perform a similar tightening procedure to the hinges. 'Mini ball' linkage assemblies are adjusted using a screwdriver, which has the great advantage that it's as easy to loosen them as it is to tighten. In the case of traditional hinges,

The points that can be tightened with linkage pliers are marked in red.

be careful not to over-tighten, as this is difficult to reverse. (If you've gone too far, one approach is to heat the hinge with a torch to boil out any lubrication, then work the linkage vigorously until you've simulated many months of use without any oil. Once the hinge has loosened, re-oil to restore a smooth action and prevent further wear.)

9 The link into the valve collar can be subject to considerable wear, but before addressing this it's usually a good idea to look at the valves themselves.

10 Remove and store the retaining screws for the collars. Remove the collars using a collar lifter and retain. Remove the screws from the cork stop plates and store them with the plates themselves, which you can simply lift off.

11 Now that you can see the bottom bearings, reassess them for play. It's probable that you'll need to use a tapered bearing reducer.

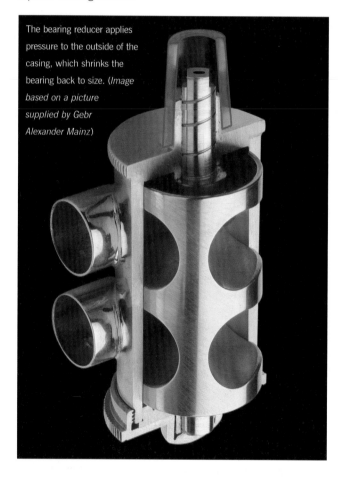

The bearing reducer applies pressure to the outside of the casing, which shrinks the bearing back to size. (*Image based on a picture supplied by Gebr Alexander Mainz*)

12 Place the bearing reducer over the bearing and tap it lightly. The further you drive the reducer down, the tighter the bearing will become, so remove it frequently and check to see if there's still play in the bearing and whether the valve rotates freely.

13 If the valve seizes as a result of tightening the bottom bearing, it'll need to be removed, which is explained in the previous procedure above. The bottom bearing will then need to be opened out slightly using a tapered reamer. (There's an argument in favour of reaming all bearings after tightening

to ensure that they're straight-sided, but not every instrument justifies repair to the highest possible standards.)

14 Once you've tightened the bottom bearings where necessary, it's time to invert the instrument and look at the top bearings. Remove the valve caps and store them.

15 Manipulating each valve by hand, examine each top bearing for play. Ideally none should be visible. If there's play, the valve will need to be removed following the steps in the previous procedure, 'Servicing rotary valve and slide systems'.

16 To tighten the top bearing in the centre of the valve plate, place it on a flat piece of solid steel and tap around the hole of the bearing with the ball of a jeweller's hammer. By thinning the plate slightly, you're automatically pushing the expelled metal towards the centre of the hole. Turn the plate over and repeat the process. Check the result by holding the valve and placing the plate on top. Repeat the process until the plate is a tight fit on the valve.

17 With the plate held upside down in soft vice jaws, remove a small amount of metal from the bearing using a tapered reamer, then place the plate on to the valve to check if it's free running.

18 Once all plates have been adjusted, clean the valve casings then clean and lubricate each valve, placing it in the relevant casing. Use a valve seater to reseat each plate, taking care to observe the correct location as marked on the plate and casing. (See previous procedure for details on this.) Be very sure each plate is correctly seated, for reasons that will become clear.

19 Check each valve, not only for smooth rotation but also for up-and-down movement. Any valve that suffers from such vertical movement to a noticeable extent will need to be taken apart again and have the plate reduced slightly in diameter, so that it sits lower in the casing, hence removing the play.

Note: If step 20 below isn't carried out successfully there's every chance that the valve plate will effectively be destroyed. We'd therefore recommend it only to repair technicians who are confident that they can fabricate a replacement plate, should they remove too much material from the original. The chance of buying a replacement plate for a vintage instrument is almost zero!

The role of the valve plate in holding the valve and top bearing can clearly be seen here, as the plate has been tinted blue. Note that most valve plates don't have the upper lip seen on this design, meaning the absolute position they assume is partly determined by the force with which they're seated.

(Based on a picture supplied by Gebr Alexander Mainz)

20 Mount the plate in the lathe chuck by the bearing chimney on top of the plate. The accuracy with which the plate is mounted is critical to the success of the operation. Following the slight taper, carefully machine a small (read 'tiny') amount of the edge of the plate, thereby reducing its circumference by a fractional amount.

21 Clean and re-seat the plate. If the valve seizes at this point you may be able to free it by tapping the shaft of the valve lightly with the wooden handle of a jeweller's hammer. However, it's quite possible that the plate will now come free, indicating that too much metal has been removed and that a new plate must be made.

22 Repeat for all valves, until every one is assembled and freely rotating, but also free of unwanted vertical and horizontal play.

23 The last hinge that needs to be adjusted is between the linkage and the valve collar. The screws have a tapered shaft, so the first thing to check is that the screws are fully tight. It's often the case that the screws are working loose with use, so it's a good idea to assess whether the threads themselves are tight enough. If not, there are two approaches:

■ Distort the thread of the screw slightly with side cutters, or…
■ Crush the reciprocal thread on the collar slightly, using the same pliers you use to tighten the hinges

24 However, it may be that tightening the screws still leaves the link too loose. There are two approaches to this and they can be used individually or in tandem. Typically, both the tapered steel screws that secure the linkage to the collars, and the steel inserts that make the reciprocal holes through the linkage more durable, will have been subject to some wear. As a result a certain amount of play can often be taken out of the system by simply replacing the screws. However, it's equally possible to tighten up the hinge without replacing the screws, which is an attractive option if you don't have a new set of screws for that particular instrument.

25 To tighten the steel insert so that it's a good fit for the screw, place it flat on a steel plate and tap it with a jeweller's hammer. Now turn it over and repeat the process.

26 Offer the lever assembly up to the screw and – if necessary – repeat step 25 until the hole through the linkage is too tight to assume its previous position on the tapered shank of the screw. (If these are the screws previously fitted to the instrument, the worn section should be clearly visible – but if not, measure the appropriate position with callipers.)

27 Hold the leg of the linkage over either a steel plate with a hole in it or on metal vice jaws that are slightly part. Open up the hole using a tapered pin reamer. Be sure to have the linkage orientated correctly, so that the taper imposed by the reamer follows that on the screw.

28 Once you've repeated steps 23–27 for all levers, you're ready to reassemble the valves and linkage systems. This is similar in some ways to the later stages of the earlier 'Servicing rotary valve and slide systems'.

29 Before you do so, it's worth considering whether to replace the cork buffers or the lever springs, as neither last for ever, and it's easier to do this while the instrument is disassembled rather than after you've put it all back together.

What can go wrong?
Just about everything! The sheer length of this particular procedure is a strong hint that experience and engineering skills are required for a successful outcome. Many of the steps above can cause the total linkage/valve assembly to seize, so you're strongly advised to check every step before moving on to the next one. Just as importantly, if you aren't a repair professional we'd urge you not to undertake this work unless you're prepared to accept that the instrument might be a write-off if you make a serious mistake.

Guards and patches

For clarity, we're going to state that a 'guard' is an extra layer of metal attached to the tubing of an instrument in order to protect it from damage, while a 'patch' is a layer of metal applied to the instrument in order to repair, or cover, damage that's already occurred. Generally speaking, patches are rarely applied these days because most players would prefer to see the component replaced, and this is often the most economical route.

From a repair point of view, the challenges presented by guards are mainly about how best to de-dent when dealing with two layers of metal. Often it makes more sense to remove the guard and repair it separately than it does to try to work with it in situ.

There are two main approaches to guard repair. One is to put the guard over a metal former and work on it from the outside using a hammer and swages, in a similar way to working on the instrument itself. The other is to use a rolling tool. In the case of high brass this is a hand-held tool, but for low brass a much larger system holds two rollers at the precise distance required to match the thickness of the material.

Often, working on a guard will change its radius, meaning that it's no longer a good fit for the instrument. Careful reworking with a roller and/or swage may be required before a good fit is achieved to both the diameter of the tube and the curvature of any bend.

Re-soldering can also be a hard task, as the length of the seam is far greater than, say, a ferrule. In addition, any air trapped under the guard will expand as it's heated and can tend to blow the solder out. Expect to use plenty of binding wire too. (These observations also apply to soldering patches.)

When it comes to making patches, the problems are much the same but there's the additional challenge of making the addition look as if it's meant to be there, rather than just covering a hole! Ugly patches can seriously ruin the look and value of an instrument.

A good strategy is to make a patch that looks like a guard, even if it means it ends up larger than is strictly necessary. A related trick when patching the frequently damaged second slide bow of a trumpet is to cut a patch from another bow that will cap the outside of the bend, leaving a clean join along each side. Visually, this is a lot less obtrusive than fashioning a patch that looks as if it belongs in a first aid kit.

What can go wrong?
The bear traps are many and range from deforming a guard so much you can't get it back on, to destroying the remaining tubing on an instrument in an attempt to patch it. Often the existing material is over-thin across a much larger area than is first apparent, so trying to patch on to it is like skating on ice.

Trombone repairs

The trombone section below was compiled with the assistance of Michael Rath Trombones. Although the procedures described aren't the only ones that need to be performed on a trombone, they're among the few that are unique to the trombone, focused as they are on the slide and on axial flow valves.

Note: Experienced trombone players may rightly express the opinion that rodding out the slide isn't the sole province of a repair pro. While we entirely agree, it appears here for two reasons: (a) because of the convenience of providing a 'trombone section' for readers; and (b) because poor rodding out can cause damage.

Rodding out trombone slide legs

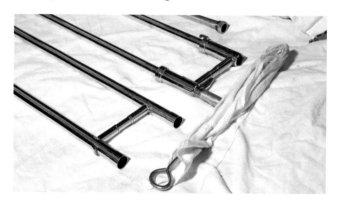

1 If the leader pipe is removable, remove it. If it isn't, be aware that this part is especially easy to distort if subjected to excessive pressure.

2 Take a strip of lint-free absorbent cloth (*eg* cotton) approximately 1.5m long and 100mm wide.

3 Thread the end of the cloth through the eye in the cleaning rod.

4 Wrap the cloth over the end of the rod. (This will help to prevent the rod causing ridges in the bow.)

5 Continue to wrap cloth around the end of the rod until the last 25mm or so forms a reasonably tight fit for the tubing. (There's no precise way of defining how tight is optimum, but the pay-off is easy enough to explain. If the cloth isn't at all tight to the tubing, it won't clean very effectively; if it's over-tight, the force required to move it along the tubing will introduce a risk of distorting the slide assembly and/or leader pipe.)

6 Wrap the remainder of the cloth round the shaft of the rod. This is simply to prevent metal-on-metal contact with the tubing. This part of the cloth wrap shouldn't be up to the diameter of the tubing.

7 Dip cleaning rod in brake and clutch cleaner.

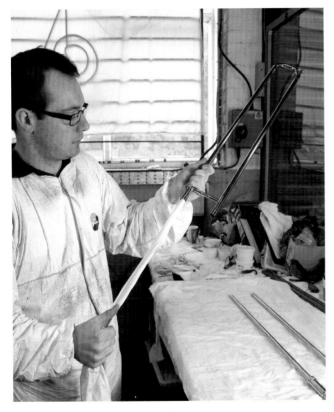

1 Slide the extractor over the first leg and move it along until it meets the felt.

2 Use a twisting action to get the tool to hook the felt, then pull it of out the barrel.

3 Repeat for second leg.

4 Clean out barrels using cloth on a rod.

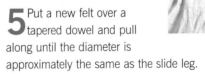
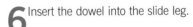

5 Put a new felt over a tapered dowel and pull along until the diameter is approximately the same as the slide leg.

6 Insert the dowel into the slide leg.

7 Pull the felt down the dowel, then down the slide leg until it reaches the barrel.

8 Repeat for second leg.

9 Put on the outer slide and use it to tamp the two felts into position.

8 Move along the tubing of the outer slide using a smooth 'ironing' action, rotating the slide around the rod as you go. Take care not to force the rod into the bow.

What can go wrong?
For a process that sounds like 'just cleaning', there are a few pitfalls. In addition to the risk of distorting the tubing, noted above, it's also possible to get the rod and cloth jammed if it's over-packed.

Replacing felts
The two felts located in the barrels on the inner slide compress and harden over time, making the slide noisier in operation. Fortunately they're cheap and relatively easy to replace, with the right tools.

What can go wrong?
Any process that involves manhandling a trombone slide needs to be done with care, but this procedure is relatively risk free. Hooking the felt can be tricky, though.

Hagmann valve – professional maintenance

Note: Hagmann recommends that its valves receive professional attention every two years for prolonged optimum performance. This service cycle will be considerably shorter if the recommended weekly care routine isn't followed. While the valve will perform poorly – and may lock up – if it's too dry, over-lubrication is also to be avoided. In particular, an excess of oil applied to the spindle and spring will attract dirt, soon forming a deposit. 'A little and often' is the key here.

1 Depress the valve before removing the slide.

2 Using a cupping action with one hand and pressing the fingers of the other hand against the rim, push the cap off the valve.

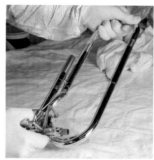
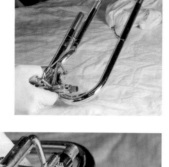

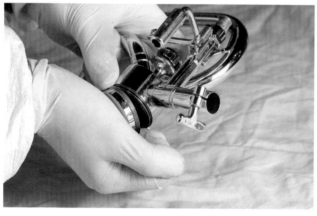

3 Remove the screw retaining the valve linkage using a flat-blade screwdriver.

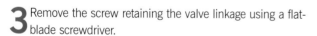

4 Remove the carriage pin, using a narrow flat-blade screwdriver, followed by a small pair of pliers for the actual withdrawal. Take care to prevent the valve lever from jumping out of position in an uncontrolled manner due to the pressure of the spring. This will help to prevent the lacquer being scratched, or tubing dented.

5 Loosen the bumper plate (which is also the valve collar in the Hagmann design) retaining screw using a 2mm Allen

key, then carefully work the plate off the valve, making sure to retain both the plate and the spring underneath it. (Rotating the valve slightly from side to side helps to ease off the plate in a controlled fashion.)

6 Gently apply finger pressure on the valve pin to slide the valve out of its casing and on to clean cloth, while using your other hand to control its movement.
Note: On no account attempt to remove a stuck valve by

pulling on it using pliers. In order to minimise weight, the tubing used for the airways is thin, and will collapse if placed under pressure. Stuck valves can only be removed safely through the use of easing oil and patient, gentle working of the valve, sometimes in conjunction with the use of heat to expand the casing.

7 Place the valve in a plastic jug of neat descaler.

8 Pour a little neat descaler into the cap of the valve.

9 Place the slide and valve casing into a tub of descaler diluted to a ratio of approximately one-third with tap water. The dilution reduces the chance of any damage occurring to the lacquered

surfaces. (Michael Rath Trombones uses Winterhalter C10 descaler, a concentrated phosphoric cleaner and descaler, with wetting agents, designed primarily to remove scale from catering equipment.) Leave for 20–30 minutes until clean.

10 All parts must now be thoroughly rinsed and brushed through using tap water. Because of the irregular shapes inside the valve, it's worth soaking it for a few minutes in water to ensure that no trace of descaler remains. Note: Failure to remove all descaler can cause a valve to seize within hours. Should that occur, the only remedy is to repeat the whole procedure, while bearing in mind the caution in step 6 regarding the use of force on stuck valves.

11 A cleaning rod and clean, lint-free cloth should be used to clean the tubing and valve casing interiors using

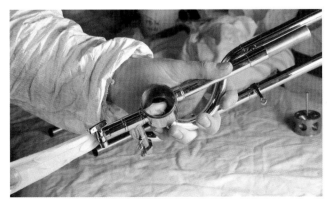

commercial brake and clutch cleaner, a formulation designed to remove oil, grease and dust safely without leaving any residue.

12 Take the Allen key and a small strip of cloth to clean out the valve bearing at the top of the casing. Use cloth to clean and dry the valve. Because of the exceptionally fine

tolerances used in a Hagmann valve, attention to detail when cleaning is critical to the performance of the valve.

13 Lubricate the body of the valve and the stem, using piston valve oil.

14 Then, holding the base of the valve, reintroduce it to the casing. Take care not to allow the valve to rest on anything beforehand, as this could introduce foreign material into the valve assembly. Gently rotating the valve at this point will help to distribute the oil and also provides an opportunity to evaluate the running of the valve. An experienced ear can detect whether the valve is rotating freely, or if it's catching slightly. Any suggestion of 'grittiness' is an indicator that the valve assembly

17 The bumper plate is returned to the spindle with the neoprene bumpers face down and the grub screw orientated so that it'll engage with the flat on the spindle once tightened. Note: Hagmann F and D valves – as fitted to bass and tenor trombones – have similar-looking but non-identical bumper plates. If these are inadvertently swapped, neither valve will function correctly, despite the fact that everything appears to be fine.

wasn't cleaned thoroughly enough and that the cleaning procedure should be repeated.

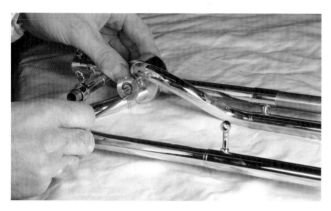

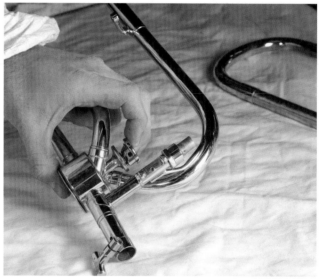

15 Check the pin that stops the bumper plate and tighten if necessary. A loose pin will result in an unnecessarily noisy valve in use.

18 The bumper plate is designed so that it'll find the correct level as it's tightened. A common mistake at this stage is to push the plate hard down towards the face of the valve casing. Not only is this unnecessary, but it will make the whole assembly too tight, impeding the free movement of the valve. The correct distance is shown here.

19 Relock the bumper plate using the Allen key.

16 Replace the spring, holding valve and spring in place as shown, while putting the bumper on to the spindle. The left hand is holding the components in place but can also orientate the work as required, making it easier for the right hand to replace the bumper plate.

20 The marks to indicate correct open and closed positions of the valve are on the valve itself. While it's important to check them at this stage, the likelihood is that they'll be correct, mainly because the factory-fitted bumpers have considerable durability. However, if the neoprene bumpers have been replaced with non-standard ones it may be necessary to trim them back to the correct positions. We haven't illustrated this process, as it's better to obtain the correct replacements.

21 Apply a small amount of slide grease to the neoprene 'O' ring that runs around the valve casing, then push the cap back into place. The grease will help to lengthen the life of the neoprene by minimising abrasion.

22 Replacing the lever back on to the carriage correctly requires that the spring be put under tension, as shown here. As with replacing water keys, this procedure takes some practice before it can be carried out with confidence, because the other hand is needed to insert the carriage pin at the same time.

23 Replace the linkage and tighten.

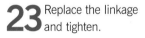

24 The final step is to lubricate the lever spring and the linkage joints with a little engine oil. Note: If the tail of the spring is the other side of the carriage to that shown here, it does nothing. This is why it must be kept under tension during assembly.

What can go wrong?
All valves are vulnerable to damage once taken apart. Although the Hagmann valve is very well designed and engineered, it isn't as simple as, say, a trumpet valve. It's best not to take it apart unless (a) there's a compelling reason to do so, and (b) you're confident that you can put it back together.

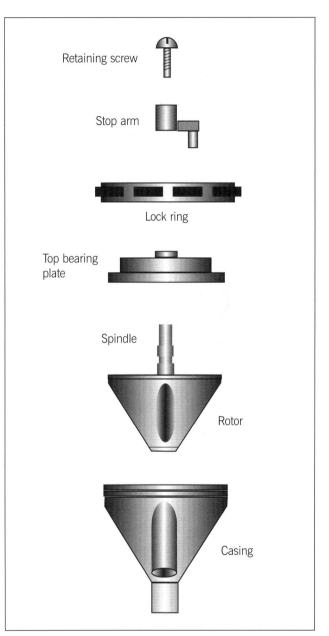

Retaining screw

Stop arm

Lock ring

Top bearing plate

Spindle

Rotor

Casing

Axial flow valves – maintenance routine

The following account is supplied by Edwards Instrument Co, which advises that its axial flow valves need be disassembled only every six months if they're oiled every two weeks through the slide receiver and main tuning slides, following the company's instructions.

Note: This procedure may not be appropriate for axial valves from other manufacturers. Always be guided by the manufacturer's instructions, if available.

Disassembly

1 Remove valve section from bell and tuning slide. Set on clean towel on the floor or a workbench.

2 Remove all tuning slides.

3 For the bass trombone you'll need to remove the second valve from the first valve section. With a common (flathead) screwdriver, remove the rod end assembly screw and set the G♭ trigger into the unengaged position. Using the Allen wrench provided, loosen the side cap screw that's between the two valves. With the trigger disconnected and the rod end assembly disconnected remove the second valve section and set it on a clean work area.

4 With all tuning slides removed take the Allen wrench and remove the top round stop arm set screw that holds the stop arm to the valve.

5 Remove the stop arm and slowly allow the spring to carry the F arm into the resting position.

6 Loosen the cross brace that connects the F and G♭ tuning slides to each other.

7 Grasp the valve lock ring completely with thumb and third finger. Be careful as you grasp the sides, as you can make the lock ring out of round, meaning it will no longer seal correctly. Loosen until the lock ring is no longer connected to the outer valve casing.

8 Carefully remove the top plate and the valve from the valve casing. Make sure not to drop the valve, as you may damage it.

9 Set the valve casing down on clean cloth.

10 Remove the valve from the top plate and set all components down. (Be sure to keep bass valves with the correct casing; don't mix up valves when reassembling).

11 Rub down all components with isopropyl alcohol and a soft cotton cloth, cleaning any and all residual elements. Use a cotton ear swab on the top plate-bearing surface, with alcohol on the swab.

12 Once all components are cleaned it's time for reassembly.

Reassembly

1 Take the valve casing and drench the inside with clear Edwards rotor oil.

2 Set the valve into the valve casing.

3 Put clear rotor oil on the spindle and top of the valve.

4 Carefully put the top plate back into the correct position and tighten the large valve lock ring into place. (Once this is tightened the risk of dropping the inner valve is greatly diminished.)

5 Reassemble in reverse order to the way you disassembled it.

6 Once reassembled use a spot of spindle oil on each side of the rod end bearings, valve springs, and both sides of the trigger spindle (the trigger spindle is what the trigger spring goes around). Don't use spindle oil on the valve spindle! This oil would slowly seep into the valve and make it sluggish and slow.

What can go wrong?

As with the Hagmann valve, all valves are vulnerable to damage once taken apart. It's best not to take it apart unless (a) there's a compelling reason to do so, and (b) you're confident that you can put it back together.

A professional slide overhaul

1 Before work can begin, the inner and outer slides must be cleaned with a commercial descaling fluid. Failure to do this will result in mineral deposits left by saliva being impacted into the walls of the tubing. Not only will this cause irregularities in the wall thickness, but in the case of the outer slide these deposits will degrade the way the slide operates. (Michael Rath Trombones uses Winterhalter C10 descaler, a concentrated phosphoric cleaner and descaler, with wetting agents, designed primarily to remove scale from catering equipment.)

2 Stop the inner legs with cork or neoprene to prevent the fluid escaping, then suspend the slides to allow the fluid to be poured in.

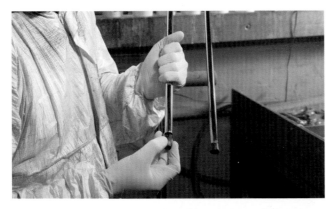

3 After 20–30 minutes, pump through the slides with warm soapy water.

4 Brush through very thoroughly to remove unwanted material, then pump with cold water.

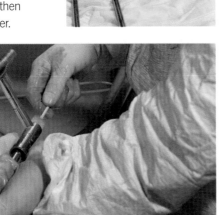

5 Repeat steps 3 and 4 three times to ensure a good result.

6 Remove water key, clean, replace cork if necessary, reassemble and oil spring.

7 Rod out the slide legs. (See separate instructions above, 'Rodding out trombone slide legs'.)

8 Remove and replace the felt bumpers, using a purpose-built extractor. (See separate instructions above, 'Replacing felts.)

9 Remove slide lock, lubricate thread with thick oil and replace.

10 If the leader pipe has been removed, grease the thread and replace it.

Note: This is the point at which enthusiasts should stop, pour themselves a drink and enjoy playing their trombone, or reading this book. The procedures detailed below take many years to master, preferably under the supervision of a skilled repair technician. Trombone slides are thin, relatively brittle, and can easily be pushed past the point of economic repair. In addition, the cost of the equipment needed to complete the steps below to a professional standard is considerable.

11 The outer slide is placed on the surface plate to check if the legs are true. In order to do this, it's necessary to get the surface of the plate at eye level, with either a light or white material in the background. The surface plate used at Michael Rath Trombones is a granite block, which has been ground flat to extremely fine tolerances. This allows the technician to detect even slight deviations in the rails.

12 By slowly rotating the slide – and careful observation – it's possible to see any bowing in the leg. The slide in this picture bows upwards slightly in the middle.

older a slide is, the more delicate it will have become. This is due to the cumulative effects of years of corrosion, and possibly thinning caused by previous repairs.

13 Correcting the bow is achieved by a combination of an ironing action across the knee…

14 …and holding the slide against one knee while ironing out the bow with one hand. (Note the cloth, which serves to reduce friction.) A good technician uses ears as well as eyes at this point. The slide is brittle and could easily snap. A slide leg that's being pushed close to the point where it'll break emits a slight creaking sound, which serves as a valuable warning not to apply further pressure. As a rule of thumb, the

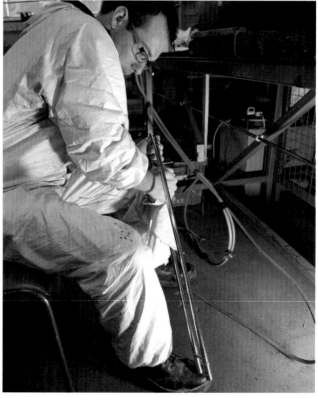

15 Constant checking of progress is vital.

16 In addition to bowing, the other common condition to check for is a twist, or warp, whereby the two legs are no longer parallel. This will manifest itself as a small amount of lift in one leg when the slide is laid flat on the surface plate. Due to the length of the legs, it doesn't take a great deal of pressure to twist a trombone slide; it can even be caused by a poorly designed case. Twisting the bow back into true requires an equally light touch.

17 Looking along the slide at a shallow angle is the best way to spot dents. (It is however, not a reliable way to check for bowing or twisting, due to the very small tolerances to which the slide must be adjusted for optimum performance.)

18 Dent removal can be performed with a small hammer working against a mandrel. It is important to polish the face of the hammer before use to minimise any scuffing to the finish. Use delicate, glancing blows to avoid thinning the wall of the slide.

19 The inner slide is cleaned, lubricated with a product such as Slide-O-Mix and, finally, reunited with the outer slide. It is now possible to consider how the inner and outer slides work together.

20 As it has only one brace holding it together, the inner slide is especially vulnerable to shift. A telltale sign is a slight spring in the inner slide when it's withdrawn from the outer. An experienced technician can often put the two legs back into parallel without re-soldering the brace, but this requires skill and judgement. As with step 14, a creaking sound serves as a warning that the slide is being pushed about as far as it can go.

21 It's now time to give the inner slide a light spray with water and check again how well the system works.

What can go wrong?
To put it bluntly, the complete destruction of the slide! It's also worth considering that the above procedures will only be effective if the slide was well made in the first place. If the slide was originally assembled with the distance between the legs at the hand brace different to the distance at the bow (*ie* the legs weren't parallel) it will be necessary to unsolder at least one joint in order to correct the condition.

Alas, that isn't always the whole story, because the inner and outer slide work together as a system. Just because the legs on both halves are parallel, it doesn't mean that they're the same distance apart. For this reason, the trombone repair technician has to look at the whole picture before deciding on the appropriate course of action.

At its extreme, rebuilding a slide is much the same process as assembling one from scratch – it's just that the component parts are no longer new. The assembly of a trombone slide is covered in the chapter *Design and manufacture*.

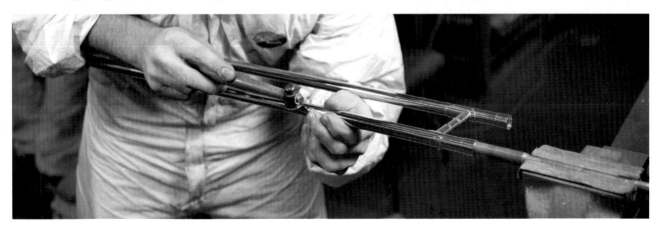

Customising your horn

While there's nothing wrong with buying a musical instrument and enjoying it the way it is, many players would like their horn to be uniquely their own. Whether you're a mild 'accessoriser' or a total hot-rodder, this chapter is for you!

A lot of trumpet players want their horn to look like a custom build from a top maker, and why not? In this chapter, Andy Taylor transforms a perfectly playable stock Vincent Bach Stradivarius into an instrument with a really contemporary vibe.

Additional information on the techniques used in this chapter can be found in the chapters *Design and manufacture*, *Maintenance and repair techniques* and *An illustrated list of tools and materials*.

LEFT Andy has already disassembled this horn and stored the valves safely. Everything else is about to get the hot-mod treatment.

1 It's off with the third valve slide ring…

2 …and goodbye to the old-style water key too.

5 There's no stopping this man! He's unsoldered the receiver from the leader pipe, and from the brace that supports it.

6 This is where the assembly starts. Andy uses emery cloth to prepare the leader pipe.

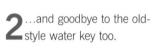

3 The next parts to go are the grip button on the first slide and the screw holder for the existing third slide finger ring.

7 If you have the skills and machinery you can make a heavier receiver, as Andy has done here.

4 A little heat from the torch and the original finger support on the leader pipe is gone too.

8 You can find tips on soldering throughout this book, but if you solder neatly there will be a lot less cleaning up to do afterwards.

13 Andy preps the first slide, removing the knob from the slide, cleaning up and replacing the thumb ring with a 'phat'-style ring.

14 The new ring is ready to fit, having been filed to maximise the surface area in contact with the leader pipe.

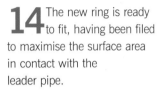

9 Re-soldering the receiver itself is best done with the instrument orientated like this. The solder needs to flow all the way through.

10 A small scraper takes off most of the surplus solder.

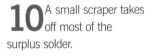

11 The remainder can be removed with emery cloth.

12 When working on tubing like this, a strap of emery is far more effective than a small square.

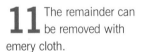

15 Before he reaches for the soldering torch, Andy checks the ring is clamped upright.

Pushing the right buttons

About the easiest way to get a custom look to your horn is to replace the finger buttons, a job anyone capable of unscrewing a ketchup bottle can attempt. For the more adventurous decorative materials, such as abalone, are widely obtainable at little cost and can be filed to fit into existing finger buttons. Providing you can get the original inlays out cleanly, all you'll need after that is a dab of glue.

Note: A word of warning – when it's thin, abalone can be razor sharp.

The buttons above are all from Vincent Bach and are a direct swap for their standard finger buttons. (*Conn-Selmer*)

These miniature works of art from Taylor Trumpets have been carefully crafted in abalone and mother of pearl.

16 With all three rings in their correct positions, it's time to get soldering again.

17 The polishing strap will get into most locations but you can always wrap it over a screwdriver for really tight spots.

18 Elsewhere, a light emery cleans things up prior to polishing.

19 Amado-type water keys are easy to obtain and will add to the new look of the trumpet.

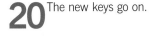

20 The new keys go on.

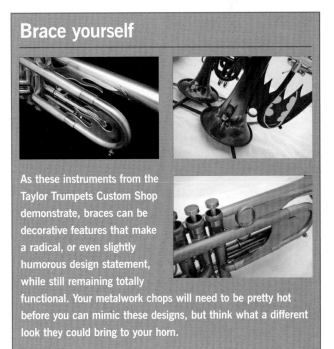

21 The second slide button gets the heavier treatment too – after all, we want the whole instrument to look as if it belongs there.

24 The new slide stop ring.

22 This stop for the third valve is a practical and visually bold addition, but Andy has to put in some work with a rat-tail file before it fits the tubing.

23 Now that it fits, soldering it into place is easy enough.

25 Water keys only work if there's a hole though the slide!

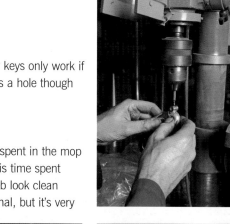

26 Time spent in the mop shop is time spent making the job look clean and professional, but it's very

important not to snag any edges on the mop, because that motor is powerful enough to hurl parts across the room. (Just one reason why protective goggles and a mask are a must.)

27 Just 27 steps in and Andy is already greasing the slides before putting them back.

28 He's also fitting neoprene 'O' rings to the first and third slides for quiet operation.

29 Now the bolt for the stop mechanism goes in for the first time.

30 You can buy heavy finger buttons and caps like these, or make your own by shaving down the old ones and sleeving them if you're clever enough. (Soldering the two parts together takes care, because if solder gets into the threads it will take a lot of work with a thread repair tool to get it out again.)

31 Fitting the top caps and finger buttons before returning the valves to the instrument is easy.

32 The bottom caps combine threaded inserts with heavy brass caps. Again, careful soldering is required when going this route.

33 They certainly look the part.

34 In fact, the whole trumpet looks very different to the one Andy started with.

After play testing, the instrument can be sent for lacquer or plate if the customer wants a mega pro finish. If not, it can be left raw for the 'lived in' look.

What can go wrong?
Too much to list here. A complete makeover like this is not for beginners, so it's best to practise small sections – such as replacing the valve caps – on a scrap instrument until you're fully confident.

Flight to the finish

Just because horns are made from brass, it doesn't mean they have to look as if they're all made from the same material. Unless you happen to have access to a pro lacquering facility, any attempt to 'do this at home' is likely to go wrong for a number of reasons, including the need to completely degrease the surface in order to get long-term adhesion, the difficulty in achieving a sag-free finish without dust trapped in it, and the dangers of getting lacquer inside valve casings and slide sleeves. But if you have the budget and the imagination, there are specialist spray shops that can deliver the goods.

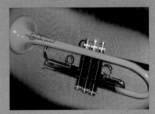

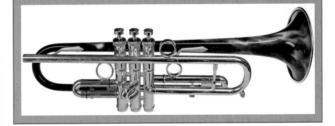

Cap in hand

Heavy replacement valve caps are almost as easy an upgrade as new finger buttons, and hold out the promise of enhanced performance as well as a cool look.

These trumpet valve caps are offered in a choice of three finishes. (*Conn-Selmer*)

Heavier valve caps aren't just for trumpet players – these valve caps are designed to fit a Hagmann valve and are said to lead to a dramatic improvement in performance in some instances. (*Michael Rath Trombones*)

An illustrated list of tools and materials

A wide array of specialist tools is used in the making and repair of brass musical instruments. Some can be bought, but many are made in the shop where they're used. As a result the designs and the names for them vary. The naming conventions used in this chapter are consistent with those in the step-by-step instructions elsewhere in the *Brass Instrument Manual*.

LEFT Tools used by David 'Satch' Botwe at Paxman Musical Instruments.

Tools

Adjustable instrument holder – See *Bell stick*.

Angle grinder – Because it's commonly available, an angle grinder can make a good ad hoc substitute for some of the more specialist bench tools used to fashion small components. Whether you decide to secure the grinder or the work depends in part on the size of the object you're working on but it is never a good idea to have both the tool and the work unclamped, because it introduces too many variables and can be dangerous.

Ball/plug set – These are a graduated set of solid metal barrels that can either be pushed through the tubing of an instrument by following it with a 'driver' plug, or fixed on to a threaded

A set of Böhm dent balls. Note the 'drivers', bottom right.

bar held in a vice (if there's sufficient access to the area to be worked on). In either case, the ball or plug has the effect of pushing out dents from the inside of the instrument. This can be enhanced by a professional repairer with the use of a specialist hammer on the outside of the tubing (see *Hammer* entries). Providing the plug is an accurate fit for the internal diameter, hammering can only induce the metal to stretch outwards. Plugs are typically supplied in sets of 100+ but even this many won't cover every instrument, as they're graduated in 0.005in/0.127mm increments. Anyone who wants to work on both high and low brass will need to make a considerable investment in plug sets.

Bandsaw – Even a hobby bandsaw is a useful tool to the musical instrument maker, as it can be used to cut raw materials such as metal rod, and in the making of wooden formers and jigs. For the repairer, a bandsaw is more likely to be used when fashioning replacement components, or as an aid to making tools.

Bearing reducer, rotary – A tapered sleeve, which is driven down on to the bottom bearing of a rotary valve casing in order to tighten it and thereby correct for wear. Böhm offers a more

A graduated set of bearing shrinkers from Böhm.

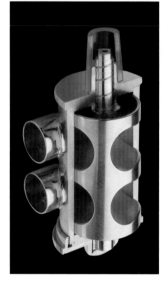

Shown here in cross-section, the bearing reducer is a piece of tapered tubing thick enough to force the sleeve of the bearing back on to the valve spindle.

This bearing shrinking tool from Böhm offers the ultimate in adjustment and is based on a collet chuck system.

advanced tool for the same job, the main advantage of which is that it shrinks the bearing along its whole length, making for a longer-lasting repair.

Bell stick – Just as a repair shop for vehicles raises cars and vans up so that the mechanics can get underneath, any brass instrument technician will want instant access to all sides of an instrument. This is usually achieved by putting a bell stick into a vice, and mounting the instrument on it. Depending on the size of the instrument, it may then require one or more restraining strings from above to hold it in a horizontal position.

A bell stick allows access to all sides of the instrument.

Although the simplest form of this device is simply a piece of wood with a tapered end covered in padding, most sophisticated adjustable holders allow for a precise fit to a variety of bell contours.

Bellows – For repairers determined to experience precise control over the air/gas mix entering their soldering torch, foot-operated bellows can represent a cost-effective alternative to an electric compressor. However, this is for the energetic only and most people would rather use a small butane torch than constantly jig up and down in an attempt to keep up a constant air supply. (See also *Torch, gas*.)

Belt sander/linisher – A machine of this type can be bought or self-built and is particularly useful for sanding curved tubing, such as instrument bells once they've been bent and had any unwanted ripples removed.

Bench vice – See *Vice*.

Bolt/rod sets for trombones – As with the rods used for drawing tubing, the bolts (or cylindrical mandrels) are designed to ensure

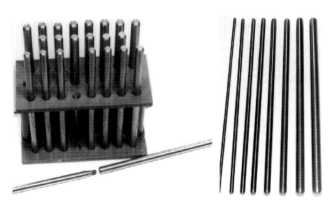

Bolt and rod sets. (*Böhm*)

that the internal diameter of the tubing is of accurate dimension and roundness. Once the appropriate bolt has been inserted into a trombone slide, a dent roller can be applied without risk of collapsing the tubing.

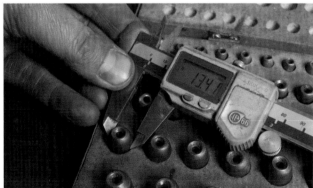

A burnisher can be made by polishing a file.

Burnisher – Often made from an old fish-tail file, from which the teeth are removed on a belt sander and the surface then polished on a mopping wheel, the burnisher is an indispensable tool when removing dents from bells and also tubing. For the burnisher to be effective, the other side of the bell needs to be pressed against either a stake or a former, both of which are normally fashioned from steel. More complex burnishing tools are available commercially, these including double-handed tools with a curved centre, suitable for burnishing the spouts of many brass band and orchestral instruments.

Callipers (Vernier gauge) – This is a measuring device that doesn't have the accuracy of a micrometer, but the better ones have more than enough resolution for most brass-making tasks, such as

Callipers are essential for accurately measuring tubing and dent balls, among many other tasks.

measuring the diameter of tubing. These days many have a digital readout, but cheap digital sets are about the worst combination because the readout is often inaccurate and is the first thing to

Clamps and clips can be your 'third hand'.

fail. Although the marks along cheaper 'mechanical' gauges can be hard to read, at least the system is inherently robust. The more expensive digital callipers have very accurate readouts to several decimal places. Callipers can be used to measure external and internal diameters, as well as the depth of holes.

NB: It's often assumed that 'callipers' is a tradesperson's colloquialism for a device that's properly known as a Vernier gauge, but the reality is slightly different. Only callipers bearing two sets of linear measuring scales – one coarse, the other fine sub-divisions – are truly Vernier gauges. Therefore the digital equivalent is just one of many types of calliper. Some callipers are hinged like a school compass and have no measuring system, being designed simply for comparative measurement.

Chuck – The component within a drill or lathe that retains either the drill bit, or the work to be turned, is a 'chuck'. Many lathe chucks have three or four jaws that are adjusted to the required diameter but these chucks have limitations, one being

A collet chuck centres the work with exceptional accuracy.

the ease with which tubing can be crushed and another the accuracy with which work can be centred.

Standard lathe chucks are generally to be used with caution, as increasing the diameter of the work they're holding also increases the protrusion of the jaws from the main chuck. When in rotation, these jaws can easily cause injury if fingers are allowed to stray too close.

A collet chuck has no protruding jaws but instead comes with a series of interchangeable rings (collets), each designed to fit a specific diameter of work. Because the great majority of the ring that forms the collet is in contact with the work, the risk of accidental crushing is minimal and the accuracy with which the work can be centred is high. In addition, the speed with which work can be mounted and demounted is greater than with a standard chuck, where it's usually necessary to check that the work is centred. (In reality, nothing can ever be absolutely centred on a three-jaw chuck for the simple reason that all three jaws are sitting in different positions on the same thread.)

However, a collet chuck with its attendant accessories can be worth more than the lathe to which it's fitted, so it's up to the individual user to decide whether the value of the work created on the lathe justifies the investment. A four-jaw chuck is something of a compromise between accuracy and cost, in that accurate centring can be achieved by careful adjustment.

Clamps/clips – When soldering components, a clamp can be a valuable 'third hand' to keep the parts in place until the process is complete. Some clamps are pre-made wire clips, but other clamping techniques – such as holding the work together with binding wire – are improvised to suit the job in hand. The other universally used type of clamp is a bench-mounted vice. For small work, pliers or Mole grips can be a useful substitute.

Collar lifter – Used on rotary valve assemblies to pull the collar from the valve shaft, these tools come in designs of varying complexity, the simplest of which is essentially a lever with a notch in it.

This collar lifter was made by David 'Satch' Botwe at Paxman.

Compressor – Professional repairers solder using a torch that mixes mains gas with compressed air. While this provides the ultimate in flame control, it must be said that compressors are large, expensive and noisy. For the non-professional, a butane gas torch designed for jewellery-making will prove suitable for most tasks, while being far more cost-effective. (See also *Torch, gas*.)

Dent balls – See *Ball/plug set*.

Dent balls, expandable – A dent removal system – especially useful for trombone slides but also suitable for the valve slides of other instruments – whereby the diameter of the ball can be increased slightly by turning a wheel at the end of the mounting rod. This circumvents the problem that the diameter of the

This expandable ball system is offered by Böhm.

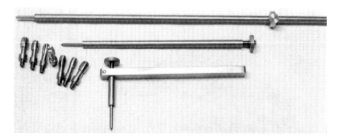

tubing at solder joints (for instance at the hand brace) will be slightly less than that of the main tubing.

Dent puller – This system reverses the logic of plugging a dent from the inside and can be handy where access is limited. At its simplest a dent puller is a length of rod with a hook at one end. The other end is soldered to the centre of the dent. Using a metal object such as an old file, the hook is then given a succession of smart strikes until the dent is slightly over-pulled. Once the dent puller is unsoldered and the area cleaned up, the dent can then be carefully levelled using a small hammer.

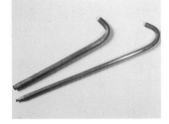

Dent pullers are easily made from nickel rod.

Dent removal, magnetic – Even in the small community of brass musical instrument repairers, magnetic dent removal is regarded as a somewhat specialist technique. This is partly because it's possible to distort the tubing if the system isn't used

ABOVE Magnetic ball system. (Böhm)
LEFT Magnetic ball inside tube. (Böhm)
BELOW Magnetic balls in use. (Böhm)

with caution, but also because it's necessary to remove ferrous objects and electronic devices from the vicinity (approximately 2m) of the very strong magnets used. Failure to do so can be dangerous. However, it has its adherents among repairers, due to the speed with which it can remove dents, especially from thick-walled tubing.

The system comprises a burnishing handle that also holds the strong magnet. This is used in conjunction with a set of spherical steel balls that are pulled and rolled against the wall of the tubing.

Dent rods – Depending on the diameter of the tubing and the tightness of the curve, it's possible to reach some of the way along the length using a bent, or jointed, rod with a smoothing ball attached to the end. Some systems employ a flexible

A Böhm dent rod system in use.

section, typically kept under tension by an inner cable, in order to extend the reach of the ball. Where applicable, dent rods are faster to use than plugs, so it's often more efficient to unsolder the legs from a slide, for example, to gain access than it is to attempt de-denting using plugs alone.

Dent roller, bell – A hand-held device used for removing dents from flares and spouts. Some repairers prefer this to a burnisher

A Böhm dent roller.

because the rotating centre section is less likely to scratch finished surfaces. It's also particularly popular for use on low brass.

Dent roller, guards – For high brass, a hand-held tool with a steel roller for smoothing guards from the inside. For low brass, a clamping system that holds two rollers a precise distance apart, this distance being equal to the thickness of the material being worked.

Dent roller, trombone – Used in conjunction with a set of cylindrical bolts (mandrels), a dent roller can be used to achieve straightening, as well as dent removal. In addition to hand-held dent rollers, Böhm offers a three-roller dent rolling machine, designed to produce superior results to hand rolling.

Dies – See *Taps and dies*.

Drawplate – This is a system of graduated holes through a single block and is an alternative to hand-draw rings for some applications, notably drawing tubing of a specific diameter. The holes are graduated in 0.1mm increments, which gives the

Böhm drawplate belonging to Taylor Trumpets.

capacity for not only considerable accuracy but also for drawing down in a series of manageable steps. For short lengths of tubing – such as might be needed for a repair – drawing down is often a hand process, and can be done against a steel rod placed inside the tube. Longer lengths – as might be required for manufacturing processes – are best created with a hydraulic or electric draw press.

Draw rings, hand – Supplied in graduated sets, these steel hand-draw rings are used to manipulate tubing. Used skilfully, they can either make the tube round or can draw it to a smaller diameter. Hence a repairer can create a good match for, say, an existing

A graduated set of draw rings.

slide leg, even though the correct diameter tube isn't held in stock. The rings are primarily used when making components, rather than in repairing an assembled instrument, when the presence of stays and other obstacles make a swage a more appropriate tool for rounding tubing. (See also *Swage*.)

Drill bits (*aka* twist bits) – Unlike drill sets from DIY stores that typically come in jumps of 1mm or more between sizes, mouthpiece makers need drill bits that graduate in increments

of 0.1mm. Before modifying a mouthpiece by drilling the throat, it's well worth bearing these small increments in mind. A typical trumpet mouthpiece throat is 3.7–3.8mm, for instance, so putting a 4mm bit through one is likely to take it outside the usable range. For more general repair work a set graduated in .5mm steps is useful. Although closely graduated drill sets are expensive (they contain more drills, for one thing), they're also available in different grades. For cutting through brass, there's no need to invest in the kind of bits that are designed for working with stainless steel.

Drill, pillar (*aka* bench drill) – When precision is a priority – for instance when holes are required to go in at right angles, or they're to be tapped for specific thread sizes – a pillar drill is a better tool than a hand-held.

A pillar drill in use.

Drill, rechargeable electric hand – In addition to the most obvious function for an electric drill, it can be used to speed up the process of 'hand' lapping piston valves. (This approach is definitely for the experienced operator only and requires a model with gearing, so that the speed can be trigger controlled.) Due to the amount of torque required when lapping a valve, a minimum power of 18V is recommended.

Engraving machine, hand-held – It's often the case with an instrument that's hand-built, or has had a fair bit of wear over the years, that parts which appear identical are not in fact interchangeable. Valve caps are an example where it's safer and easier to discreetly number them 1, 2, 3 on the inside than it is to try to work out where they went at the end of the process.

Similarly, before removing valves it's worth checking that there are manufacturer's marks indicating which position each belongs to – and that the plastic locating keys are different sizes on either side of the valve (not always the case on a cheap instrument). It can also be worth engraving a small 'nick' before removing tubing that could conceivably go back in more than one position. Tubing may seem perfectly round, but if it's been worked on before it probably isn't.

File brush/card – An essential tool for cleaning out clogged files.

The fish-back file is a specialist tool.

File, fish-back (*aka* tongue-shaped) – Unlike most files, which can be obtained from general engineering suppliers, the fish-back file is a specialist musical instrument tool. With two curved sides, both of which are shallower than the half-round file, the fish-back is suitable for working on gentler contours.

File, half-round – A good general-purpose tool for smoothing brass and related metals, this has one flat and one rounded side. As brass isn't difficult to abrade and the wall thicknesses involved are small, a fine-cut file is preferred. A rough-cut file will get through the material

A half-round file is a versatile tool.

slightly faster but will leave deeper gouges that will take longer to remove with abrasive cloths and polishing.

File, needle – The small size and fine cut of these files makes them suitable for work on very small components.

File, quarter-inch flat – This file is useful for tasks such as recutting the key slot on the older type of piston valve. Over time the slot becomes wider in the middle, so needs to be filed straight and the key itself replaced with a larger one.

File, rat-tail – Available in various sizes, these are more suitable for components, where their ability to get inside tight apertures makes them useful for enlarging holes or describing shapes that aren't circular.

A rat-tail file.

Former – There are two applications for formers. They're used in the manufacture of bells, initially when beating the metal into a close approximation of the final shape with a mallet and then on the lathe, where wooden, followed by steel burnishing tools – sometimes referred to as 'spoons' – are used to spin the metal into the exact profile dictated by the former, prior to finishing with a variety of scrapers and a succession of emery clothes, of which the last is fine enough for the bell to be polished, if required.

This bellmaker at Taylor Trumpets is using a former with a drawplate to shape the spout.

The second application for formers is in the removal of dents from bells under repair. Here, the metal of the bell is pushed against the former using a burnisher (see also *Burnisher*). Generally speaking, the bells of high brass are repaired by burnishing against a former, while the larger brass instruments are repaired using a stake.

NB: The terms 'former' and 'mandrel' are frequently interchanged in everyday use. For the sake of clarity, we have reserved the term 'former' for symmetrical solid metal shapes that precisely match the internal profile of an actual bell, or other component. When we use the term 'mandrel', we mean a metal shape that's useful when working with a component but doesn't match any particular design and isn't suitable for lathe turning.

Gauge, bell thickness – There are many commercially available thickness gauges that can be adapted to the task of measuring the wall thickness of bells and spouts (typically somewhere in the region of 14 thousandths of an inch, in the case of a French horn bell). The only adaptation required is for a frame to be built of sufficient size and curvature that the gauge and its reciprocal reference point can be passed along the entire length of the bell.

Gauge, mouthpiece shank – In commercial custom mouthpiece building, a durable gauge is used to ensure that the taper and length of the shank are correct. For the enthusiast, an old receiver from a scrap instrument will work just as well, though it will prove less durable under constant use. For anyone who already possesses the appropriate mouthpiece reamer, making a mouthpiece gauge is an easy task. (See also *Reamer, receiver*.)

Grinder, rotary bench – Although an electric grinder isn't specifically required to make or repair musical instruments, it is required for sharpening tools (an ongoing need in any workshop). With practice and skill it's possible to sharpen a range of tools, including drill bits, by hand and eye. **NB:** Grinders should not be operated without safety goggles and prior instruction from qualified personnel.

Hammer, dent – While dents on the externals of bends can be addressed by a ball or plug inside the tubing and tapping the outside with a jeweller's hammer, the internals of bends often require a hammer with a more tightly radiused head. Dent hammers are typically double-headed and are available in a variety of sizes.

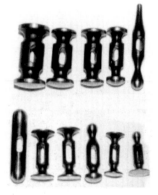
A variety of dent hammers from Böhm.

Hammer, jeweller's – A lightweight hammer used to tap the dents out of tubing, or to smooth high spots back down, a jeweller's hammer is designed to manipulate the metal without bruising it unduly. Many experienced repairers will grind and linish the face of the hammer to best suit the types of instrument they work on and their individual technique. The

A jeweller's hammer is a useful dent removal tool.

opposite side of the hammer's head comprises a ball. This is useful when tightening the linkage that joins the collar of a rotary valve, as the screw through the collar will wear the reciprocal lever bearing over time. Tapping the face of the bearing against a solid surface, such as a vice head, will close the hole up again. The taper of the hole can then be restored with a pin reamer.

Hammer, pegging – A hammer that can be used inside an instrument's bell during manufacture to increase its bore somewhat. Typically this is done to pre-spun bells in order to make them an exact match for a specific model. The bell will then be beaten on to a former with a mallet and the spinning process will be repeated. (See also *Sandbag*.)

Planishing hammer reducing seam thickness.

Hammer, planishing – A heavy hammer, often pneumatically powered, designed to reduce the thickness of an overlapped seam on a spout back to that of the original material.

Hand chuck (*aka* hand wrench/vice) – When lapping valves by hand, the chuck will grip an adaptor that replaces the stem of a piston valve. This gives the operator a T-shaped handle that's easy to manipulate without becoming excessively tiring. The same holder is used when tapping threads. (See also *Taps and dies*.)

Hook scraper – See *Scraper, solder*.

The hand chuck used to lap a piston valve.

Lathe – Anyone hoping to customise mouthpieces, or to make parts for brass instruments, such as ferrules, will need a lathe. A small and reasonably accurate hobbyist lathe popular in the UK is the Myford Super 7. While it lacks the engineering precision and versatility demanded of professional applications such as cutting screw threads, such a lathe can certainly be

This lathe is being used for mouthpiece making.

used to increase the throat bore of a mouthpiece, for instance. (Attempting the same task with a hand-held electric drill will turn a mouthpiece into a new object known as an 'ornament'.)

Exactly how suitable a given lathe is to the task in hand depends on a number of factors, including its overall condition. No matter how precise a lathe was on the day it was made, once the bearings have worn it will no longer work to the same tolerances. (While bearings can be restored, that's a subject well beyond the scope of the *Brass Instrument Manual*.)

A modern, small industrial lathe, such as made by Harrison, comes equipped with bearings that are designed for duty cycles and tolerances massively beyond anything the hobbyist is likely to expect or afford. These are the machines of choice for cutting accurate threads, and tidy knurlings, amongst other applications including mouthpiece making. (See also *Chuck*.)

The type of lathe used for spinning instrument bells is almost the opposite to the modern engineering lathe, in that it needs to offer almost nothing in the way of facilities beyond the mounting for the rotating former and an adjustable rest on which the operator can steady the hand tools used to flatten the sheet metal against the former. Mechanical tolerances aren't massively critical, unlike size and robustness, the need for which obviously increases in line with the scale of the formers and the bells they produce. As most formers are cut from solid steel, large bearings and heavy-duty motors are the most important attributes of a spinning lathe.

An even more specialised form of lathe is the turret lathe, used in the manufacture of valves. Rather like a milling machine (*qv*), a turret lathe is a large piece of machinery that's potentially useful for only a small fraction of the overall musical instrument-making process. Because of this and the very specific skills required to make high-performance valves, there has been an increasing trend to outsource the supply of these from specialist companies. (This isn't unlike building a high-performance car around a Lotus engine, or an electric guitar around Seymour Duncan pickups.)

Lead-pouring ladle – Used to pour molten lead into small-bore tubing to prevent it from collapsing when being bent to shape. **NB:** Working with molten metal is potentially extremely dangerous and should only be attempted by trained personnel wearing the appropriate safety gear. Even the synthetic substitutes can burn skin.

Lifter, valve collar – See *Collar lifter*.

Magnetic dent removal – See *Dent removal, magnetic*.

Mallet – Designed to shape metal without bruising or thinning it, the mallets used in brass instrument manufacture were traditionally of leather, but these days nylon is preferred because of its durability. In addition, some mallets have replaceable heads. These can be bought from car accessory shops.

A mallet won't bruise metal.

Mandrel – A tapered (usually) solid steel shape, the mandrel is an important tool in the manufacture of the spout part of the

A tapered mandrel allows a variety of shaping and hammering processes.

bell. It's the mandrel over which the sheet metal of the spout is folded prior to brazing the joint. Once the seam has been brazed, the spout is returned to the mandrel in order that the overlapping join can be reduced to a single sheet thickness using a planishing hammer. (See also *Former* and *Hammer, planishing*.)

Mandrel sets for trombones – See *Bolt/rod sets for trombones*.

Milling machine – A machine tool designed to cut through solid material, a milling machine is similar in some ways to a hand-held router in action. The biggest difference is that the cutting blade on a milling machine is static while the work is advanced in a controlled fashion on a moving bed below. A milling machine is a frustrating proposition for the small-scale musical instrument maker because it's a device that's extremely useful for a tiny proportion of the process. It is, for instance, ideal for fashioning the plate that retains the finger levers on a rotary-valved horn but possibly nothing else on the instrument. For practical reasons, milled parts are often bought in from a specialist fabricator.

Mirror, piston valve inspection – A small mirror, mounted on a stick, used to inspect the alignment of piston valves. A useful accompaniment to this is an LED torch. Some people use a fibre optic probe, rather than a mirror, but this is an expensive way of achieving the same result. However, a probe will allow internal inspection of the entire instrument.

Mopping wheel – Polishing emery marks from bells and other components requires a soft, cloth mopping wheel powered by an electric motor. The wheel is covered in mopping 'soap', which contains the polishing abrasive. This is available in a selection of grades of which

Mopping is dirty work but the results are beautiful.

the finest is 'rouge', a finishing grade that leaves an exceptionally high gloss.

A purpose-built polishing machine is a somewhat specialist item but it's possible to make a medium-duty version by modifying a bench grinder. The spindle needs to be swapped for one that has a pointed, threaded end, which engages with the polishing wheel. Having a slightly underpowered motor is actually an advantage because the sound of the motor labouring slightly provides a clear warning that too much pressure is being applied to the work. There's also a tendency for the mop to occasionally 'grab' the work as it rotates. Again, a less powerful motor gives the operator a better chance of keeping hold of the work, rather than it ending up wrapped around the spindle of the machine.

Because it's necessary to hold the work – especially a bell – at a variety of angles and positions, it's worth pointing out that there has to be clearance below the mop right down to floor level. Therefore anyone considering modifying a bench grinder should think in terms of mounting the motor on a plinth, or at least on the absolute edge of a bench. **NB:** A powered mopping wheel is a device that should only be operated after supervision by a qualified technician.

A mouthpiece cutter in action.

Mouthpiece cutter – A tool designed to be mounted into the tailstock chuck of a lathe in order to remove the bulk of material required to make the cup of a mouthpiece. (See also *Scraper, mouthpiece*.)

Mouthpiece puller/extractor – Jammed mouthpieces are a common problem, not least because the Morse taper used on most mouthpieces was originally developed to create a force fit. A mouthpiece extractor is a specialised clamp that can be expanded to exert pressure between the leader and mouthpiece.

Böhm offers this mouthpiece puller.

Mouthpiece reamer – See *Reamer, receiver*.

Pliers, cork (*aka* flat-nosed pliers) – Used to insert the buffer corks into rotary valves, these have wide, flat, smooth jaws.

Flat-nosed pliers. (*Böhm*)

Pliers, cutting – See *Side cutters*.

Pliers, linkage – These are designed for use primarily with the older-style linkage using non-adjustable hinge points. Over a period of time the linkage between the levers and the collars of rotary valves

Linkage pliers, *aka* shrinking pliers. (*Böhm*)

wears loose. Gripping the nickel silver outer casing with linkage pliers and rotating has the effect of pushing the metal back towards the steel inner pin – a repair that potentially puts years of additional use into the valve system.

Pliers, modified round-nose – By heating and bending one of the rounded 'noses' of round-nose pliers (*qv*), so that its end comes down vertically on the other face, the brass instrument maker creates a useful tool for holding together small components, such as flanges, during silver soldering. The modified pliers give a firm grip, with minimal contact, so that heat isn't unduly diverted from the work. Also, the pinpoint contact from one side of the pliers makes it possible to hold flat, or curved, work against the second part of a component.

These pliers have been modified for silver soldering.

Pliers, parallel jaw – The vast majority of pliers use jaws attached to a central pivot, meaning that the angle between the jaws increases as the pliers are opened. As their name implies, the more

Parallel pliers. (*Böhm*)

complex construction of parallel jaw pliers allows them to act more like a mini-vice. This can be useful when holding tubing, for instance, as it allows for firm retention of the work with minimum risk of damage.

Pliers, round-nose – A pair with long, narrow jaws are best for pulling springs, as you can get them into the ring at the end of the spring. It's

Round-nosed pliers. (*Böhm*)

then possible to increase the tension exerted by the spring by tightening the winding on the post. There's a variety of round-nose pliers, some with considerably fine and extended jaws, while others have jaws that are bent to make it easier to access springs when levers, tubing and the like are in the way.

Pliers, toothing – These are used to cut a series of 'teeth' into the sheet that forms the spout of an instrument. Once gently folded over with a small hammer, these will then hold the two edges together, with a controlled overlap, until they're braised together permanently.

Böhm toothing pliers in use at Taylor Trumpets.

The superior grade of toothing pliers have a precision-made tooth cutter that's adjustable for position and will give long service without requiring sharpening.

Pliers, tubing – Useful for gripping tubing or sheet. Actually made for gripping slide legs and the like, they're better than pliers when dealing with sheet material because their smaller faces make for a firmer grip, and also makes them act less like a heat sink when work is to be heated. When gripping a

Tubing pliers. (*Böhm*)

stuck tube, they can be struck with a hammer in order to free it up without applying a percussive force to the tubing itself.

Puller for stop arm – See *Collar lifter*.

Push-back ball – See description of 'driver' under *Ball/plug set*.

A backbore reamer forming a mouthpiece.

Reamer, backbore – A tool used to shape the interior profile of a mouthpiece within the shank. These are prohibitive for an enthusiast to buy but they can be made relatively easily from case-hardened steel. (However, it's up to the toolmaker to ensure the relevance of the reamer's profile.)

Reamer, pin – Used for adjusting the size of the bearing in the collar of old-style rotary valves. (See also *Hammer, jeweller's*.)

Reamer, receiver (*aka* mouthpiece reamer) – Available in a variety of sizes for different instruments, these are used to cut the straight-sided taper in the receiver that accommodates the mouthpiece.

Two of several designs of mouthpiece reamer available from Böhm.

Rod, draw – Designed to be used with drawplates in the making of tubing of specific diameter, these are similar to the cylindrical bolts/mandrels used in trombone repair but usually have a turned section at one end that's used to create a positive lock with the draw press.

Rolling dent tool – See *Dent roller* entries.

A rotary sander is a handy machine.

Rotary/disk sander – Traditionally a woodworking tool, this machine can be adapted to various uses in the brass-making shop, including fashioning and rough-finishing solid parts.

Rotary valve bearing shrinking tool – See *Bearing reducer, rotary*.

Rounding irons – See *Draw rings, hand*.

Rounding tools – These are hand-held devices for restoring roundness to slide legs. They're best made, rather than bought, because the optimum tubing for the tool is the actual slide sleeve tubing used by a specific manufacturer, albeit with a certain amount of reinforcement.

These tools are used to restore the roundness to slide legs.

Ruler, steel – Made from 'stainless' steel (something of a misleading name), these have an obvious application as a measuring device but are frequently multifunctional in the workshop environment, where they tend to be used for wedging and holding small objects during soldering. Unfortunately, this leads to the ruler being splashed with acid flux, causing a significant degree of corrosion. Although this reduces the ruler's usefulness for measuring, what it teaches us is that no steel is truly 'stainless', no matter how much chromium has been added to it. Rulers

Even stainless steel corrodes when faced with heat and acid flux.

are also sometimes used by musical instrument makers as impromptu 'feeler gauges'. Although the information that an aperture is 'two rulers thick' has no absolute value, it can be quite useful as a comparative guide.

Sandbag – Usually fashioned from two stout disks of leather to form a pouch that's filled with sand, a 'sandbag' is useful for partially supporting sheet-work while performing operations such as pegging. Although there's sufficient resistance in the bag to prevent much movement in the work as a whole, there's also enough give to allow the hammer to indent, or deform, the profile of the metal. (See also *Hammer, pegging*.)

Scraper, flat bell – This tool is used to smooth the external surface of a horn bell while it's mounted on a former and spinning on a lathe. It's invariably made by the bellmaker, rather than bought, for the simple reason that it's easy and inexpensive to fashion from the blades used in stationary electric hacksaws.

This bell is being shaved with a recycled hacksaw blade.

Scraper, mouthpiece – A hand-held cutter with a rounded end used to refine the cup of a mouthpiece on the lathe. Although it's possible to create the entire cup using a scraper, it's a slow technique compared to using a dedicated mouthpiece cutter to remove the bulk of the material first. A mouthpiece scraper can be fashioned from an old file using a grindstone. (See also *Mouthpiece cutter*.)

A mouthpiece scraper in action.

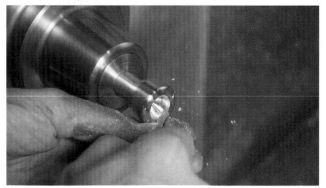

Scraper, solder – Various scrapers can be used for removing surplus solder but the most common can be made from an old screwdriver by bending the blade while it's red hot. The tip can then be re-hardened by quenching the red-hot end in cold water, after which a cutting edge is formed using a grindstone.

Careful scraping off of surplus solder is one of the keys to a pro-looking job.

Scraper, triangular bearing – Traditionally used in the engineering industry for the hand-shaping of bearings and the removal of unwanted burrs, the triangular scraper is a useful tool for shaving the interior of a bell until it's been reduced to the required thickness. The conventional triangular bearing scraper requires constant sharpening on a rotary bench grinder, but the modern alternative has a replaceable tip. Which of these is more preferable depends in part on the operator's sharpening skills, but also on the value assigned to the operator's time versus the cost of the blades.

Screwdrivers – There aren't many screw heads to be found on brass instruments but a medium-sized flat-bladed screwdriver is useful for adjusting the linkage hinge-points on rotary valves. A medium-sized Pozidriv for general-purpose use and a set of jeweller's screwdrivers is also useful. While very small screws don't often feature on brass instruments, when a larger screw sheers the remaining shaft can often be removed by scoring a line across it, then unscrewing it by using the largest jeweller's screwdriver blade that will fit.

Shears – Used for cutting sheet metal, these come in a variety of sizes and also in curved or straight configurations, depending on the line to be cut. As the handles of shears are asymmetrical (to take them away from the sharp edges of the sheet as it's cut), they're also available in a left-handed version.

Cutting sheet metal to the line is a skill best acquired early on.

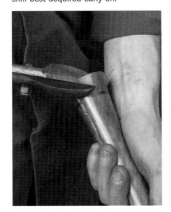

Shovel-shaped bell iron – See *Stake*.

Shrinking die for valve bearings – See *Bearing reducer, rotary*.

Shrinking pliers – See *Pliers, linkage*.

Side cutters (*aka* wire cutters or cutting pliers) – In addition to their obvious use when cutting wire, side cutters can be used to gently distort threads as a cure for loose bolts. This technique should be used with caution, as overuse can simply strip the female thread.

Slide holder/rack – A device designed to hold slides securely during polishing etc.

Spoon, bell – Once a bell/ spout has been beaten into as accurate a shape as possible using a mallet against a former, it must be spun on a lathe to make it smoother. This is usually done with

This slide holder at Paxman is probably 50 years old and still sees daily use.

The bell spoon is a smoothing tool.

first a wooden and then a metal spoon, the pressure and linear progress of which is adjusted by the operator, who levers it between the rotating work and a long hand-rest.

Spoon, spelter – A small spoon is used to apply a paste of borax and spelter in a neat row along a spout or bell prior to braising it with a torch. (See *Spelter* in the 'Materials' section.)

Stake – Similar in appearance to a refined anvil top, a stake is a steel shape designed to support the inside of a bell while a burnisher is applied to the outside, in order to

Stakes of different sizes from Böhm.

iron out creases. It's more suited to larger brass instruments, whereas trumpets and instruments of a similar size are better dealt with using a symmetrical former. (See also *Former*.)

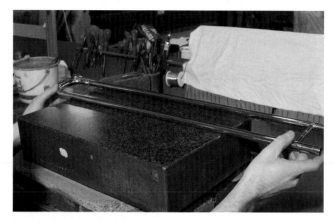

The 'stone' or 'surface plate' at Michael Rath Trombones was fashioned from solid granite by scientific instrument makers.

Stone – A solid slab, made either from stone or steel, used to ascertain whether the slides of a trombone are straight and parallel. Also known as a 'surface plate'.

Surface plate – See entry above.

Swab (*aka* cleaning rod) – A metal rod over which cotton cloth is wrapped for the purposes of cleaning piston valve casings. Longer variants are used for cleaning trombone slides.

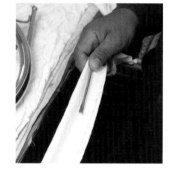

A swab or cleaning rod.

Swage – This device is used with an ironing action to restore a cylindrical profile to tubing after it's been worked on. Most repair shops will have a number of swages of varying sizes to accommodate different diameters of tubing.

NB: To an extent, the meaning and use of a 'swage' overlaps with that of a 'drawplate' (*qv*). For the sake of clarity we've reserved the use of the word 'drawplate' for a solid steel plate containing one or more enclosed holes of set diameter. When we refer to a 'swage' we mean a hand-held tool that covers approximately a semi-circle, making it useful when repairing instruments that are already fully assembled. (See also *Draw rings* and *Drawplate*.)

Tapered mandrel – See *Mandrel*.

Taps and dies – Taps and dies are cutting tools used to create screw threads. These are common operations in manufacture and also repair procedures, as threads wear over time, holes become enlarged, corroded threads cause bolts to break… and parts on vintage instruments have to be crafted by hand as there's no commercial equivalent available.

A tap is used to cut the female portion of the pair (typically, a nut). A die is used to cut the male portion of the pair (a bolt). The process of cutting threads using a tap is called 'tapping', whereas the process using a die is called 'threading'. Both tools can be used to clean up a thread, which is called 'chasing'.

When tapping a 'blind' hole (*ie* one that doesn't go all the way through the material) it's often necessary to use three taps in succession: tapered, intermediate and plug (or 'bottoming'). Add to this the need to keep taps and dies for a variety of diameters and thread standards, along with the hand wrenches needed to use them, and it's no surprise that busy repair shops soon collect an impressive array of taps and dies.

Templates – Many a visitor to a brass workshop has asked what the 'metal kipper ties' are on the wall. The answer is, they're the templates that are scribed around before the sheet metal is cut to make a spout or bell for an instrument. Once the sheet has been joined to form a three-dimensional object, the shape of the template starts to make sense. Until then the contour described by the

This template describes the shape that will become part of a trumpet bell.

template seems to contain an extreme amount of flare to the untrained eye.

Thread repair tool – A hand-held tool designed to repair damaged threads on valve casings and caps.

Top slide, lathe (*aka* tool slide) – The assembly that sits on top of the saddle of a lathe and holds the tool post. This is required for mouthpiece making, as setting it at an angle will cause the cutting tool to create a tapered shank when the handwheel is rotated.

Torch, gas – There are two types in common use for the purpose of soldering and braising brass sheet and other parts. The type found in professional workshops has independent inlets for mains gas and compressed air, each with its own valve. This allows for an exceptional degree of

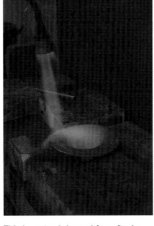

This large torch is used for softening and braising instrument bells.

Pre-made felts are readily obtained, but these cutters from Böhm allow them to be made to any thickness or diameter.

control, because the size of the flame and the intensity of the flame can be set separately. For instance, a large amount of gas and small amount of air produces a relatively unfocused flame that's useful for the general heating of a wide area of metal, while a lesser amount of gas but a greater amount of air produces a smaller, hotter flame more suited to soldering. (See also *Compressor*.)

For occasional use, a gas torch powered by a disposable canister is a good alternative, especially when the main requirement is for high-precision soft and silver soldering. As well as presenting an economical alternative, this type of gas torch has the added advantage that it can be used in a variety of positions, without the need to cope with two trailing tubes. (See also *Soldering* in the 'Materials' section.)

Tube-bending jig – These come in as many shapes and sizes as the instruments they're used to form tubes for, and serve as an aid to bending tubing to the required shape. Small-bore tubing is traditionally filled with lead to prevent it collapsing, while spouts and larger bore tubing are filled with a mixture of coal tar pitch and resin. *NB:* Working with molten metal is potentially extremely dangerous and should only be attempted by trained personnel wearing the appropriate safety gear.

Valve casing mandrel, expandable – A tool for pushing the dents out of piston valve casings.

This expandable valve casing mandrel from Böhm can undo distortions to valve casings caused by physical impact.

Valve felt cutting tools – Can be used with felt or card to create felts of various diameters and depths.

Valve seater – The retaining plate that sits at the top of a rotary valve is held into the casing by force, as it has a slight taper to the edge that engages with the casing. The valve seater allows the plate

It's essential to replace the top plate of a rotary valve using a seater, not direct hammer action.

to be tapped into position with a small hammer, without having to tap the plate itself, an action that could otherwise damage the top bearing. These are easily made from a cotton reel.

Vice and vice jaws – A bench-mounted vice is essential for holding either complete instruments or components. Because brass and related metals are easily marred, a pair of fibre-lined or plastic vice jaws is another must-have.

To the right of this picture is a set of vice jaws, leaning on a gas torch. Just to the left is a sandbag.

Materials

Acid – Although flux will remove a certain amount of oxide, and prevent further oxidisation during soldering and braising processes, it's usually necessary to remove grease and oxide from the work first. Oxide must also be removed to prevent unnecessary blunting of tools, especially when turning bells.

An acid mix is used to remove oxide, and also the flux left after 'hard' soldering.

For professional brass instrument manufacturers, this is most efficiently achieved through dipping the work in a dilute mix of nitric and sulphuric acid. The traditional mixing method is as follows. (1) Put five parts water in a non-reactive (ie acid-proof) container. (2) Add one part nitric acid. (3) Add two parts sulphuric acid. The chemicals must be added in the order specified and each should be added slowly. The mix is usually a little vicious in action at first but will calm down. If the mix is actually fizzing, it's necessary to add more water, again slowly.

NB: The above information is provided for interest only. The safe handling, storage and use of acids requires training. Overalls, goggles and gloves are the minimum safety wear required. For many repair processes, a solvent or descaling product is a more appropriate material than acid. (See below for advice on solvents).

Braising rod – See *Spelter*.

Emery cloth – The finishing of brass and related components is achieved by smoothing with a graduated series of abrasive sheet materials, of which the most common is emery cloth. (Because the material in use doesn't have clogging problems, this is a process that can be done dry.) The abrasiveness of emery cloth is defined by the amount of grit particles in a given area, meaning a lower number denotes a bigger grit size and therefore a rougher cloth. When finishing a horn bell, the grades of 100 grit, 180 grit, 240 grit and 320 grit are used in succession, after which the finish should be fine enough for polishing, if desired. The additional use of 600 grit is by no means obligatory but will reduce buffing time where a high shine is required.

Polishing cloths – Commercially produced impregnated cloths designed to restore the shine to silver are a good bet when working with silver-plated instruments, as more abrasive techniques may wear through the plate. (Although re-plating is always an option, it has an associated cost and increases repair time.) Small pieces of silver polishing cloth are available from supermarkets but tool suppliers sell similar products on a roll.

Ragging tape – When covered in either mopping soap (*qv*) or a liquid metal cleaner such as Brasso, ragging tape makes fast work of cleaning and polishing an instrument's tubing. About 600mm/2ft of tape is enough to hook over the tubing, which can then be cleaned by an alternating up/down motion. Although the disadvantage of this technique is that the instrument must be suspended to give free access to the underside, the technique is vastly more efficient than trying to polish the instrument as if it were a complicated pair of shoes! Commercially made ragging tape is available in a variety of widths suitable for everything from a trumpet to a tuba. Similar results to pre-made

Ragging tape can help to achieve a professional finish without an electric mop.

ragging tape can be obtained using torn-off strips of old shirts or sheets. Mopping soap is better than Brasso because it doesn't splash. However, the end result is much the same.

Soap, mopping – Where large surfaces of metal – such as a horn bell – are to be brought to a high gloss, the best tool for the job is a free-standing electric mopping machine. The mops themselves are made from cloth and are available in a variety of hardnesses and diameters to suit different applications. (A very hard mop isn't a good choice for a thin horn bell, because it's likely to cause damage, but that same mop will make fast work of polishing solid components.)

The abrasive used for polishing is called mopping soap, and is applied to the edge of the mop while it's rotating. Despite its solid consistency when cold, mopping soap softens considerably when warmed by the friction of the mop and still further when actually polishing. As a result mopping soap flies out from the mop to cover walls, floors and ceilings. For this reason, mopping

Mopping soap is not unlike 'Brasso in a bar'.

machines are usually placed in a 'mop shop', in a bid to prevent the soap spreading throughout the workshop.

NB: It's essential to wear a face mask when operating an electric mop. Training is also required. (See also *Mopping wheel* in the 'Tools' section.)

Solder – Broadly speaking, solder has been divided historically into 'soft' and 'hard', where soft solders were based on a mix of lead and tin, whereas hard solders were based primarily on silver, copper and zinc. Traditionally, 'silver solder' and 'hard solder' have meant much the same thing in brass musical instrument making. (Other hard solder formulations are available but that needn't concern us too much, as they're mainly used in other industries such as jewellery making.)

The development that has complicated this once simple division between 'soft' and 'hard' is a worldwide move away from the use of lead-based solder in favour of less polluting alternatives. Many of the new 'soft' solder formulations involve the use of a certain amount of silver in place of lead as a flowing agent. However, this doesn't mean the new lead-free formulations should be regarded as 'hard solder' or 'silver solder'.

Probably the best way to explain the different types of solder is to look at the traditional formulations, and then look at the effect international legislation has had on the solder types now available to musical instrument makers and repairers.

Soft soldering is used to join ferrules, flanges and other parts.

Soft solders have conventionally been available in five different 'melting grades', which describe the level of heat that needs to be applied to the surfaces to be joined before the solder becomes liquid. Essentially, the more lead there is in the solder, the lower the temperature at which it melts. Manufacturers of cheap instruments invariably use high-lead solder because it runs freely and it's easy to clean off. Sadly, that's precisely the reason why such instruments are forever falling apart. High-lead solder is easy to work with, but the joins it makes are weak.

As a guide to lead/tin ratios, 60/40 is easy to work but 70/30 produces a stronger join. However, the stronger 70/30 puts extra demands on the technician. The 'flux' used to keep the surfaces to be soldered oxide-free has to be clean and fresh. (In contrast, flux that's been sitting in an open container for days on end will usually work well with a 60/40 solder.)

For manufacturers, lead-free solder is now a reality, as there are legal restrictions on the use of the old leaded solder. Doubtless, better formulations will be developed but the current generation of silver-based solders are more difficult to work with. Partly this is because the new solders don't flow as well as the traditional ones, but also because any surplus is far harder to scrape off.

At the time of writing there's no restriction on the use of leaded solders for musical instrument repair work in Europe and these solders continue to be freely available. The amount of solder used by the musical instrument industry is, in any case, tiny compared to, say, consumer electronics, or even plumbers.

All solders require flux to remove from – and prevent the formation of oxide on – the metals to be joined. (This is even true of electrical solder, but in that instance the solder has tiny cores of flux within it.) The soft solders used for brass instruments need to be used in conjunction with either a paste or a fluid flux, such as Baker's No 3. Liquid fluxes tend to splash more than the paste varieties but are easier to wash off afterwards, so there's an element of personal preference here. Flux is irritating to the skin, so it's better to avoid getting it on your hands or, worse, absent-mindedly rubbing an eye with unwashed hands.

Silver soldering is a much more demanding process than soft soldering. On the one hand, this is because soft solder has a much lower melting point than brass, so there's little danger of accidentally burning the work during the soldering process; on the other, silver solder will only run when the work is red hot, so burning a hole in it is a possibility. Fortunately most silver soldering is carried out on stays and other components made of nickel silver, which has a higher melting point than brass and therefore a greater margin for error.

Silver soldering is a more permanent way of making braces and other components.

Be careful not only to keep containers well away from naked flames but also to remember to leave plenty of time for evaporation before starting any process involving a gas torch.

Spelter – Traditionally, musical instrument makers have another trick up their sleeves that makes for even stronger joints than soldering – braising. The difference between soldering and braising is that the formulation of the braising metal and the material to be joined is very close. This makes for a join that is, to all intents and purposes, as strong as the material itself. Also, when the join is hammered flat and the work is rubbed down and polished, it can be close to invisible. The downside is that the difference between the melting point of the material to be joined and that of the braising metal itself is also very close, so the risk of destroying the work by overheating is very high.

A granulated brass, the spelter has a slightly higher zinc content than the material to be joined, which is how the melting point is reduced. The flux is simply borax, which is mixed in with the spelter and some water to form a paste. This paste is lined up along the seam and – once dry – is heated with a torch until the spelter melts into the seam.

In mainstream engineering, the braising material is supplied in the form of 'braising rods', and the use of these is becoming increasingly common in musical instrument making, as they're easier to obtain. However, an understanding of how spelter works is a useful introduction to the subject of braising and silver soldering. Today, there is an array of braising rod formulations, designed for different melting points and therefore suitable for use with different alloy formulations. Not only is it advisable to know which are suitable for a particular application, it's also necessary to know which of the modern fluxes work with that braising rod, as they aren't interchangeable.

The correct flux for silver soldering is a white powder, typically sold under the Easy-flo brand. The silver solder is heated somewhat and dipped in the powder, which is than applied to the work as the metal heats. The most common mistakes would-be silver solderers make in their early days are failing to heat the work enough to melt the solder and/or leaving a gap between the two surfaces to be joined. Unlike soft solder, silver solder won't fill a gap, so it's best to think of tolerances in terms of microns, rather than millimetres.

To compound the problem, the hot flux is capable of bridging much larger gaps than silver solder, and once cold is hard enough to present quite a convincing impression of a good solder joint. It's only during the subsequent cleaning process, when the work falls back into bits, that the truth is revealed.

Solvent – For cleaning components, particularly during repair and maintenance, a degreasing agent is often more appropriate than using acid. (For instance, when dealing with a sticky valve, removing all traces of existing lubricants and whatever contaminants they may contain is a good starting point. However, taking off the outer layer of the valve's surface at this point using acid is not recommended.)

Solvents conventionally used in the engineering and musical instrument industries include trichloroethylene. However, the use of these substances is increasingly limited to organisations that have invested in complex, sealed systems that will avoid fume emissions. For the hobbyist, good substitutes include electrical switch cleaner, lighter fuel or isopropyl alcohol.

NB: Unlike 'trike', lighter fuel is obviously very inflammable.

Braising rod has increasingly taken over from spelter in instrument making.

Appendix

Further reading and resources

Readers seeking additional information, spare parts or tools will find the following online resources, books and suppliers useful:

Books

Stan Bray. *Metalworking Tools and Techniques* (Crowood Press, 2003).

Doug Briney. *The Home Machinist's Handbook* (TAB Books, 1983).

Mark J. Fasman. *Brass Bibliography: Sources on the History, Literature, Pedagogy, Performance, and Acoustics of Brass Instruments* (Indiana University Press, 1990).

Allen B. Skei. *Woodwind, Brass & Percussion Instruments of the Orchestra: a Bibliographic Guide* (Garland, 1984).

Magazines and journals

The American Musical Instrument Society (www.amis.org) produces an annual journal of about 160 pages, as well as a newsletter.

Brass Bulletin 'the international magazine for the brass player' can be bought from www.editions-bim.com/brass-bulletin.html.

The Brass Herald, 'the magazine for the brass'. Subscription details can be found at www.thebrassherald.com.

Jazz Improv Magazine covers all instruments, and comes with one or sometimes two CDs. Details can be found at www.jazzimprov.com.

British Bandsman, 'the leading international brass magazine'. Subscription details can be found at www.britishbandsman.com.

The *Historic Brass Society Journal* is produced annually. See www.historicbrass.org.

Forums and information websites

www.bandsman.co.uk –
    'The Brass Band Portal – helping brass bands since 1995'.
brassmusician.com –
    'The online magazine for brass players'.
www.brassreview.com –
    'The largest source for brass instrument reviews on the Internet'.
www.britishtrombonesociety.org –
    'A properly constituted association for trombonists'.
www.4barsrest.com –
    'Brass band news, information and shopping'.

www.hornmatters.com –
    A variety of resources related to the French horn.
www.hornsociety.org –
    Online home of The International Horn Society.
www.ibew.org.uk –
    'The information resource for brass bands world-wide'.
www.iteaonline.org –
    The International Tuba Euphonium Association.
www.rjmartz.com –
    'Dick Martz, his collection of strange and wonderful horns'.
www.trombone.net –
    Home of the International Trombone association.
www.trombone.org –
    'Online Trombone Journal – A free Internet resource for, and by, trombonists'.
www.trumpetguild.org –
    The Trumpet Guild produces a journal.
www.trumpetherald.com –
    'The largest and oldest community site for trumpet players on the Internet'.
www.trumpetmaster.com – Forum, wiki and galleries.
www.vintagecornets.com.

Parts and tools suppliers

www.band-supplies.co.uk.
www.brass-fix.co.uk.
www.brasswarehouse.co.uk.
www.dawkes.co.uk.
www.jlsmithco.com.
www.mouthpieceexpress.com.
www.musiciansfriend.com.
www.normans.co.uk.
www.thebandroom.biz.
www.thomann.de.
www.trevadamusic.co.uk.
www.windcraft.co.uk.
www.windplus.co.uk.
www.wwbw.com.

Tool manufacturers

www.alliedsupplycorp.com.
www.boehmtools.de.
www.cat-sys.co.uk.
www.ferreestools.com.
www.votawtool.com.

Index

Simon Croft and Andy Taylor would like to thank the following:

Forewords

Tony Fisher, trumpet

Winston Rollins, trombone

Cindy Bradley, trumpet

Giles Whittome,
writer and collector

Additional technical input:

David 'Satch' Botwe,
Paxman Musical Instruments

Tim Sidwell, Michael Rath
Musical Instruments

Photographers Tim Coppendale (main image, this page)
Richard Ecclestone, Charlotte Godfrey,
Dave Harrington, Dean Smith

For additional images etc and sharing their collections/product ranges with us:

Alexander (Gebr. Alexander Musikinstrumentenfabrik), Böhm (Josef Böhm), British Museum, Marc Caparone, Richard Church, Conn-Selmer, Mike Corrigan (BAC Horn Doctor), Nick DeCarlis, Edwards Instrument Co, Rene Hagmann (Servette Music), Horniman Museum and Gardens, Hoxon Gakki, JHS (John Hornby Skewes), Trevor Jones, Kelly Mouthpieces, Michael Rath Musical Instruments, Paxman Musical Instruments, Chris Tyle, Gerard Westerhof, HN White Company, Giles Whittome, Yamaha